Paleo
~Home~
Cooking

Flavorful Recipes for a Healthy,
Gluten-Free Lifestyle

by
Sonia Lacasse

author of
The Healthy Foodie

Victory Belt Publishing Inc.

Las Vegas

First Published in 2015 by Victory Belt Publishing Inc.

ISBN-13: 978-1-628600-68-1

This book is for entertainment purposes. The publisher and author of this cookbook are not responsible in any manner whatsoever for any adverse effects arising directly or indirectly as a result of the information provided in this book.

Book design by Yordan Terziev and Boryana Yordanova

Printed in the U.S.A.

RRD 0115

To my daughter, my best friend in the entire universe, who has turned my world upside down on more than one occasion and without whom I wouldn't be where I am today. Thank you for being such an amazing woman, for being such a breath of fresh air, and for rocking my world day after day after day.

I love you with all my heart, today, tomorrow, and for eternity.

TABLE OF CONTENTS

introduction

MY STORY—
HOW PALEO FOUND ME

For as long as I can remember, I have struggled with my weight. As such, I have fallen victim to the diet syndrome more times than I can count on my fingers. In an effort to rid my body of unwanted pounds, I would starve myself and eat "rabbit food" for months. Sure, the fat would come off, and fairly quickly, too, but it was only a matter of time before I gained it all back because I never knew how to feed my body properly and, more importantly, make it stick.

THEN I MADE A NEW YEAR'S RESOLUTION...

Several years ago, I decided that I not only wanted to shed some (*ahem*—fifty to sixty) pounds, but also wanted to get in better shape physically. I had already quit smoking two years prior and dramatically lowered my alcohol consumption the year after that, going from several drinks a day to drinking only on the weekends. Eventually, under that new regimen, the need to drink alcohol completely subsided, and now I only indulge in the very occasional drink.

I figured that if I'd been able to quit smoking *and* drinking, two things that I thought were impossible for me to do, then surely I would be able to adopt better eating habits as well as learn to move my body a little bit. My official resolution that year was to be active for a minimum of thirty minutes a day, at least six days a week. I invested in an elliptical machine and a couple of sets of dumbbells and started training at home. I was extra motivated, and that half hour a day soon became an hour. The pounds started to come off, and I felt so much better, so energized, so pumped! I looked forward to my exercise sessions, but before long I began to feel like I needed more, like I needed a tangible goal.

That's when I started running and set a goal to run a 10K at the Marathon de Montréal in September 2010. Not only did I achieve that goal, I surpassed it! I actually ran a half-marathon that year, which I completed in 2 hours, 1 minute, and 40 seconds. I will never, ever forget that time.

TO RUN, TO CYCLE, TO ROW...

Truth is, though, I really hate running. It is much too slow and monotonous for my taste. Plus, I tend to get bored when I do the same thing over and over, day after day after day. So I started cycling instead, but then I got bored with that, too. But over the years, I've always found new ways to stay motivated and keep my body active by trying all kinds of different exercises, such as resistance training, yoga, Zumba, rowing, and, more recently, CrossFit and weight lifting. The latter I absolutely adore; I think I've finally found something that I won't get bored with anytime soon. I've even invested in a small home gym and hired a personal coach so I can work out in the comfort of my own home. To this day, I still make it my business to be physically active at least five days a week, for a minimum of sixty minutes per day. Another resolution that stuck!

For sure you must think that I absolutely *love* exercising! Well, the truth is, I don't always enjoy it and oftentimes would gladly skip it, but I love the results. I know just how good it is for me, for my body and for my health, and how it makes me feel so much better about myself. Plus, I must admit, it feels great to be in good shape.

Now that exercise is a part of my daily life, I wouldn't dream of quitting. I'm no athlete and I struggle sometimes, but I know that the only way I will improve is if I keep going. And that is exactly what I intend to do.

I'm convinced of the importance of exercise and think that everyone should move their body on a daily basis. The key is to experiment with different sports until you find one that you enjoy. Whether it's swimming, tennis, racquetball, lacrosse, squash, badminton, basketball, skiing, hockey, ballet, tap dancing, karate, kickboxing, spinning, aerobics, or power walking around the neighborhood, there's simply no way you won't be able to find a sport that fits your budget, interests, and lifestyle.

Get out there and get movin'!

EXERCISE ISN'T EVERYTHING

Being active is just one part of the equation. Back then, my food choices weren't always optimal. I realized that I also had to relearn how to nourish my body, and to learn how to cook healthy yet tasty and appetizing meals for myself and my family. That's when my blog, *The Healthy Foodie*, came into existence. It was a way for me stay on track and to keep a record of recipes I'd created and meals I'd eaten. What started as a simple online food diary soon became a real passion. It inspired me and helped me expand my boundaries and make tons of new discoveries through sharing recipes, ideas, and information with other like-minded people.

For most of my life, I've been what I humorously refer to as a *Hard-Corus Humanus Carnivorous*. I bet you can tell that I really, really *love* meat. A meal without at least some kind of animal protein was a concept I could barely grasp. I kept telling all who would listen that I could *never, ever* become a vegetarian.

But then the funniest thing happened: When I decided to turn my life around and take a walk down the "healthy" path, I practically became a vegetarian, mainly for ethical reasons—I couldn't stand the way the poor animals were being treated—but also because I wanted to do what I believed at the time was best for my health. I gave up on eating meat, with the exception of the occasional lean chicken and fish. Whey protein powder and dairy products, namely low-fat cottage cheese and Greek yogurt, became my preferred sources of protein.

I would eat six times a day, at regular intervals, and kept track of every single calorie that passed my lips. And yes, I kept that number low—way too low for my actual requirements. My meals and snacks were small and unsatisfactory, and I constantly found myself looking at the clock, obsessing about my next meal. I was hungry all the time. But I did lose a bunch of weight, so I was happy with that.

Sort of…

MY FIRST GLIMPSE OF PALEO

It was about this time when I first heard about the Paleo diet, and I remember thinking, *"OMG, I wish I had discovered this diet back when I was still digging meat! I would've loved filling up on meat and animal fat while calling it healthy!"* But given my convictions at the time, I couldn't bring myself to switch back and give it a try. I was convinced that red meat and saturated fat were evil and would only make me fat and clog my arteries. The way I saw it, the Paleo diet was about nothing but worshiping bacon and eating meat galore, so I pretty much ruled it out as totally unhealthy.

Plus, I was nowhere near ready to give up my precious whole grains, whey protein, and dairy!

That is, until I took a thirty-day clean eating challenge that basically removed any and all forms of grains, dairy, refined sugar, alcohol, and processed food. For thirty days, I ate nothing but meat, healthy fats, plenty of vegetables, some fruits, and a few nuts and seeds. In other words, nothing but real food!

Little did I know that the cleansing diet I was following was, in a nutshell, what the Paleo diet is all about…and I got completely hooked on it! I loved it so much and felt so great that, from that day on, I never looked back or felt the need to reintroduce any of the non-Paleo foods that I'd been eating all my life and thought I could never do without.

Paleo-friendly foods include meat, fish and seafood, eggs, and tons of fresh vegetables, as well as some fruit, nuts, and seeds. I realized that my first conception of Paleo was misguided.

It's about much more than gorging on fatty cuts of meat.

PALEO IS THE BEST THING THAT EVER HAPPENED TO ME

For me, this new lifestyle proved to be a total liberation: no more calorie and macronutrient counting, no more eating small, unsatisfying meals at regular intervals, no more staying slightly hungry all the time, no more stepping on the scale every week and obsessing over that number—and out the window went my fat phobia! I felt so much better physically, too. My all-too-familiar migraines soon became a thing of the past, and my legs no longer swelled up to twice their normal size every other week or so, for no apparent reason. The pitting edema that I'd been battling for years finally seemed to be under control. So was my rosacea: My skin cleared up, as if by miracle.

Many people will argue that the Paleo lifestyle is incredibly restrictive. For me, it ended up being quite the opposite: It opened up a whole new world of possibilities in the kitchen. Now that my beloved meat had been reinstated and I'd finally come to realize that fat is not the enemy—it's what keeps me full and satisfied—I felt inspired to come up with new, tasty, and healthy Paleo recipes nearly every day.

I began researching the lifestyle more extensively, and the more I read about it, the more I fell in love with it. I soon learned that the source of my food is almost as important as the food itself: Whatever my food eats, I end up eating, too. Same goes for what ends up *on* my food and where my food is grown…it all ends up in my body.

The way I see it, the Paleo diet is all about feeding on the highest possible quality of plants and animals that you can find and afford, and filling your plate with food from sustainable sources that has undergone as little processing as possible.

Now, I'm not saying that Paleo is the only truly healthy diet out there, nor am I trying to convince you that you absolutely must switch, lest your health will suffer a terrible blow. All I'm saying is that it has done wonders for me, and I like to spread the word.

Thank you for reading my story, and please feel free to take whatever you want from it.

THE INS AND OUTS OF THE PALEO DIET

The fundamentals of what constitutes a real, authentic Paleo diet aren't necessarily black and white. If you do a little bit of research on the subject, chances are you'll find quite a few different interpretations.

Truth be told, there really isn't an official, be-all-and-end-all definition of what constitutes the Paleo diet. However, the general consensus is pretty much the same: Feed your body real, nutrient-rich food that is as close as possible to what nature intended it to be, and keep it whole, unprocessed, and unrefined.

As a general rule, these are the guidelines that I personally adhere to. Note that these lists are in no way exhaustive. They are intended to give you an idea of what can be included in each category and what should be avoided.

EAT PLENTY OF:

ANIMAL PROTEIN

- Eggs (and by all means, eat that yolk!)
- Beef
- Lamb
- Pork
- Chicken
- Turkey
- Salmon
- Tuna
- Mackerel
- Sardines
- Herring
- Shrimp
- Scallops
- Rabbit
- Duck
- Wild boar
- Bison/ buffalo

As much as possible, consume the meat of animals that have been raised on pasture and have never been given hormones, antibiotics, or commercial feed. Grass-fed meat is much higher in nutrients than the meat of animals that come from commercial operations.

The same principle applies to fish and seafood. Always opt for wild-caught, and buy from certified, sustainable fisheries.

Oh, and don't forget organ meats! Liver, kidney, heart, and other organs from organically raised, grass-fed animals are some of the most nutrient-rich foods you can eat. Organ meats are said to be between 10 and 100 times higher in nutrients than muscle meats. That's reason enough to make an effort to include them in your diet.

VEGETABLES

- Arugula
- Asparagus
- Beets
- Bell peppers
- Bok choy
- Broccoli
- Brussels sprouts
- Cabbage
- Carrots
- Cauliflower
- Celery
- Collards
- Cucumber
- Eggplant
- Endive
- Garlic
- Kale
- Lettuce/leafy greens (the darker, the better)
- Mushrooms
- Onions
- Parsley
- Spinach
- Squash (acorn, butternut, delicata, pumpkin, spaghetti)*
- Sweet potatoes/ yams*
- Swiss chard
- Tomatoes
- Turnips/rutabaga
- Watercress
- Zucchini

Due to their higher carb content, it's best not to go overboard with starchy vegetables such as winter squash and sweet potatoes, especially if you're trying to lose weight.

Loaded with vitamins and minerals, vegetables— especially dark, leafy greens—should make up a big chunk of your daily diet. If you can, buy local, organic vegetables and opt for those that are in season.

HEALTHY FATS AND OILS

Cooking Fats/Oils

- Animal fat (such as lard, tallow, and duck fat)
- Ghee (clarified butter)
- Avocado oil
- Coconut oil
- Extra-virgin olive oil (will tolerate only low to moderate heat)
- Cacao butter

Nonheat Oils (For Salads, Etc.)

- Avocado oil
- Extra-light-tasting/mild olive oil (when a mild flavor is desired, such as when making mayo)
- Extra-virgin olive oil

Eating Fats

- Avocados
- Coconut (milk, fresh meat, unsweetened dried flakes, butter, and oil)
- Olives
- Nuts and seeds (go easy on these)
  Best choices: almonds, Brazil nuts, cashews, hazelnuts, macadamia nuts, pecans, pistachios, and walnuts. Stick with raw. Limit to one to two handfuls per day. Avoid if trying to lose weight.

Fat is not the enemy and, contrary to popular belief, will not make you fat. Indeed, fat is a critical part of a healthy diet: It provides essential fatty acids, keeps skin soft, delivers fat-soluble vitamins, and is a great source of energizing fuel.

Make sure to include some healthy fat in every one of your meals. Not only will it supply your body with valuable energy, but it will also keep your tummy fuller, longer. In addition to using healthy fats or oils when cooking or preparing meals, eating any of these is an excellent and easy way to up the quantity of healthy fat in your diet: avocados, olives, coconut products (any form, but always unsweetened), and raw nuts and seeds.

When it comes to animal fats or ghee, it is especially important to opt for sources that are organic, grass-fed, and/or farm-raised or pastured.

EAT IN MODERATION:

NUTS AND SEEDS

- Almonds
- Brazil nuts
- Cashews
- Hazelnuts
- Macadamia nuts
- Pecans
- Pistachios
- Walnuts

Stick with raw. Limit to one to two handfuls per day. Avoid if trying to lose weight.

FRUITS

- Apples
- Apricots
- Bananas
- Berries (blackberries, blueberries, raspberries, etc.)
- Dates
- Figs
- Grapefruit
- Grapes
- Kiwi
- Lemons/limes
- Mangoes
- Melon (cantaloupe, honeydew, watermelon)
- Oranges
- Papaya
- Pears
- Peaches
- Pineapple
- Pomegranates

Fresh fruit is very good for you, but keep in mind that it's also high in natural sugar. Limit consumption to one or two servings per day, especially if you're trying to lose weight.

ENJOY ON OCCASION:

DAIRY AND DAIRY PRODUCTS

- Butter (except for clarified butter or ghee, which may be consumed in greater quantities)
- Cheese (all types)
- Heavy cream
- Kefir
- Milk
- Sour cream
- Yogurt

Dairy is one of those gray areas of the Paleo diet. Some people tolerate it, and others don't. Some choose to include it, and others don't.

If you decide to consume dairy, steer clear of commercial products. Not only do they come from animals that have been poorly fed and raised, but most undergo so much processing, such as pasteurization, that the majority of the enzymes and beneficial bacteria are destroyed, resulting in nothing more than a processed food.

Instead, aim for raw, unpasteurized, organic, pasture-raised, grass-fed, and full-fat products. Bonus points if you can get them from a local farmer or artisan!

REFRAIN FROM CONSUMING:

ALCOHOL

This one is a no-brainer. Alcohol does absolutely nothing for your body from a nutritional standpoint. That said, no one is saying that you can't ever enjoy a drink in good company.

If you're going to indulge, refrain from drinking alcohol that contains grains or gluten, such as most beers, or that is very high in sugar, like most mixers, mixed drinks, and liqueurs.

Your best options include wine (preferably red), champagne, and hard cider. If hard liquor is more your thing, opt for tequila, potato vodka, or rum.

ABSOLUTELY, POSITIVELY STAY AWAY FROM:

GRAINS AND PSEUDO-GRAINS

- Wheat (also known as bulgur, couscous, durum, farro, graham [flour], kamut, seitan, semolina, spelt, and triticale)
- Amaranth
- Barley
- Bran
- Buckwheat/kasha
- Corn (all forms)
- Millet
- Montina
- Oats
- Quinoa
- Rice/wild rice
- Rye
- Sorghum
- Teff

Grains are sneaky and can hide in the most unsuspected places, such as:

- Alcohol/beer
- Baking powder (contains cornstarch)
- Condiments, salad dressings, and sauces
- Mirin
- Soy sauce/tamari
- Store-bought broths and stocks (cans and bouillon cubes)
- Most commercially prepared foods

Make sure to read labels carefully!

LEGUMES

- Beans (all kinds, except for fresh green beans, which are more vegetable than legume)
- Chickpeas
- Lentils
- Peanuts (yes, they're legumes, not nuts)
- Peas (except for snow peas and sugar snap peas, which are more vegetable than legume)
- Soy (including soy sauce, tofu, miso, tempeh, edamame, and lecithin, which is commonly added to prepared foods; again, read labels carefully!)

REFINED AND ARTIFICIAL SUGARS

Including, but not limited to:

- Aspartame
- Brown sugar
- Caramel
- Corn syrup
- Dextrose
- Fructose
- Glucose
- Malt syrup
- Maltitol
- Saccharin
- Stevia
- Sucralose
- White sugar
- Xylitol

If you must use a sweetener, stick to dried fruit (especially dates), natural fruit juices, raw honey, pure maple syrup, and blackstrap molasses. Coconut sugar is also an acceptable choice.

REFINED OILS AND FATS

Including, but not limited to:

- Canola oil
- Corn oil
- Margarine
- Peanut oil
- Safflower oil
- Soybean oil
- Sunflower oil
- Vegetable oil
- Vegetable shortening

FAKE AND PROCESSED FOODS

Pretty much everything that comes in a box— man-made, manufactured, foodlike products. Avoid them like the plague.

IN A NUTSHELL

EAT PLENTY OF

Animal protein   **Healthy fats**   **Vegetables**
(other than starchy)

ENJOY IN MODERATION

Starchy   **Nuts and seeds**   **Fruits**
vegetables

INDULGE ON OCCASION

Dairy and dairy
products

REFRAIN FROM CONSUMING

Alcohol

ABSOLUTELY,
POSITIVELY STAY AWAY FROM

Grains and   **Legumes**   **Refined and**   **Refined**   **Fake and**
pseudo-grains   **artificial sugars**   **oils and fats**   **processed foods**

MY SHADES OF PALEO

Having the lists on the preceding pages handy when first adopting the Paleo diet is extremely helpful. They will help you keep track of what's okay to consume and what's not okay. But lists alone are not a guarantee for success. Everyone needs guidance, encouragement, and a strategy to help make the changes stick. Most of all, you need to know that...

PALEO NEED NOT BE PERFECT

I'm not a Paleo purist...far from it.

Though I try to adhere to the food guidelines put forth by the lifestyle and practice that I preach, I understand that it's not possible to be 100 percent perfect 100 percent of the time.

The best approach is to develop what I like to think of as Paleo wisdom.

Indeed, you need to take many factors into consideration when purchasing food, such as your budget and product availability. For instance, if you have to drive for hours to get your hands on farm-fresh eggs, then you may be better off buying organic eggs from your local health food store. And if your budget won't allow that, then perhaps you should consider getting conventional eggs from the grocery store. Though conventional eggs are the least preferable option, a meal of fried conventional eggs is still better than a bowl of organic granola.

Likewise, in the dead of winter, buying fresh produce directly from the producers might be darn near impossible for you. Even finding local produce at the grocery store can prove to be quite a mission. If such is your case, don't fret; do what you can. Buy local as much as possible, and stick with organic if your budget allows it, but don't go without vegetables and fruits because you can't find or afford "acceptable" products.

When it comes to meat, though, I admit that I'm a little pickier. For me, eating the flesh of animals that have been treated with love and respect throughout their lives is of utmost importance. Not only that, but I like to know that they have been fed right, too. Let's face it: Whatever foods or "supplements" they were fed while they were alive are going to wind up in my body. It's also been proven that the meat of grass-fed or pasture-raised animals is much higher in nutrients.

Considering this, I have invested in a chest deep freezer and now purchase meat by the whole animal directly from local farmers. That said, I can still be seen buying meat at the grocery counter from time to time, if only for the sake of convenience, although I really try to make it the exception.

Let's be honest here: It's not always easy or even possible to provision happy meat. Again, always do the best *you* can, and if that means buying meat from your local grocery store, so be it.

The way I see it, you're much better off enjoying a conventionally raised steak with a side of nonlocal asparagus and mushrooms for dinner than opting for organic tofu served over a bed of organic couscous and lentils. Likewise, a trio of supermarket eggs, some fresh coleslaw, a handful of olives, and a few slices of avocado (and by the way, unless you live in California or Mexico, I dare you to try and find a local avocado!) would make a far superior breakfast than organic granola with organic low-fat milk or a couple of slices of whole-wheat toast with all-natural peanut butter.

In sum, always do the best you can given your circumstances and beliefs, and do what it takes to make Paleo a viable, simple, and, most of all, *sustainable* long-term solution for you.

With that in mind, you will rarely see me specify food grade such as "organic" or "all-natural" in my recipes. I used the best-quality food that I could afford or get my hands on at the time I created the recipes in this book, and I expect you to do the same.

PALEO NEED NOT HAPPEN OVERNIGHT

No one says that you have to wake up one morning and go, "BOOM, from now on, I'm Paleo!" The switch certainly did not happen overnight for me.

Start by making small changes on a regular basis, like every other week or every month, and make each of those changes durable. What you want to do is create new, permanent habits for yourself, so make sure you don't bite off more than you can chew, or you might get discouraged.

The changes could be things like eating no grains whatsoever during the week, living without bread and pasta for a full month, cooking all your meals at home from fresh ingredients six days a week, replacing dessert with fresh fruit for a couple of weeks, or making a conscious effort to introduce a new Paleo food that you're not familiar with every week. This will force you to change your mindset and will help transform your habits over time.

At first, you may find yourself struggling, and you may need to carry a list of "approved" ingredients in your purse or pocket. But the more often you eat Paleo dishes and prepare your own delicious Paleo meals at home, the easier it will become. Soon, you'll become really familiar with Paleo ingredients, and the decisions about what to cook and eat will come naturally. You won't even need to think about it.

And if you fall off the wagon? No biggie! Just brush yourself off and get right back on. We all slip from time to time. You totally got this!

GUIDE TO USING THIS BOOK

As a French Canadian from Québec, I feel that I bring a distinct touch to the Paleo world. Not that the ingredients I use are really so different—the cuisine in my part of the world is fairly similar to that of the rest of North America—but my Québécois approach to various common and popular dishes presents a refreshing variant to what other Paleo chefs have to offer. For instance, I like to work with lots of fresh herbs, make frequent use of ginger, cinnamon, and nutmeg, and often incorporate fruits or coconut into my savory dishes to give them a touch of sweetness; sometimes I even hit them with a touch of fresh vanilla to give them that little *je ne sais quoi*—that intriguing flavor that you can't quite put your finger on but adds so much depth to a dish.

Reflecting my heritage, within these pages you will find several regional Québécois classics, such as French Canadian meat pie, or *tourtière*, which is a pie filled with nothing but delicious meat, usually pork, beef, rabbit, or wild game; *Cretons à la Québécoise*, a tasty concoction of minced meat, typically pork and beef, and spices transformed into a super creamy and spreadable topping; and salted herbs, a brilliant blend of fresh herbs and finely chopped vegetables that, being preserved in salt, can be kept in the fridge for months and used to quickly and easily season just about any dish. These foods can be found on the shelves of basically any grocery store around here, but sadly don't seem to exist in other parts of the world. Then there's *Pouding Chômeur*, a staple here in Québec. Literally "unemployed man's pudding," this dessert consists of a simple cake batter that gets doused with a hot caramel sauce made with maple syrup, resulting in a rich cake that bakes and rises right through the syrup, which in turn settles at the bottom of the pan to create a thick, sweet sauce underneath the cake. Can you say decadent?

I also happen to be a real fan of nut butters. Over the years, I've developed a veritable passion for them. I love to come up with all kinds of delicious flavor combinations that not only call for different varieties of nuts, but also include various spices, dried fruits, coconut, natural sweeteners, and even…bacon! As such, I have dedicated an entire chapter to them, where you will find more than twenty recipes for making your own nut butters at home, as well as useful tips and a troubleshooting guide.

One thing you won't really see me do is desperately try to recreate the "junk food" items that plague the Standard American Diet, so you won't find recipes for corn dogs, French fries, or pizza in this book. I'm all for a little treat from time to time (more on that later), but for the most part, I strongly believe in eating nothing but real, unprocessed food. As such, I tend to transform my food as little as possible and make practically everything from scratch.

SEEING MEALS IN A WHOLE DIFFERENT WAY

I now see food for what it is: fuel for my body! But this didn't happen overnight; it was an evolution in thinking.

After eating Paleo for a couple of years, I pretty much stopped referring to my meals in the conventional ways. Oh, I still do eat what's known as breakfast, usually in the morning, and still refer to it as such, too. Then I sometimes do lunch a little later in the afternoon, followed by dinner, which typically seals the deal near the end of the day. Occasionally, I'll snack a little, too.

Only the way I think of these meals has changed. No longer do they have to fit a certain standard. Breakfast doesn't have to be cereal or toast or pancakes or bacon and eggs anymore. To me, breakfast is just another meal, and as such, my breakfast plate may contain just about anything, so long as the food is nutritious and will support me until my next meal. Same goes for lunch and dinner. Lunch need not be a sandwich with soup or salad, and dinner doesn't have to equal steak, potatoes, and veggies. As well, snacks no longer equate to muffins and granola bars. I regard and handle all my meals equally. Yes, that means I might have steak, sauerkraut, and sweet potatoes first thing in the morning. In fact, one of my favorite foods to eat in the morning nowadays is beef liver. And no day would start right if there weren't some kind of meat on my plate.

With that in mind, you won't find breakfast or lunch or snack recipes in this book. Instead, you will find recipes to prepare all kinds of delicious meals that you can enjoy at any time of the day, whenever you feel like it!

Before long, I bet you too will start thinking of meals as fuel for your body, rather than as fitting into stale notions of breakfast, lunch, and dinner.

THE PLACE OF TREATS IN A PALEO LIFESTYLE

I've just gone on for several pages about how the Paleo lifestyle focuses on putting real, whole, nutrient-dense foods into your body. Food that's as close as possible to what nature intended.

Yet, in the last two chapters of this book, you will find quite a few recipes for sweets and treats. Isn't that a bit contradictory? After all, I've never seen a cake grow from a tree!

Well, I am in no way suggesting that treats should be included in your everyday diet as part of a healthy lifestyle, but let's face it: We're all bound to get cravings for something sweet or feel the need for a tasty treat from time to time. It is human nature to want to satisfy your sweet tooth, and I don't think this is necessarily an evil thing, so long as it remains the exception.

Holidays, anniversaries, birthdays, family gatherings…there are so many social occasions that lead us to want to splurge a little bit. I say that when such an opportunity arises, there's no need to run and hide under a rock until it passes. Just go with it and indulge—enjoy the treat. Only do your darn best to keep it healthy!

Plus, in case you didn't know, I'm a certified baker. When the itch to bake hits, there's simply no controlling it!

HOW TO USE THE ICONS IN THIS BOOK

To help you navigate your way around this book and determine at a glance which recipes will work for you, depending on how much time you have to spend in the kitchen and what your dietary needs are, I've created several icons, explained below.

Recipe Categories

 quick & easy

Quick & Easy: These recipes will be ready in no time at all, usually in 15 minutes* or less.

 under 30

Ready in Under 30: As the name implies, 30 minutes* is all you will need to get these tasty dishes on your table.

 time intensive

Time Intensive: You might want to save these recipes for the weekend or for special occasions, as they require either a somewhat lengthy cooking time or a commitment to spend a fair amount of active prepping time in the kitchen.

 plan ahead

Plan Ahead: These recipes may require steps such as marinating or chilling. Or they may call for subrecipes, such as mayonnaise, date paste, or stock, that will take extra time to prepare. You may need to start working on these recipes the previous day, or even several days in advance.

 make ahead

Make Ahead: These recipes can be made ahead of time and either cooked, baked, or reheated at the last minute.

 freezer friendly

Freezer Friendly: The name says it all. These recipes can easily be frozen and thawed to be enjoyed at a later time.

In calculating time, I counted only the making of the recipe at hand, not the time to make any subrecipes used in the main recipe.

Special Dietary Needs**

 squeaky clean

Squeaky Clean: These recipes are safe to eat during an elimination diet, such as the Whole30 program created by Melissa and Dallas Hartwig, or pretty much any other clean eating/detox challenge.

 keto friendly

Keto Friendly: These recipes are in line with a ketogenic diet, which is high in fat and low in carbohydrate. Nutritional ketosis varies from person to person; please work with your healthcare practitioner to determine what is best for you.

 nut-free

Nut-Free: These recipes don't contain any nuts or nut products.

 egg-free

Egg-Free: These recipes are entirely free of eggs.

*** All of the recipes in this book are dairy-free, so if you do not tolerate dairy, you may safely consume all of them.*

NUTRITIONAL INFORMATION

The Paleo movement isn't really in favor of counting calories, and I totally stand behind that. In fact, not counting calories anymore was one of the things that I found extremely liberating when I decided to fully embrace the lifestyle. The idea is that if you stick to eating real food, including good-quality animal protein, healthy fats, and nonstarchy vegetables, at each and every one of your meals, as well as listen to your body's satiety signals, there is absolutely no need to count calories.

Sometimes, though, I still feel the need to get a sense of what is going into my body, especially in terms of macronutrients. As such, I like to have a way to track that information. Also, I realize that for certain people, calorie and/or macronutrient counting is absolutely crucial, and they will go so far as to deny themselves the right to enjoy a certain dish if they don't have access to that information. I can very well understand this impulse; I used to be exactly like that.

With that in mind, and because I would hate for anyone to pass on any of my recipes strictly on that account, I chose to include the nutritional facts for the majority of the recipes in this book. If I didn't include them, it's because I couldn't calculate them with enough accuracy. Keep in mind, however, that although I made every effort to be as precise as possible, the nutritional information supplied in this book was calculated using a free online tool and as such cannot be regarded as scientifically accurate.

HOW THIS BOOK WAS MADE

Every single recipe in this book was developed and photographed by a real person, in a real home environment, in a very normal, functional kitchen, and photographed on the corner of a real dining room table.

It goes without saying that every single dish in this book was made using nothing but real food and was devoured by that same real person after it was done being pretty for the pictures. Sometimes, though, good friends and family members, including my dog, Shamba, did their part to help out with that final task....

Needless to say, the making of this book has been a real pleasant experience for all. Now I can only hope that you will have just as much fun recreating the recipes I've shared in this book in your very own kitchen!

GUIDE TO KITCHEN TOOLS

Let's face it: If you're going to adopt a healthy lifestyle, you're going to need to spend a chunk of time in the kitchen and cook your own meals from fresh ingredients. Truth be told, real food does not come in a box. There will be no popping frozen pizza in the oven or throwing TV dinners in the microwave. Pretty much everything that will go into your body, you'll have to create from scratch. And if you're going to do that, having the proper equipment will make your life a whole lot easier.

I'm not going to list every single tool and gadget that I have in my kitchen (that would probably take up an entire book!), but I want to share a list of those must-have tools that I feel I could never be without. These are all very handy pieces of equipment, and I believe that you should seriously consider equipping your own kitchen with them.

MY ABSOLUTE MUST-HAVES

Quality Knives and Cutting Board

This is where it all starts. You wouldn't be able to do much in a kitchen without a knife and a cutting board!

You don't need to invest in a full block of knives, though. In fact, you're better off buying fewer, better-quality blades. All you really, truly need is a sturdy 8-inch (20-cm) chef's knife and a trusty paring knife.

Keep in mind that a sharp blade is much safer to use than a dull blade, so you'll want to keep your knives nice and sharp. The best tools for the job are a whetstone and honing steel, but if you're like me and you aren't too confident in your knife honing skills, you'll be happy to know that there are several decent electric knife sharpeners available.

Also, know that nothing will ruin a blade faster than marble, stone, or glass, so stay away from cutting boards made from those materials. The best choice you can make to preserve your blades' edges is wood. Contrary to popular belief, wood does not harbor more bacteria than plastic, probably even less so, and truly is your knives' best companion. Oh, and one more thing: Don't be afraid to go big. Choose a board that gives you ample room to work.

Pots and Pans

If you're going to be cooking your food, you're not gonna get by without a good set of pots and pans. The following is a good starting point:

- ***8-inch and 10-inch (20-cm and 25-cm) nonstick skillets***

  Perfect for pan-frying eggs and omelettes, I wouldn't dream of being without my nonstick skillets. They can't handle much heat, though, so reserve them for more "delicate" dishes.

- ***12-inch (30.5-cm) stainless-steel skillet***

  For browning and searing large roasts and pieces of meat, nothing beats a large stainless-steel skillet. Look for one that has a helper handle; you will no doubt find it very handy, as these pans can be fairly heavy and hard to manipulate without one.

- ***10-inch (25-cm) cast-iron skillet***

  This one can handle some serious heat. A cast-iron skillet is perfect for cooking up a nicely crusted steak when the outdoor grill is retired for the cold season, or for any task where scorching heat is in order. In fact, I use mine for everything and anything "meat," so it gets used pretty much every day!

- ***Cast-iron grill pan***

  If you don't have a gas or charcoal grill, or if outdoor grilling isn't an option on the day you plan to make one of the grilled recipes in this book, a cast-iron grill pan is a good substitute.

- ***Small and medium saucepans (1½ to 3 quarts/1.4 to 2.8 L)***

  You're gonna use these. A lot. For pretty much everything.

- ***Large stockpot (8 quarts/7.5 L)***

  To make stocks, soups, and stews on the stovetop, a stockpot is an absolute must.

Mixing Bowls

Stainless-steel mixing bowls are my absolute favorites. Not only are they super stylish, but they're also unbreakable and will not harbor bacteria. Look for sets of five or six different sizes, and favor those that come with tight-fitting lids. They will soon become your best friends in the kitchen!

Bakeware

Bakeware isn't just for baking sweets and treats. Some of these you're going to use for meatloaf, roasted vegetables, casseroles, gratins, etc.

- *Ceramic baking dishes*—Get at least one square dish and one rectangular. The sizes I use are 9-inch (23-cm) square and 13 by 9 inches (33 by 23 cm).

- *Rimmed baking sheets*—18 by 13 inches (46 by 33 cm) is a good size.

- *Square/round cake pans*—Go with the 8- or 9-inch (20- or 23-cm) size.

- *Springform pan*—Go with the 8- or 9-inch (20- or 23-cm) size.

- *Muffin pan*—A standard 12-cup pan is a good one to get.

- *Loaf pan*—9 by 5 inches (23 by 12.75 cm) is a pretty standard size.

- *Deep-dish pie pan*—Go with the 8- or 9-inch (20- or 23-cm) size.

- *Wire cooling rack*

Measuring Spoons and Cups

You will need to measure ingredients while cooking. Invest in the following measuring devices:

- *Measuring spoons*—Usually come in sets of ¼ teaspoon, ½ teaspoon, 1 teaspoon, and 1 tablespoon.

- *Measuring cups (for dry ingredients)*— Usually come in sets of ¼ cup, ⅓ cup, ½ cup, and 1 cup.

- *Measuring cups (for liquid ingredients)*— Get the following sizes: 1 cup (240 ml), 2 cups (475 ml), and 4 cups/1 quart (950 ml).

Whisks, Spoons, and Spatulas

Essential for mixing, beating, whisking, scraping, flipping, spreading, and more. Get at least the following:

- *Flat whisk*—I use this whisk for little jobs, like whisking a couple of eggs for a single-serving omelette. Go for the 8-inch (20-cm) size.

- *Balloon whisk*—This whisk is for bigger jobs and for incorporating air into whatever you're whisking (without pulling out the stand mixer), such as when making larger omelettes or light batters. I own a 10-inch (25-cm) and a 12-inch (30.5-cm) balloon whisk, but the 10-inch (25-cm) size is the one I go to for most tasks.

- *Wooden spoon*

- *Slotted and serving spoons*

- *Rubber spatula*

- *Ladle*

- *Turner/spatula*

Parchment Paper

Though not technically a tool, parchment paper will no doubt become your best ally in the kitchen. It does not burn in the oven, and nothing sticks to it. Use it to line your baking dishes; not only will it prevent food from sticking, but it will make cleanup a breeze, too!

Colander and Sieve

Get a good-sized, standard colander to drain and rinse ingredients under cold running water. A fine-mesh sieve is good at catching smaller particles, so you'll want to use it to strain stocks, broths, and other concoctions that you want to be extra creamy and velvety.

Food Processor

This is the one kitchen "toy" that I could not be without. Though not mandatory, a food processor will make your life a lot easier when it comes to chopping, shredding, grating, and pureeing. Plus, it's the king when it comes to making nut butters.

Kitchen Scale

A kitchen scale can be had for such a small price nowadays; I think it is well worth the investment, especially if you're planning on doing some baking. Often, in baking recipes, quantities need to be extremely precise; otherwise, delicious experiments can easily turn into total disasters. The only way to ensure that you get it exactly right is to weigh your ingredients.

OTHER NICE-TO-HAVE KITCHEN GEAR

Blenders

To me, an immersion (stick) blender is an essential, if only for making mayonnaise and salad dressings. If you're a fan of these foods, too, you'll want to move this tool to the must-have list!

A high-speed blender is the ultimate kitchen toy! It can make velvety soups, silky sauces, creamy nut butters, and even frozen desserts, all at the touch of a button. You won't find a better tool for grinding coffee beans or coarse salt or for making your own flour from whole nuts.

Coffee Grinder

Ideal for grinding spices or nuts when making small amounts of flour.

Dutch Oven

The best tool for slowly roasting and braising meats to perfection, as well as for making delicious hearty stews. I use both the 3-quart (2-L) and the 4-quart (3.8-L) size.

Food Processor (Small)

Handy to have if you're going to process or puree small quantities of food.

Mandoline

If you want to make paper-thin slices, very thin julienne strips, or evenly sized matchsticks, this is the tool that you need. While I don't use my mandoline every day, I absolutely could not part with it.

Mason Jars

Useful for storing all sorts of foods, from mayo, salad dressings, and nut butters to dried fruit and spices.

Meat Mallet

Tenderize your meat or make it really thin by pounding it with one of these.

Melon Baller

Not just for making cute little melon balls or Parisian potatoes, this is by far the best, most convenient tool for quickly, easily, and cleanly coring apples and pears.

Microplane Zester

This sharp stainless-steel zester grates your favorite citrus quickly and effortlessly; it's also the perfect tool for grating nutmeg, garlic, and ginger.

Mixer (Hand Mixer or Stand Mixer)

Almost any batter will require the use of either a hand mixer or a stand mixer. Though more affordable, a hand mixer isn't as powerful and doesn't offer as many possibilities as its standing counterpart. Another great advantage of a stand mixer is that you don't need to hold it, so you can get busy doing other things while it does the work for you!

Mortar and Pestle

My tool of choice for grinding small amounts of whole spices, especially black peppercorns. It gets the job done much faster and more efficiently than any pepper mill out there!

Nut Milk Bag

Almost essential for making nut milk, a nut milk bag is also the best tool for squeezing liquid out of vegetables like cauliflower and spinach.

Offset Spatula

When it comes to putting icing on a cake, no other tool will serve you better than this one.

Pastry Bag with Decorating Tips

For much more than decorating cakes, a pastry bag with tips is a super neat tool to have if you want to, say, deliver mousse cleanly and prettily into a small vessel, or make your shepherd's pie super fancy by making the top all decorative and swirly. It's very handy if you're going to make your own chocolate chips, too! You may not use this tool every day, but once it's a part of your arsenal, you'll wonder how you ever lived without it.

I recommend that you get a decent-sized plastic-coated bag (12 inches/30.5 cm is a good size to start with), as well as a few different sizes of round and star tips. I prefer the larger tips that go inside the bag and don't require the use of a coupler.

Potato Masher

Not just for potatoes! This tool works great with cauliflower, squash, and even egg salad.

Rolling Pin

If you're going to bake pies, then you're going to need one of these. I always use a straight French rolling pin, which is basically a long wooden dowel without handles. I find that it gives me a much better feel for the dough and yields more even results.

Slow Cooker

Perfect for those times when you can't be there to attend to your meals, or for making dishes that require long, slow cooking (bone broth comes to mind).

Spiral Slicer

Make long noodlelike strands out of all kinds of vegetables, such as zucchini, carrots, turnips, cucumbers, parsnips, and butternut squash.

Spring-Loaded Ice Cream Scoop

So helpful when it comes to shaping perfect, evenly sized meatballs or scooping evenly sized portions of cookie dough. I mainly use two sizes: a small 1¼-inch (3.25-cm) scoop (about 1½-tablespoon capacity) for small meatballs and cookies, and a larger 2-inch (5-cm) scoop (about 3-tablespoon capacity) for larger meatballs, muffins, and cupcakes.

Steamer Basket

A must if you're going to steam vegetables, which I bet you will; a steamer basket is well worth the investment.

Tongs

Unless you have bionic fingers and feel comfortable flipping steaks with your bare hands, or you don't mind poking holes in them with a fork and losing all those precious juices, you will want a set of tongs. They are indispensable for flipping anything that's cooking in a pan, especially meat and vegetables.

Vegetable Peeler

You simply can't be without one of these. Just as with knives, it's worth investing in a good-quality vegetable peeler. Skip the dollar-store junk and get a peeler that will give you years of easy peeling satisfaction.

GUIDE TO COMMONLY USED INGREDIENTS

I believe that real food and quality ingredients are the foundation of healthy eating. As such, I always use the best ingredients I can afford or get my hands on in my recipes.

ANIMAL PROTEIN

Meat and Seafood

Though I didn't feel the need to mention it in every single recipe, the animal protein that I used to make the recipes in this book was the best I could get—organic, grass-fed, pastured-raised, or wild-caught. I trust that you will do the same: Always buy the best meat and seafood that you can afford.

Eggs

I purchase my eggs directly from a local farm, and as such, they tend to vary greatly in size. However, when creating the recipes for this book, I made a conscious effort to select eggs that were as close as possible in size to a standard large egg, which weighs 2 ounces (56 g).

SWEETENERS

Maple Syrup

Québec being the world's largest producer of maple syrup, it's only natural that maple syrup is my top choice when it comes to selecting a sweetener. It's easy for me to get my hands on high-quality, locally produced, organic maple syrup at an affordable price. I always use Canadian grade Medium, which is the equivalent of what is now labeled grade A "dark" or "very dark" in the United States, replacing the old U.S. grade B. Not only is this grade much more flavorful, but it also has more nutrients and minerals than the lighter grades of maple syrup.

Honey

Honey is another sweetener that is largely produced here in Québec, but it's widely available in many other parts of the world. Stick to raw, unpasteurized honey in order to fully benefit from all the nutrients it offers. Indeed, in its raw state, honey is a powerful antibacterial and contains a fair amount of vitamins, namely B2, B3, B5, and C.

Date Paste

Using homemade date paste is a convenient, delicious way to sweeten just about anything naturally. Not only that, but date paste is one of the healthiest sweeteners, too. Dates are rich in dietary fiber, are an excellent source of iron and potassium, and are packed with an impressive list of essential nutrients, vitamins, and minerals, such as calcium, manganese, and copper.

Date paste can be used in just about any baked good. It helps keep baked goods moist and imparts a rich, deep flavor to cakes and cookies.

Although ready-made date paste can be purchased in some specialty stores, it can be hard to find and is somewhat pricey. However, date paste is extremely easy and cheap to make at home; see my recipe on page 82.

Coconut Sugar

Coconut sugar (also known as coconut palm sugar) is a rich granulated sugar with a brown color and a deep caramel flavor. It is produced by tapping the sweet nectar from the coconut palm tree flower and drying the sap in large open kettle drums.

Although I prefer using less processed sweeteners such as date paste, raw honey, and pure maple syrup, coconut sugar is my number-one option whenever the use of a dry or granulated sugar is crucial to the success of a recipe.

SPICES AND SEASONINGS

Cinnamon

Milder, sweeter, and more complex in flavor than the more common cassia variety, Ceylon is the only true cinnamon for me. As a great antioxidant and a source of many vitamins and minerals, Ceylon is said to be superior to cassia from a nutritional standpoint. It's also said that using cinnamon daily will aid greatly in lowering your blood sugar. So go ahead, sprinkle it liberally!

In the United States and many other countries, cassia cinnamon is sold simply as "cinnamon." Read labels closely to determine whether the cinnamon you are considering buying is Ceylon.

Nutmeg

I remember hating the taste of nutmeg. I simply could not stand it…until one day I got to taste the real thing! Freshly grated nutmeg tastes so much better than the preground stuff; there is simply no comparison.

Now I absolutely adore the sweet spice, but I buy it whole and grate it as needed. It's a bit harder to measure with precision, but you'll quickly get the hang of it and know exactly how much you need to add and when you need to stop grating. Besides, nutmeg is one of those spices that people seem to add more or less of, depending on their own personal taste.

Himalayan Salt

Himalayan salt is an unrefined, unprocessed natural salt that is hand-mined from abundant salt caves formed millions of years ago around the earth. It is the only salt that contains the full spectrum of 84 minerals and trace elements, just like Mother Nature intended.

With the exception of a pinch of fleur de sel here and there for garnish, fine-ground Himalayan salt is the only salt that I use and call for throughout this book. If you can't get your hands on it, fine-ground Celtic sea salt is an excellent alternative.

Bird's-Eye Chili Peppers

Bird's-eye chili peppers are fairly hot, tiny red peppers commonly found in Asian food markets. They are usually available either fresh or dried. If you can't get your hands on them, you can easily substitute any other hot chili pepper, fresh or dried, or even leave them out entirely if heat is not your thing.

Vanilla

I love working with fresh vanilla beans. To me, nothing even comes close to matching the flavor of the real thing. Vanilla adds so much depth to the flavor of almost any dessert—and can add a surprisingly distinctive touch to many savory dishes, too! Plus, I adore the tiny little black specks you see in foods made with vanilla beans. Purchased individually, the pods tend to cost an arm and a leg. Luckily, there are many online sources, such as eBay and Amazon, where you can buy them in bulk for a much more affordable price. Vanilla beans keep for a very long time provided that you store them in an airtight container, so you need not fear that they will go bad on you.

Since vanilla can be a tad costly even in bulk, I like to make the most of every pod.

For starters, I use pods to make my own vanilla extract (page 84).

I also like to use vanilla powder in my cooking, and quasi-exclusively when making nut butters. You can purchase vanilla powder, but it's rather pricey. I strongly suggest that you make your own instead; it's incredibly easy to do, and such a great way to make use of seeded vanilla bean pods!

To make vanilla powder:

Whenever you use fresh vanilla seeds in a recipe, hold on to the empty pod and place it in a brown paper bag to dry out. When you have collected a dozen or so empty pods, and they are fully dried and brittle, break them into little pieces, throw them in a coffee or spice grinder along with two or three whole vanilla beans, and whizz the whole lot into a fine powder. Transfer that powder to a small airtight container and store it in the pantry, where it will keep indefinitely.

BAKING INGREDIENTS

Almond Flour

Almond flour is extremely versatile and can be used in almost any baked good, just like you would use wheat flour. It has a subtle flavor that blends well in both sweet and savory baked goods.

You can save tons of money by making your own almond flour at home. Simply buy whole or sliced blanched almonds in bulk (the sliced variety works especially well for this purpose) and grind them in a food processor, a high-speed blender, or even a coffee grinder, then sift the flour to remove the larger pieces. Process a small amount at a time so that the nuts have plenty of room to fly around, and be careful not to grind them for too long, or you'll end up making nut butter!

Note that you can make flour with just about any kind of nut, so long as the nuts are free of skin. Next to almonds, the most popular nut for making flour is the hazelnut. Store nut flour in an airtight container in a cool, dry place, or in the refrigerator, for up to a few months.

Tapioca Starch

This high-carb flour is made from the starch that is extracted from the cassava plant. It acts as a binding agent in gluten-free baked goods and helps make cakes, breads, and other baked treats much lighter and fluffier. It's also an awesome thickener for stews and sauces.

If you can't find tapioca starch, you can use arrowroot powder instead. The two are completely interchangeable and play the exact same role in both cooking and baking. I tend to favor tapioca over arrowroot simply because it's easier to source in my part of the world, and it's a tad less expensive, too.

Coconut Flour

High in fiber, manganese, and protein, this low-carb flour is obtained by grinding dried, defatted coconut meat. As such, it does have a light coconut flavor, but that flavor blends harmoniously in most sweet and savory baked goods. Coconut flour does not perform like regular flour, though, in the sense that it is extremely absorbent, so you use a lot less to get similar results. Still, it's an excellent choice for baking, and one that I use often. It also makes a great filler in meatloaf, meatballs, and hamburger patties.

Cacao Butter

Cacao butter is the fat that is extracted from cacao beans. It provides a healthy dose of omega-6 and omega-9 fatty acids and contains natural antioxidants as well as many nutrients that support mood and the immune system. It also contains oleic acid and theobromine—the potent alkaloid that makes chocolate unique.

Though cacao butter is more commonly used in the making of chocolates, baked goods, and other sweet treats (I use it in my White Chocolate Macadamia Nut Butter on page 330), it would, theoretically, make a very good cooking fat for savory dishes, as it happens to be very heat stable. It does, however, have a mild, creamy, and almost sweet flavor that may not pair so well with certain foods. Though I imagine it might work fantastically well with sautéed apples, it may not be the best choice for pan-frying a piece of salmon.

Raw Cacao Powder

There are many different kinds of cacao powder out there, so be especially careful when making your selection. Some products are highly processed, rendering them extremely bitter, and some contain unwanted additives and even sugar. For best results and for optimal health, always opt for raw cacao powder, which is made by grinding raw cacao beans at a low temperature to turn them into a very fine powder. Raw cacao powder is a powerful antioxidant, and it contains a fair amount of iron and magnesium. Plus, cacao is known to make you feel good, so don't be afraid to use it liberally!

Cacao Paste/Liquor

Cacao paste, also referred to as cacao liquor, is nothing more than chocolate in its purest form, without anything else added to it. It can be used just like regular dark chocolate, except that you need to make up for the lack of sweetness somehow.

Since I've yet to find a brand of dark chocolate that doesn't contain any form of refined sugar, I always use cacao paste in my recipes and adjust the sweetness by adding raw honey or pure maple syrup. I even make my own honey-sweetened chocolate chips; the recipe is on page 80.

Coconut Milk

Anytime you see coconut milk mentioned in this book, assume that I am referring to the delicious, super thick and creamy full-fat stuff that comes in a can or carton.

Pay extra close attention when purchasing coconut milk, as the vast majority of products contain an impressive list of unwanted additives and preservatives. Look for a label that lists nothing but coconut meat and water as ingredients. A good ratio is 70 percent coconut to 30 percent water.

Note that coconut milk will separate after a while, so make sure to give the can or carton a good shake before you open it.

HEALTHY COOKING FATS

Ghee

Ghee is my favorite cooking fat. Not only does it have a fantastic, rich, buttery flavor, but it's also abundant in medium-chain fatty acids, which are absorbed directly into the liver and burned as energy. Although it is made from butter, all traces of milk solids (casein and lactose) have been stripped from it, leaving behind nothing but the fat. As a result, ghee becomes highly digestible even by those who are dairy intolerant; as such, it is not regarded as a dairy

product by the Paleo community, but as a valuable source of healthy fat. Furthermore, it has a very high smoke point, which means that it can handle serious heat, and it is shelf stable, so there's no need to refrigerate it; it will keep in the pantry for up to several months.

I've included the names of a few recommended brands at the end of this book (see page 373), but you can make your own ghee at home if you prefer. You can find detailed instructions and step-by-step photos on my blog, *The Healthy Foodie*, in the DIY subject category under "Paleo Recipes" (or go to thehealthyfoodie.com/homemade-ghee/).

Oh, and know that butter and ghee are completely interchangeable, so don't hesitate to replace butter with ghee in recipes that you find in books or online.

Coconut Oil

Rich in medium-chain fatty acids, coconut oil is another excellent choice to use as a cooking fat. It will not only boost the nutritional value of your dishes, but also pass on its rich yet subtle coconut flavor. You'd be surprised at how good a steak pan-fried in coconut oil tastes. Just like ghee, coconut oil has a very high smoke point and can be stored at room temperature. Note that coconut oil melts at about 76°F (25°C). Below this temperature, it's solid, white, and opaque; any warmer than that, and it'll turn into a crystal-clear liquid.

Lard or Tallow

Lard or tallow is obtained by slowly rendering pork or beef fat, respectively. When I purchase meat by the whole animal, I always ask the farmer to give me every edible part, including the fat, so I can render my own, but it's often possible to buy lard or tallow from your butcher or local farmer. Rendering your own lard is fairly easy; if you want to give it a try, you can find detailed instructions and step-by-step photos on my blog, *The Healthy Foodie*, in the DIY category under "Paleo Recipes" (or go to thehealthyfoodie.com/how-to-render-your-own-lard/).

When it comes to fat, it's especially important to consume only the fat of grass-fed or pastured-raised animals that were fed a healthy diet free of grains, growth hormones, and antibiotics.

OTHER INGREDIENTS

Coconut Butter

I used to spend a fortune on ready-made coconut butter, until I realized just how easy it is to make it at home, and for a fraction of the price. Now I use homemade coconut butter exclusively (I show you how to make it on pages 296 to 298), but if you'd rather not go to the trouble and opt for the ready-made stuff, Artisana and Nutiva are two very good brands. There are other great products out there, but as always, make sure to read the labels carefully and choose one that is free of added preservatives, especially sulfites, and preferably is organic.

Coconut butter is also referred to as coconut manna, so look for it under that name, too.

Dried Fruits and Shredded/Flaked Coconut

This is one area where I *always* buy organic and inspect labels very carefully. Most manufacturers sneak in all kinds of additives, preservatives, highly processed oils, and even sugar. Read the labels before purchasing, and make sure that the products you buy list just one ingredient.

Mustards, Vinegars, Hot Sauces, and Other Condiments

You would be surprised by the unwanted ingredients that can hide in commonly used basics like vinegar and Dijon mustard. Read the labels very carefully when purchasing. Watch for added sugar, caramel, high fructose corn syrup, MSG, sulfites, carrageenan, soy, wheat, artificial flavoring, colorant, and other nasty ingredients with names you can't pronounce.

If, like me, you prefer to know exactly what goes into your food, you can always make your own condiments. It really isn't that complicated, you'll see! In the Basics chapter of this book, you'll find an array of easy recipes to get you started, such as salad dressings (pages 54 to 63), barbecue sauce (page 68), and my famous Foolproof Mayonnaise (page 64).

Unseasoned Rice Vinegar

Although rice vinegar is typically made from grain, the fermentation process is said to destroy all the antinutrients that it contains and, as such, eliminates the reason to avoid consuming it in the first place. In fact, fermented foods have been shown to possess many health benefits, and vinegar is no exception, be it rice vinegar or any other kind.

When purchasing rice vinegar, make sure to get the unseasoned variety, and read labels carefully to avoid added sugar, sulfites, and other preservatives.

White Balsamic Vinegar

White balsamic vinegar is a blend of white grape must and white wine vinegar that is cooked at a low temperature to prevent darkening. The flavor is very similar to that of regular balsamic vinegar, although the dark variety tends to be slightly sweeter and a tad more syrupy.

My reason for choosing white balsamic over its dark counterpart is mostly aesthetic: When added to lighter-colored foods, sauces, or dressings, white balsamic vinegar does not cause any unappealing discoloration.

White balsamic vinegar can be a little harder to find than the regular variety. Look for it in the gourmet section of your grocery store or in specialty gourmet food stores.

CHAPTER 1

basics

quick & easy
 keto friendly
 make ahead
 egg-free
 squeaky clean
 nut-free

SPICE AND HERB MIXES

Instructions for all blends

Place all the ingredients in a mixing bowl and mix until very well combined. Store in an airtight container away from direct light for up to 6 months.

Montreal Steak Spice

Makes ¾ cup (90 g)

Despite the name, this spice blend goes well with just about anything. Add some to soups, stews, and sauces, or sprinkle it over grilled vegetables, chicken, pork chops, or sautéed shrimp. Sometimes I even like to add a dash or two to mayonnaise and salad dressings.

- 2 tablespoons paprika
- 2 tablespoons coarsely ground black peppercorns
- 2 tablespoons Himalayan salt
- 1 tablespoon garlic powder
- 1 tablespoon granulated onion
- 1 tablespoon coarsely ground coriander seeds
- 1 tablespoon coarsely ground dill seeds
- 1 tablespoon red pepper flakes
- 1 tablespoon dried chives

Chili Moka Steak Rub

Makes a scant ½ cup (60 g)

This steak rub confers a deep, rich, and intricate flavor to grilled meats. Don't be afraid to use a generous amount and really take the time to massage it into the meat. For even better results, let the meat rest for at least an hour after it's been rubbed before throwing it on the grill.

- 2 tablespoons finely ground espresso or instant coffee powder
- 1 tablespoon cacao powder
- 1 tablespoon Himalayan salt
- 1 tablespoon freshly ground black pepper
- 1 teaspoon dry mustard
- 1 teaspoon ground Ceylon cinnamon
- ½ teaspoon ginger powder
- ½ teaspoon freshly ground nutmeg
- ½ teaspoon red pepper flakes
- ¼ teaspoon cayenne pepper
- ¼ teaspoon ground clove

Ras el Hanout

Makes ⅓ cup (40 g)

A classic of Moroccan and North African cuisine, this warm and pungent spice blend works fabulously well in stews and tagines but also makes a fantastic rub or marinade flavoring for fish, seafood, beef, lamb, or even chicken.

- 2 teaspoons ginger powder
- 2 teaspoons ground cardamom
- 2 teaspoons ground mace
- 1 teaspoon ground Ceylon cinnamon
- 1 teaspoon ground allspice
- 1 teaspoon ground coriander
- 1 teaspoon freshly grated nutmeg
- 1 teaspoon turmeric powder
- ½ teaspoon freshly ground black pepper
- ½ teaspoon ground white pepper
- ½ teaspoon cayenne pepper
- ½ teaspoon ground anise seeds
- ¼ teaspoon ground clove

Tex-Mex Seasoning

Makes ⅔ cup (80 g)

Turn any dish into a Mexican fiesta by adding a pinch or two of this hot and spicy seasoning. It works great in guacamole and salsas and is especially delicious with ground beef. Try adding some to your next batch of hamburgers or meatballs!

- 3 tablespoons ground chipotle pepper
- 2 tablespoons ground cumin
- 1 tablespoon paprika
- 1 tablespoon freshly ground black pepper
- 1 tablespoon Himalayan salt
- 1 tablespoon garlic powder
- 1 tablespoon onion powder
- 1½ teaspoons red pepper flakes

Chai Spice

Makes ⅔ cup (80 g)

Use in desserts, baked goods, nut milks, smoothies, tea, and coffee. Replaces cinnamon beautifully!

- 2 tablespoons ground Ceylon cinnamon
- 2 tablespoons ground cardamom
- 2 tablespoons ginger powder
- 2 tablespoons Chinese five-spice powder (see Notes, page 162)
- 1 whole nutmeg, grated
- 2 teaspoons ground coriander
- 1 teaspoon ground clove
- 1 teaspoon freshly ground black pepper
- 1 teaspoon vanilla powder

Herbes de Provence

Makes about ¾ cup (90 g)

This blend works great in salads or sprinkled over fish, seafood, and poultry. The lavender adds a nice touch of exoticism and freshness to dishes.

- ¼ cup dried oregano leaves
- ¼ cup dried thyme leaves
- ¼ cup dried savory
- 1 teaspoon dried basil
- 1 teaspoon dried rosemary leaves
- 1 teaspoon dried rubbed sage
- 1 teaspoon dried lavender

Italian Seasoning

- Use equal parts dried basil, thyme, oregano, marjoram, sage, and rosemary leaves.

Poultry Seasoning

- Use equal parts ground dried sage, thyme, and oregano.

make ahead

 egg-free

 squeaky clean

nut-free

 keto friendly

Makes about 4 cups (840 g)

- 1½ cups (90 g) finely chopped fresh parsley
- 1½ cups (340 g) finely chopped leek (1 medium)
- 1 cup (140 g) peeled and finely diced carrots (2 medium)
- 1 cup (100 g) finely chopped white onion (1 small)
- 1 cup (100 g) finely chopped celery (2 medium ribs)
- ½ cup (15 g) finely chopped fresh chives
- ¼ cup (8 g) finely chopped fresh tarragon
- ¼ cup (8 g) finely chopped fresh oregano
- 3 tablespoons finely chopped fresh thyme
- 2 tablespoons finely chopped fresh rosemary
- 1 tablespoon finely chopped fresh sage
- ¾ cup (210 g) Himalayan salt

SALTED HERBS

Salted herbs are very popular here in Québec, and I can't quite understand why they haven't hit the shelves of every store around the world. Once you get a taste, you won't know how you were able to live without them for so long. You won't believe the amount of flavor that these herbs pack under their hood. I guarantee that they will soon find their way into all your favorite dishes!

1. Place all the ingredients in a large mixing bowl and mix until very well combined, then gently pound the herbs with a pestle or large wooden spoon to bruise them a little bit and get some of the moisture out. You don't want to completely destroy them; you just want them to release a little bit of their water and flavor.

2. Transfer the herbs to an airtight container with a tight-fitting lid and refrigerate. Give them a good stir every day for the next 7 days, then store in the refrigerator in mason jars for up to 6 months.

NUTRITIONAL FACTS (per tablespoon)

Calories: 6   Total fat: 0.1 g   Total carbs: 1.2 g   Net carbs: 1.2 g   Protein: 0.2 g

make ahead
 egg-free
 squeaky clean
nut-free
 keto friendly

Makes 3 heads

- 3 large heads garlic
- Extra-virgin olive oil
- Himalayan salt and freshly ground black pepper

ROASTED GARLIC

Make a habit of keeping roasted garlic in your refrigerator. It'll keep for up to two weeks, and you can use it as desired to add tons of flavor to your favorite recipes. Simply squeeze out a couple of cloves and throw them right into your dish, or go all out and use the whole head—why not? Roasted garlic is good in mayonnaise, salads, vinai-grettes, and scrambled eggs and is particularly spectacular in Roasted Garlic Cauliflower Mash (page 278).

1. Preheat the oven to 400°F (205°C).

2. Remove most of the papery outer peel from the heads of garlic and trim about ¼ inch (6 mm) from the top of each head.

3. Set each head of garlic on a piece of aluminum foil that's large enough to wrap completely around it. Drizzle generously with olive oil (I use about 2 tablespoons per head), then sprinkle just as generously with salt and pepper.

4. Wrap each head of garlic individually in the foil and bake for 35 to 50 minutes, until the cloves are super soft, can very easily be pierced with the tip of a knife, and have turned an incredibly beautiful golden cara-mel color. Your home will be filled with the most intoxicating aroma you could possibly imagine.

5. Open up the foil packets and let the garlic cool slightly before using.

NUTRITIONAL FACTS
(based on 1 head of garlic prepared with 2 tablespoons of oil)

Calories: 73 · Total fat: 2.0 g · Total carbs: 13.0 g · Net carbs: 11.7 g · Protein: 2.4 g

quick & easy

 make ahead

 squeaky clean

 keto friendly

egg-free

 nut-free

Makes about 1 cup (240 ml)

- ½ cup (120 ml) extra-virgin olive oil
- ¼ cup (60 ml) balsamic vinegar
- 2 tablespoons fresh lemon juice
- 1 clove garlic, minced
- 1 teaspoon freshly ground black pepper
- 1 teaspoon finely chopped fresh thyme (see Notes)
- ½ teaspoon Himalayan salt

BASIC BALSAMIC VINAIGRETTE

This is one of those recipes that you should know by heart. In fact, I bet this will quickly become your go-to salad dressing and, after tasting it, you'll never feel the need to go for store-bought again.

1. Place all the ingredients in a glass jar with a tight-fitting lid and give it a vigorous shake. That's it, you're done! Your vinaigrette is ready to be drizzled over your favorite salad.

2. Keep any leftovers in an airtight glass container in the refrigerator for up to a few weeks. Shake vigorously before each use.

Notes: *The olive oil will solidify somewhat when refrigerated. To bring your vinaigrette back to a liquid state, you'll need to take it out of the fridge ahead of time. If you're in a pinch, you can place the jar in warm water for a couple of minutes or pop it in the microwave for a few seconds.*

If fresh thyme isn't available, feel free to use dried, or substitute any other fresh or dried herb you have on hand. Have fun playing with different flavors!

NUTRITIONAL FACTS (per tablespoon)

| Calories: 56 | Total fat: 6.3 g | Total carbs: 0.2 g | Net carbs: 0.2 g | Protein: 0.1 g |

quick
& easy

keto
friendly

make
ahead

egg-
free

squeaky
clean

nut-
free

Makes about 1 cup (240 ml)

- 2 cloves garlic, minced
- 2 tablespoons Dijon mustard
- Juice of 1 lemon or lime
- 2 tablespoons white balsamic vinegar
- 1 tablespoon finely chopped fresh thyme
- 1 tablespoon finely chopped fresh oregano
- ½ teaspoon Himalayan salt
- ½ teaspoon freshly ground black pepper
- ½ cup (120 ml) extra-virgin olive oil

CLASSIC DIJON HERB DRESSING

If you could have only one salad dressing for the rest of your life, this should definitely be the one. Bursting with flavor, it goes well with just about any salad, comes together in no time, and keeps in the fridge for a couple of weeks! Feel free to play around with the herbs, too. Try using fresh sage, savory, parsley, rosemary, or basil. And if fresh herbs aren't readily available at the time you make this dressing, you can always substitute the dried variety (using only one-third as much of the dried kind).

1. Place all the ingredients except for the olive oil in a medium mixing bowl and whisk until well combined.

2. Slowly add the olive oil in a steady stream while whisking constantly to create an emulsion.

3. Drizzle liberally over your favorite salad. Keep any leftover dressing in an airtight glass container in the refrigerator for up to 2 weeks.

NUTRITIONAL FACTS (per tablespoon)

Calories: 59　Total fat: 6.5 g　Total carbs: 0.7 g　Net carbs: 0.7 g　Protein: 0.2 g

quick & easy

 keto friendly

 make ahead

nut-free

 squeaky clean

Makes about 1 cup (240 ml)

- 1 large egg
- Juice of 1 lemon
- 3 cloves garlic, smashed with the side of a knife
- 3 or 4 anchovy fillets in olive oil, chopped
- 1 tablespoon Dijon mustard
- 1 tablespoon capers
- ½ teaspoon freshly ground black pepper
- ½ cup (120 ml) avocado oil or extra-light-tasting olive oil
- 1 tablespoon bacon drippings (optional)

Equipment needed:

Immersion blender

Tall, narrow glass jar barely wide enough to accommodate the head of your immersion blender (a 1-pint/475-ml wide-mouth mason jar works wonders, or you can use the container that came with your immersion blender)

CREAMY CAESAR DRESSING

Though the addition of bacon drippings isn't absolutely necessary, they add a lot of flavor and depth to this dressing. So go ahead and throw some of that tasty fat in there! Try this dressing with my Grilled Caesar Salad on page 126.

1. Place all the ingredients in a tall glass jar and let them sit for a few seconds, just long enough for the egg to settle comfortably at the bottom of the jar, underneath the oil.

2. Insert your immersion blender and push it all the way down until it makes contact with the bottom of the jar. Push the power button and do not move the blender for a full 20 seconds. This will cause the dressing to emulsify and become lusciously thick and creamy. After 20 seconds, start moving the blender around and up and down to make sure that every last bit gets well incorporated.

3. Drizzle liberally over your favorite Caesar salad.

4. This dressing will keep in an airtight glass container in the refrigerator for up to a week.

NUTRITIONAL FACTS (per tablespoon)

Calories: 76 | Total fat: 7.9 g | Total carbs: 0.5 g | Net carbs: 0.5 g | Protein: 1.3 g

quick & easy

egg-free

make ahead

nut-free

CREAMY HONEY DIJON DRESSING

Makes about 1 cup (240 ml)

Sweet, creamy, velvety smooth, and oh so tasty, this quick and easy dressing will turn any ordinary salad into a veritable delight. And you know what? It's also delicious served over grilled meat and makes a fabulous dipping sauce for shrimp. Hey, who says salad dressing is only good for dressing salads?

- 2 tablespoons Dijon mustard
- 2 tablespoons raw honey
- 2 tablespoons apple cider vinegar
- Juice of ½ lemon
- 2 cloves garlic, minced
- ½ teaspoon Himalayan salt
- ½ teaspoon freshly ground black pepper
- ¼ teaspoon freshly grated nutmeg
- ½ cup (120 ml) avocado oil or extra-light-tasting olive oil

1. Place all the ingredients except for the avocado oil in a medium mixing bowl and whisk vigorously until well combined.

2. Slowly add the avocado oil in a steady stream while whisking constantly to create an emulsion.

3. Pour generously over your favorite salad.

4. This dressing will keep in an airtight container in the refrigerator for up to 2 weeks.

NUTRITIONAL FACTS (per tablespoon)

Calories: 65　　Total fat: 6.4 g　　Total carbs: 2.5 g　　Net carbs: 2.5 g　　Protein: 0.1 g

quick & easy

 keto friendly

 make ahead

 egg-free

 squeaky clean

nut-free

Makes about 2 cups (475 ml)

CREAMY RANCH DRESSING

This creamy dressing came to life one day as I was trying to save a failed attempt at making hollandaise sauce. I had to make it a few times to perfect it, but boy, am I glad that hollandaise sauce didn't cooperate with me that day—this dressing is good stuff! I'm telling you, once you've tried this homemade version, you'll never buy store-bought ranch dressing again.

- 1 cup (240 ml) avocado oil or extra-light-tasting olive oil
- ¼ cup (60 ml) water
- 2 tablespoons fresh lemon juice
- 2 tablespoons white wine vinegar
- 2 tablespoons Dijon mustard
- 2 tablespoons sliced green olives
- 1 tablespoon olive brine (from the jar of olives)
- 1 tablespoon minced dehydrated onions
- 1 tablespoon dehydrated chives
- 2 cloves garlic
- 1 teaspoon fresh thyme leaves
- ½ teaspoon celery seeds
- ½ teaspoon red pepper flakes
- ¼ teaspoon Himalayan salt
- ¼ teaspoon freshly ground black pepper

1. Place all the ingredients in a tall glass jar.

2. Insert your immersion blender and push it all the way down until it makes contact with the bottom of the jar. Push the power button, slowly lift the blender, and move it around and up and down until the dressing is fully emulsified and turns a beautiful shade of creamy white.

3. Drizzle liberally over your favorite salad.

4. This dressing will keep in an airtight container in the refrigerator for up to a week.

Equipment needed:

Immersion blender

Tall, narrow glass jar barely wide enough to accommodate the head of your immersion blender (a 1-pint/475-ml wide-mouth mason jar works wonders, or you can use the container that came with your immersion blender)

Tip: Say you tried making homemade mayonnaise, but for some reason it refused to emulsify. The solution? Turn it into creamy ranch dressing instead! Simply add all the ingredients listed in this recipe, except for the oil and lemon juice, and follow the same instructions. While you may not end up with the unctuous mayonnaise that you were dreaming of, at least you won't have to throw anything out, and you'll get to console yourself with a deliciously creamy ranch dressing!

NUTRITIONAL FACTS (per tablespoon)

Calories: 63 | Total fat: 6.9 g | Total carbs: 0.4 g | Net carbs: 0.4 g | Protein: 0.1 g

quick & easy

 make ahead

 squeaky clean

 keto friendly

 nut-free

Makes about 1½ cups (300 g)

FOOLPROOF MAYONNAISE

I used to think that making mayo at home was nearly impossible. All the fuss with tempering the egg yolk, then drizzling in the oil super slowly while whisking at just the right speed to create the perfect emulsion…. I'd tried different methods but failed miserably each time, so I'd pretty much given up on the idea. That is, until I discovered the immersion blender method using the whole egg! With this technique, making mayo is so easy, you can almost do it with your eyes closed. Plus, the process is so cool to witness; I sometimes want to whip up a batch of mayo just for the sake of watching it go. I promise you that after giving this recipe a try, you'll never, ever buy store-bought mayo again.

- 1 large egg, taken straight out of the fridge
- Juice of ½ lemon
- 1 clove garlic
- 1 tablespoon Dijon mustard
- ¼ teaspoon Himalayan salt
- ¼ teaspoon freshly ground black pepper
- 1 cup (240 ml) avocado oil or extra-light-tasting olive oil (see Note)

Equipment needed:

Immersion blender

Tall, narrow glass jar barely wide enough to accommodate the head of your immersion blender (a 1-pint/475-ml wide-mouth mason jar works wonders, or you can use the container that came with your immersion blender)

1. Place all the ingredients, in the order listed, in a tall glass jar and let them sit for a few seconds, just long enough for the egg to settle comfortably at the bottom of the jar, underneath the oil.

2. Insert your immersion blender and push it all the way down until it makes contact with the bottom of the jar. Push the power button and do not move the blender for a full 20 seconds. Almost instantly, you'll see magic take place right before your eyes: The oil will begin to emulsify and turn into a lusciously creamy and thick concoction, slowly making its way to the top of the jar.

3. After 20 seconds, the transformation should be pretty much complete, so start moving your blender around and up and down to make sure that every last bit of oil gets well incorporated.

4. Store the mayo in an airtight container in the refrigerator for up to 2 weeks.

Tip: *Make this mayonnaise your own by adding herbs, spices, and aromatics to it. Don't be afraid to experiment!*

Note: *If using olive oil, it is imperative that you stick with the extra-light, mild-tasting variety. Never use extra-virgin olive oil; it tastes way too strong, and when emulsified, its flavor seems to intensify and becomes highly unpleasant.*

NUTRITIONAL FACTS (per tablespoon)

Calories: 76   Total fat: 8.7 g   Total carbs: 0.1 g   Net carbs: 0.1 g   Protein: 0.3 g

quick
& easy

 keto
friendly

 plan
ahead

nut-
free

make
ahead

Makes about 1 cup (200 g)

FIERY BUFFALO MAYO

If you're a fan of heat, then you will definitely fall in love with this zesty mayo. It will set your mouth on fire, all right, but not without simultaneously delivering an utter eruption of flavor to your taste buds! Try it as a condiment on your favorite meat, or use it instead of regular mayo in your next egg, tuna, or chicken salad to give it some kick.

- ½ cup (120 ml) Frank's RedHot Sauce
- ¼ cup (55 g) ghee
- 2 cloves garlic, minced
- ½ cup (100 g) Foolproof Mayonnaise (page 64)
- 2 tablespoons Dijon mustard
- ½ teaspoon cayenne pepper
- ½ teaspoon ground chipotle pepper

1. In a saucepan, bring the hot sauce, ghee, and garlic to a boil, then reduce the heat and simmer for about 5 minutes, whisking from time to time, until the sauce has thickened and reduced by almost half.

2. Kill the heat and let the sauce cool to room temperature, then refrigerate until completely chilled, at least 2 hours.

3. Place the chilled hot sauce mixture, mayo, mustard, cayenne pepper, and chipotle pepper in the bowl of a small food processor or blender and process until smooth and fully combined.

4. Store the mayo in an airtight container in the refrigerator for up to a week.

NUTRITIONAL FACTS (per tablespoon)

Calories: 72 | Total fat: 7.8 g | Total carbs: 0.6 g | Net carbs: 0.6 g | Protein: 0.3 g

plan ahead

egg-free

make ahead

nut-free

freezer friendly

Makes about 3 cups (710 ml)

HOT AND SPICY BBQ SAUCE

I'll admit, this sauce involves quite a few ingredients and requires a little more work than cracking open a jar of ready-made barbecue sauce. But I urge you not to let that scare you away from trying your hand at making BBQ sauce from scratch. I'm telling you, once you've had a taste of this, you'll want to lay it on thick over every single piece of meat you throw on your grill; you'll find yourself adding it to hamburgers, meatballs, and meatloaf for a quick flavor boost and even using it to give a whole lot of character to your favorite slow-cooked meat recipes.

- 1 medium onion, minced
- 2 cloves garlic, minced
- 1 (6-ounce/170-g) can tomato paste
- 1 (14-ounce/400-g) can crushed tomatoes
- ½ cup (125 g) unsweetened applesauce
- ¼ cup (75 g) Date Paste (page 82)
- ¼ cup (60 ml) balsamic vinegar
- ¼ cup (60 ml) apple cider vinegar
- 3 tablespoons Dijon mustard
- 2 tablespoons blackstrap molasses
- 1 teaspoon Himalayan salt
- 1 teaspoon freshly ground black pepper
- 1 teaspoon smoked paprika
- 1 teaspoon onion powder
- 1 teaspoon ground chipotle pepper
- 1 teaspoon red pepper flakes
- 1 teaspoon ground Ceylon cinnamon
- ½ teaspoon ground white pepper
- ½ teaspoon ginger powder
- ¼ teaspoon ground clove
- A few drops of all-natural liquid smoke

1. Place all the ingredients in a blender or food processor and process until completely reduced to a fine, liquidy puree.

2. Transfer the puree to a medium saucepan and bring to a boil. Lower the heat, partially cover, and simmer for 25 to 30 minutes, stirring from time to time, until the sauce is nice and thick and darker in color.

3. Kill the heat and let the sauce cool to room temperature, then refrigerate until completely chilled.

4. If you want a really smooth BBQ sauce, pass it through a fine-mesh sieve (you will have to help it through by swirling it around with a ladle); otherwise, just transfer it straight to an airtight container and refrigerate.

5. This BBQ sauce gets better after sitting in the fridge for a few days. It will keep for 2 to 3 weeks in the refrigerator or for up to a few months in the freezer.

NUTRITIONAL FACTS (per ¼ cup/60 ml serving)

Calories: 84 · Total Fat: 0.4 g · Total carbs: 14.4 g · Net carbs: 11.0 g · Protein: 8.8 g

quick & easy
 plan ahead
 make ahead
 squeaky clean
 keto friendly
 nut-free

Makes about 1½ cups (330 g)

TARTAR SAUCE

It's a well-known fact that tartar sauce goes superbly well with fish, but have you ever thought of trying it atop your favorite beef burger? How about as a substitute for tzatziki with pork or chicken souvlaki? And why not use it as a dipping sauce for crudités, or even as a salad dressing? These are all fantastic options, I swear!

- 1 cup (200 g) Foolproof Mayonnaise (page 64)
- 1 large dill pickle, finely chopped
- 2 tablespoons finely chopped preserved lemon rind (see Notes)
- 1 tablespoon finely chopped fresh dill
- 1 tablespoon Dijon mustard
- 1 tablespoon dried chives
- 1 teaspoon freshly ground black pepper

1. Place all the ingredients in a bowl and mix until well combined. If time permits, refrigerate the sauce for a couple of hours to allow the flavors to meld before serving.

2. Store the sauce in an airtight container in the refrigerator for up to a few days.

Note: Preserved lemon is a commonly used condiment in Indian and North African cuisine, on top of being a key ingredient in many Moroccan dishes. Lemons are pickled in a salty brine and then allowed to ferment at room temperature for weeks or months before being used. The pureed pulp makes a fantastic addition to stews and sauces, but it's the chopped rind that gets the most attention, with its slightly tart and explosive lemony flavor.

Preserved lemon can be a little hard to source in this hemisphere, however. Try your local ethnic food store, look online, or better yet, make your own super easily. You will find detailed instructions on my blog at thehealthyfoodie.com/make-preserved-lemons.

If you don't have preserved lemons on hand for this recipe, try using the grated zest of one lemon, or substitute a tablespoon of roughly chopped capers.

NUTRITIONAL FACTS (per ¼ cup/55 g serving)

Calories: 211 · Total fat: 23.3 g · Total carbs: 2.0 g · Net carbs: 1.3 g · Protein: 1.1 g

PORT WALNUT CRANBERRY SAUCE

Makes about 4 cups (1 kg)

Although cranberry sauce is a condiment that is typically served around the holidays, I believe it should find its way to our plates much more regularly. While I totally agree that its sweet and tangy flavor goes particularly well with turkey, it's also fabulous with lamb, pork, and even beef. Try it over a burger with caramelized onions and sautéed mushrooms…to die for!

- 2 (12-ounce/340-g) packages fresh cranberries
- Grated zest of 2 oranges
- Juice of 2 oranges
- 1 cup (240 ml) port wine (see Note)
- ½ cup (120 ml) pure maple syrup (dark color or Canadian Medium)
- ¼ cup (28 g) finely chopped raw walnuts
- 2 tablespoons finely chopped raw pistachios
- 1 tablespoon pure vanilla extract, homemade (page 84) or store-bought
- ¼ teaspoon Himalayan salt

1. Place the cranberries, orange zest, orange juice, port wine, and maple syrup in a medium saucepan and bring to a boil over medium-high heat.

2. Reduce the heat to a simmer, then add the walnuts, pistachios, vanilla extract, and salt. Continue cooking until most of the cranberries have popped, 5 to 7 minutes. You don't really need to stir it, but you probably won't be able to resist the urge to do so from time to time.

3. Turn off the heat and let the sauce cool to room temperature, then transfer it to the fridge to chill completely, at least 4 hours but preferably overnight. The sauce is much thicker and tastier when cold, and even more so after it's had a couple of days to mature.

4. Store the sauce in an airtight container in the refrigerator for up to a month.

Note: If you'd rather not use port wine, you can substitute unsweetened apple juice or pomegranate juice.

NUTRITIONAL FACTS (per ¼ cup/62 g serving)

Calories: 86   Total fat: 1.7 g   Total carbs: 15.5 g   Net carbs: 12.7 g   Protein: 1.1 g

time intensive

keto friendly

make ahead

egg-free

freezer friendly

nut-free

squeaky clean

Makes about 5 cups (1.2 L)

BROWN BONE BROTH

I like to roast bones before throwing them in the slow cooker, because this extra step adds so much flavor and color to the final product. That especially holds true if I'm planning on drinking the bone broth by itself, with a mere handful of finely chopped fresh herbs for garnish. If you're in a pinch or want a lighter-colored broth, you can skip the roasting step and add the bones directly to the slow cooker. Oh, and if you're a fan of lamb, feel free to swap those beef or pork bones for lamb bones!

- 3 pounds (1.4 kg) beef or pork marrow bones
- 2 large carrots, cut into big chunks
- 2 celery ribs, cut into big chunks
- 1 large onion, skin on, washed and quartered
- 4 cloves garlic, peel on, smashed with the side of a knife
- 1 teaspoon Himalayan salt, plus more for seasoning the bones
- 1 teaspoon freshly ground black pepper, plus more for seasoning the bones
- A few sprigs fresh thyme
- 2 tablespoons apple cider vinegar
- 10 cups (2.3 L) cold water

1. Preheat the oven to 475°F (245°C).

2. Lay the marrow bones on a rimmed baking sheet and sprinkle them generously on both sides with salt and pepper.

3. Switch the oven to broil and place the bones directly under the broiler for 5 to 7 minutes, until they turn golden and start to bubble. Flip them over and broil on the other side for 3 to 5 minutes, until golden.

4. Transfer the bones and rendered fat that has accumulated on the baking sheet to a 6.5-quart (6.2-L) slow cooker; add the rest of the ingredients and cook on low for 24 to 72 hours.

5. Pour the broth through a fine-mesh sieve into a large container and use as desired. Keep it in an airtight container in the refrigerator for up to 3 days or in the freezer for a few months.

Tip: The minimum recommended cooking time is 24 hours, but you can cook your broth for up to 72 hours if you want to. The longer you cook it, the more goodness you will extract from the bones.

time intensive · keto friendly · make ahead · egg-free · freezer friendly · nut-free · squeaky clean

BROWN CHICKEN STOCK

Never throw away another chicken carcass. Instead, turn those carcasses into a super tasty and nutritious brown stock!

Makes about 6 cups (1.4 L)

- 3 or 4 chicken carcasses, raw or previously cooked, trimmed of excess fat
- 3 large carrots, chopped or broken into 2 or 3 pieces
- 3 celery ribs, chopped or broken into 2 or 3 pieces (don't bother removing the leaves)
- 2 medium onions, skin on, washed and cut into 4 to 8 pieces
- 4 cloves garlic, peel on, smashed with the side of a knife
- 3 sprigs fresh thyme
- 1 tablespoon Italian Seasoning (page 49)
- 1 teaspoon Himalayan salt
- 1 teaspoon freshly ground black pepper
- 1 teaspoon coriander seeds
- 2 or 3 bay leaves
- 1 star anise
- 4 quarts/16 cups (3.8 L) cold water

1. Preheat the oven to 475°F (245°C).

2. Place the chicken carcasses in a broiler pan and roast for about 30 minutes, turning them a few times, until golden brown on all sides.

3. Transfer the bones to a large stockpot, add the rest of the ingredients, and slowly bring to a boil over medium-high heat. Reduce the heat, partially cover, and simmer for about 4 hours, until the stock is reduced by about half and deliciously fragrant.

4. Remove from the heat and let cool slightly, then strain the stock through a fine-mesh sieve into a bowl. Press down on the veggies and bones so you get every last bit of liquid out of them, then discard them.

5. Use the stock immediately or cover and refrigerate for up to 3 days. You can also freeze the stock for up to 3 months.

Tip: *Refrigerate your stock overnight so it gets gelatinous, remove the fat if you prefer a lighter stock, and then ladle it straight into resealable plastic bags. Lay the bags flat on a baking sheet and place the whole rig in the freezer. Once the stock is frozen solid, it takes up very little storage space and is super easy to use.*

time intensive

 freezer friendly

 make ahead

 squeaky clean

Makes 4 crusts

PALEO PIE CRUST

Every time I make this pie dough, I think to myself: NEVER AGAIN! Mind you, working with pie dough has always been one of my biggest pet peeves in the kitchen. I have no patience for it. And this Paleo version is particularly testing. I'm not gonna lie to you; it's not what I would call a pleasant experience. Without the presence of gluten to hold it together, the pastry will crack and break on you, forcing you to do lots of reconstruction work after you flip it into the pie dish. It'll probably have you cursing through your teeth, too! But honestly, it's soooo good and light, so flaky and buttery, and so unbelievably true to the real thing that even I can't help but come back to this recipe every time I make pie. Then I think to myself once more: NEVER AGAIN...until the next time!

- 2 cups (230 g) almond flour, sifted
- 2 cups (240 g) coconut flour, sifted
- 1 cup (115 g) tapioca starch
- 1 teaspoon Himalayan salt
- 1 cup (224 g) lard, frozen and grated
- 1 cup (220 g) ghee, frozen and grated
- ½ cup (120 ml) ice-cold water, plus more if needed
- 2 teaspoons apple cider vinegar
- 2 large eggs

For the egg / milk wash (optional)
- 1 large egg, beaten, or 2 to 3 tablespoons full-fat coconut milk, or a mixture of both

1. In a large bowl, whisk together the flours, tapioca starch, and salt. Add the grated lard and ghee and, using your fingers, gently mix and rub the fat in until the mixture resembles fine crumbs with a few larger pieces.

2. In a measuring cup, whisk together the cold water, vinegar, and eggs. Pour over the dry ingredients, stirring briskly with your fingers until some kind of a ragged dough starts to form. If you find that your dough is too crumbly, add a little more ice-cold water, 1 or 2 tablespoons at a time, until it sticks together when you press it in the palm of your hand.

3. Turn the dough onto a work surface and gently press it into a ball. Cut into 4 wedges and, being careful not to overwork the dough, form each wedge into a disc. Wrap each disc in plastic wrap and refrigerate until chilled, about 30 minutes. (You can safely refrigerate the dough for up to 3 days if you like.)

4. At least 30 minutes prior to rolling out the dough, take it out of the fridge to give it a chance to get back to room temperature. This will help it roll better and not crack so much.

5. To roll out the dough, remove the plastic wrap from a dough disc and place it between 2 sheets of parchment paper. Roll out the dough, taking care to flip it over from time to time as you work. If the dough starts to adhere to the paper and not expand all that well, peel off the paper, scrape it clean with a plastic scraper, and then place the paper back over the dough.

6. When the disc is large enough to fit into your pie dish, slide it with the parchment paper onto a pizza plate or other plate that's at least 12 inches (30 cm) in diameter. Peel off the top sheet and place the pie dish over the dough. Flip the whole thing upside down so that the dough falls into the pie pan. Peel off the remaining sheet of parchment paper, reposition the dough, if necessary, and fix the inevitable cracks and breakage. Yes, I did say "inevitable." There will be some of that. Maybe even LOTS of that. But don't worry; it's fairly easy to fix.

7. Preheat the oven to 375°F (190°C).

NUTRITIONAL FACTS (per crust)

Calories: 1,709 · Total fat: 141.3 g · Total carbs: 81.9 g · Net carbs: 51.6 g · Protein: 26.8 g

8. If blind-baking the crust prior to adding a filling that does not require cooking, prick the crust with a fork to prevent it from puffing up, then bake for 20 minutes or until golden.

9. If baking a filled pie, pour the desired filling into the crust. If you want to add a top crust, roll out another dough disc as described opposite, then remove the top sheet of parchment paper, slide your hand underneath the dough, and flip the rolled-out dough onto the pie filling with the bottom sheet of parchment paper still attached to it. Once the dough is correctly positioned, peel off the parchment. Trim off any excess dough, then seal by crimping the edges together with your fingers. For better adherence, brush the edge of the bottom crust with an egg/milk wash before adding the top layer.

10. Cut little vents in the top crust with the tip of a sharp knife. If you wish to give your crust a nice shiny look, brush the egg/milk wash all over the top crust. Bake the filled pie for 25 to 30 minutes, until golden brown.

Tip: *In its raw state, this pie dough will keep in the refrigerator for up to 3 days and in the freezer for up to several months. You can freeze individually wrapped discs of dough or roll out a portion of dough and place it in a pie dish, then wrap it well in plastic wrap. Thaw completely before using.*

time intensive

egg-free

make ahead

nut-free

freezer friendly

Makes about 1 cup (168 g)

EXTRA DARK CHOCOLATE CHIPS

Good-quality chocolate chips are fairly hard to find, especially when you're looking for dark chocolate that's entirely free of refined sugar. Solve the problem and make your own, why don't you? It's not that complicated, and there's something extremely rewarding about making those cute little chocolate hats yourself. You'll probably find yourself staring at them for a wee while thinking that they're so darn cute, and that you won't ever be able to eat them…but that won't last long, trust me! Soon you'll have one, and that'll be the end of it!

- 4½ ounces (128 g) cacao paste, finely chopped
- 2 tablespoons raw honey, melted
- Pinch of Himalayan salt

1. Melt the cacao paste in the microwave: Because chocolate is extremely fragile, you need to be extra careful with this step. Make sure that your chocolate is chopped very finely and evenly; the finer it is, the quicker it will melt. Place it in a microwave-safe bowl, then microwave it on high, checking on it and stirring very well (for a good 10 to 15 seconds) every 30 seconds or so, until it's completely melted. Chocolate will fully melt long before it gets truly hot, so check it often and STIR! This is very important; you do not want to burn your chocolate, and that can happen very quickly in the microwave.

2. When the chocolate is fully melted, add the honey and salt and stir gently until smooth.

3. Let the chocolate cool down for 15 to 20 minutes, until it has the consistency of soft buttercream, then transfer it to a pastry bag equipped with a ³⁄₁₆-inch (5-mm) round tip. Pipe little dollops of chocolate onto a piece of parchment paper; you might want to place the parchment paper on a baking sheet for easier transport.

4. Place the chocolate chips in the fridge to set for about an hour. Once they're completely set, store them in an airtight container in a cool, dry place, where they will keep for up to several months, or use them immediately in any recipe that calls for good-quality bittersweet, dark, or 70-percent-cacao chocolate chips.

Variation: Extra Dark Chocolate Chunks

To make chocolate chunks instead of chips, pour the melted chocolate with the honey and salt mixed in onto a rimmed baking sheet lined with parchment paper and spread it to a thickness of about ¼ inch (6 mm). Place in the fridge to chill for about 30 minutes. When set, chop coarsely into small chunks, and use them just as you would chocolate chips.

NUTRITIONAL FACTS (per batch)

Calories: 931 · Total fat: 67.0 g · Total carbs: 65.9 g · Net carbs: 48 g · Protein: 18.0 g

plan ahead · egg-free

make ahead · nut-free

Makes about 2 cups (600 g)

- 1 pound (455 g) pitted dates
- ¾ cup (180 ml) water
- 1 teaspoon pure vanilla extract, homemade (page 84) or store-bought
- ¼ teaspoon Himalayan salt

DATE PASTE

All you need to make this little marvel of a natural sweetener is a bunch of pitted dates, some water, and a good food processor. So easy to make and delicious to eat, it's by far my favorite sweetener for making all kinds of baked goods and other sweet treats.

1. Pack the pitted dates really tightly in a 1-pint (475-ml) mason jar.

2. Pour the water over the dates, cover, and let soak overnight. If you have too much water, don't worry about it; just add as much as will fit in the jar. Alternatively, you could cover the jar loosely with a nonreactive lid and pop it in the microwave for about 2 minutes. You don't want to cook the dates; you just want to soften them up a little.

3. After the dates have soaked or have been softened in the microwave, transfer the entire contents of the jar, including the water, to the bowl of a food processor. Add the vanilla extract and salt and process for 5 to 8 minutes or until really smooth and creamy.

4. Transfer the date paste back to the jar and keep it in the refrigerator for up to 3 months.

NUTRITIONAL FACTS (per ¼ cup/75 g serving)

Calories: 159 · Total fat: 0.2 g · Total carbs: 42.2 g · Net carbs: 37.7 g · Protein: 1.4 g

time intensive

egg-free

make ahead

nut-free

keto friendly

Makes about 1 cup (240 ml)

- 8 vanilla beans (or more, if you like)
- 1 cup (240 ml) good-quality vodka, preferably nongrain, such as potato

VANILLA EXTRACT

Because it's so hard to find a store-bought vanilla extract that's really pure and doesn't contain any and all kinds of sugar, caramel, artificial coloring and/or flavoring, and/or other ingredients whose names I can't pronounce, I decided to make my own at home. And I've never looked back. The key to making good vanilla extract is to use lots of fresh vanilla beans and to give it plenty of time to age.

1. Cut the vanilla beans to the length of your jar(s) or bottle(s) and slice them lengthwise, not quite all the way to the end. You want to expose the seeds but keep the ends attached.

2. Place the beans in the jar and cover them completely with vodka. Put the lid on and shake gently.

3. Put away in a cool, dark place (such as a cupboard) and give the jar a couple of gentle shakes every day for about a week or so. You can leave the jar on the counter if it helps you remember to shake it.

4. After a week, you can start shaking less often, like once or twice a week, for about a month. Your vanilla extract will be ready to use after 6 to 8 weeks, but for full flavor, let it sit for at least 3 months before you use it. Just make sure to give it a little shake once in a while.

5. When your bottle of vanilla extract is down about 25 percent, you can top off the bottle with fresh vodka without affecting the flavor all that much. Ideally, though, you'll want to let your vanilla sit again for a couple of weeks. For that reason, I prefer to have two bottles going simultaneously; when I top one off, I can use the other one until it too needs to be topped off, at which point I switch back to the first one. This allows your vanilla to develop to its full potential without you ever having to hang dry! Of course, you can't just top off forever…or else you'll end up with vanilla-flavored vodka. When you find that your vanilla starts to become a little weak on vanilla flavor and a little strong on booze, it's time to start a new batch and let those old bottles go completely dry.

Note: Feel free to double or even triple this recipe; just make sure to keep this same ratio of at least 8 vanilla beans to 1 cup (240 ml) of alcohol. Use any less vanilla than that and you'll end up with vanilla-flavored vodka.

appetizers

make ahead
 keto friendly
 squeaky clean
 egg-free

Makes about 2 cups (400 g), 8 servings

BABA GHANOUJ

Fire-roasted eggplant is the key ingredient that gives this dish its distinct smoky flavor. To get the eggplants cooked just right, you need heat, and lots of it! A lot more than what you can get from your oven. In ancient times, eggplants were dropped directly into the fire to cook, so I think it's safe to say that the intense heat generated from an outdoor grill is in order here. Bonus points if you can get them roasting on an open flame!

- 2 large eggplants (about 1 pound/ 455 g each)
- ¼ cup (60 g) tahini
- 4 cloves garlic, finely chopped
- Juice of 1 lemon
- ½ teaspoon Himalayan salt
- ½ teaspoon freshly ground black pepper
- ½ cup (30 g) fresh parsley leaves, finely chopped

For garnish
- Handful of chopped fresh parsley
- 2 tablespoons raw pistachios, chopped
- 1 tablespoon extra-virgin olive oil

1. Preheat a grill to high heat.

2. Prick the eggplants with a fork in several places and place them directly on the grill. Cook for about 30 minutes, turning often, until the skin becomes crispy, charred, and loose and the eggplants look like deflated balloons.

3. Remove the eggplants from the heat and let them cool until they can be handled safely. Scoop the pulp into a fine-mesh sieve and let it drain for about 5 minutes.

4. Transfer the drained pulp to the bowl of your food processor. Add the tahini, garlic, lemon juice, salt, and pepper and process until smooth and creamy. Add the parsley and pulse a few times until just incorporated.

5. Transfer to a serving bowl and garnish with parsley and chopped pistachios, then drizzle with olive oil.

6. This dish will keep in the refrigerator for up to a few days.

NUTRITIONAL FACTS (per serving)

Calories: 104　　Total fat: 7.0 g　　Total carbs: 9.6 g　　Net carbs: 4.6 g　　Protein: 3.1 g

Makes 16 pieces

GRILLED PROSCIUTTO E MELONE

Dare to be different: Surprise your guests by serving them a unique twist on a firmly established classic! Instead of merely wrapping slices of melon in prosciutto and serving them as is, this recipe has you marinate the wrapped melon slices for a few hours and then briefly throw them on the grill. This marinating-grilling combo not only brings out the sweetness and creaminess in the melon, but also accentuates the saltiness and chewiness of the meat, creating an explosion of flavors and a contrast in textures that you won't soon forget.

For the marinade

- 2 tablespoons avocado oil
- 1 tablespoon balsamic vinegar
- 1 teaspoon Dijon mustard
- 1 clove garlic, minced
- 1 tablespoon fresh rosemary leaves, finely chopped
- 1 teaspoon fresh thyme leaves, finely chopped
- ½ teaspoon Himalayan salt
- ½ teaspoon freshly ground black pepper
- ½ teaspoon red pepper flakes
- ¼ teaspoon freshly grated nutmeg

- ½ large cantaloupe
- 16 slices prosciutto

1. Place all the ingredients for the marinade in a small mixing bowl and whisk until well combined; set aside.

2. Slice the cantaloupe into 8 equal wedges and then cut each wedge in half crosswise. Trim off the curvy end and remove the peel. You should be left with 16 fairly equal rectangular-shaped pieces of cantaloupe.

3. Wrap each piece with a slice of prosciutto and secure with a toothpick, then place on a flat plate or small rimmed baking sheet.

4. Brush the prosciutto-wrapped cantaloupe with the marinade, making sure that the pieces get covered on all sides, and place them in the refrigerator to marinate for at least 2 hours.

5. When you are ready to grill your appetizers, oil the cooking grate well, then preheat the grill to high heat.

6. Grill the prosciutto-wrapped cantaloupe for about 45 seconds per side, until it gets nice grill marks all around.

7. These are equally good served hot, warm, or cold and will keep in the refrigerator for up to a few days.

NUTRITIONAL FACTS (per piece)

Calories: 38 · Total fat: 1.2 g · Total carbs: 3.2 g · Net carbs: 2.7 g · Protein: 3.6 g

quick & easy

 make ahead

 squeaky clean

keto friendly

nut-free

Makes about 2 cups (400 g), 8 servings

GUACAMOLE

Guacamole is traditionally served as a dip with corn chips, but since I gave up corn chips, I've discovered so many other brilliant ways to use it. For instance, have you ever tried garnishing your favorite beanless chili with a generous dollop of guac? How about topping your scrambled eggs with it? It's phenomenal piled high over a grilled beef patty, with caramelized onions and crispy bacon. In fact, guacamole is now one of my favorite condiments to have around the house.

- 2 ripe avocados, halved and pitted
- 1 small tomato, seeded and finely chopped
- 2 jalapeño peppers, seeded and finely chopped
- 2 tablespoons finely chopped white onion
- 1 clove garlic, minced
- Juice of 1 lime or lemon
- ¼ cup (50 g) Foolproof Mayonnaise (page 64)
- ½ teaspoon ground cumin
- ½ teaspoon Himalayan salt
- ¼ teaspoon freshly ground black pepper
- ¼ teaspoon ground chipotle pepper

1. Scoop the flesh of the avocados into a medium mixing bowl. Add the rest of the ingredients and mash loosely with a fork until well combined.

2. It is best to serve guacamole immediately, but it will keep in the refrigerator for a couple of days. See the tip below to help keep it from browning.

Tip: Not serving your guac right away and want to prevent it from turning brown on you? Simply place it in a suitably sized container, smooth the top as best you can, and carefully pour water over it, a tablespoon at a time, until the top is completely covered. This creates a barrier that will prevent air from getting to your precious dip and turning it brown. When ready to serve, simply tip your container to drain the water, stir well, and serve your beautiful, bright green guacamole!

NUTRITIONAL FACTS (per ¼ cup/50 g serving)

Calories: 148 | Total fat: 14.4 g | Total carbs: 5.6 g | Net carbs: 1.9 g | Protein: 1.3 g

plan ahead

 make ahead

 squeaky clean

 keto friendly

egg-free

NONDAIRY CHIVE AND ONION DIP

Makes about 2 cups (400 g), 8 servings

When I was a kid, and even later in my adult life, sour cream and onion dip was THE classic that was always served at parties and other social gatherings. Our not-so-secret recipe had only two ingredients: sour cream and dry onion soup mix. Tasty, it sure was. But healthy? I think not. Having wised up since, I've come up with an alternative that is not only much healthier, but also packs a serious flavor punch. It is guaranteed to turn any boring crudité into a tasty and nutritious snack!

- 2 cups (240 g) raw cashew pieces, soaked for at least 8 hours
- ¼ cup (60 ml) apple cider vinegar
- Juice of 1 lemon
- ½ teaspoon Himalayan salt
- ½ cup (120 ml) water
- 3 tablespoons dehydrated minced onions
- 2 tablespoons finely chopped fresh chives, plus more for garnish
- 2 tablespoons extra-virgin olive oil, plus more for drizzling
- 1 tablespoon Dijon mustard
- ½ teaspoon freshly ground black pepper
- Assorted crudités for serving

1. Drain the soaked cashew pieces and rinse them really well under running water. Place them in the bowl of a food processor along with the vinegar, lemon juice, salt, and water. Process until smooth and creamy, about 5 minutes, stopping to scrape the sides of the bowl from time to time.

2. Transfer the pureed cashew mixture to a large mixing bowl and add the dehydrated onions, chives, olive oil, mustard, and pepper. Stir with a rubber spatula until well combined, then place the bowl in the fridge for at least 2 hours to allow the onions to rehydrate and the flavors to meld.

3. Scoop the dip into a serving bowl and garnish with chopped chives and a drizzle of olive oil. Serve with crudités.

4. This dip will keep in the refrigerator for up to 5 days.

NUTRITIONAL FACTS (per serving)

Calories: 211 | Total fat: 16.6 g | Total carbs: 11.0 g | Net carbs: 9.7 g | Protein: 5.3 g

plan ahead
 squeaky clean
 make ahead
 egg-free

SCALLOP AND PINK GRAPEFRUIT CEVICHE IN AVOCADO BOATS

Serves 4

Served in avocado boats, this scallop ceviche makes a refreshing and visually stunning appetizer. However, you could easily turn it into a great salad by dicing the avocados and adding them directly to the ceviche as opposed to using them as serving vessels. Despite being extremely fragile once the dish is constructed, the ceviche itself, without the avocados, can be made up to a day in advance. In fact, the longer you leave it in the fridge, the more cooked your scallops will be.

For the ceviche

- 1 pink grapefruit
- 7 ounces (200 g) scallops, cut into ½-inch (1.25-cm) pieces
- Grated zest of ½ lemon
- ½ teaspoon grated fresh ginger
- ¼ teaspoon Himalayan salt
- ¼ teaspoon freshly ground black pepper
- 10 to 12 fresh basil leaves, chopped
- 10 to 12 fresh mint leaves, chopped
- 2 tablespoons chopped raw pistachios

For the avocado boats

- 2 ripe avocados

For garnish

- Chopped raw pistachios
- Extra-virgin olive oil

1. With a sharp paring knife, peel the grapefruit all the way down to the flesh, then, working over a bowl to catch the juice, carefully carve out the fruit segments from between the membranes and allow them to drop into the bowl. Cut the grapefruit supremes into bite-sized chunks and put them back in the bowl with all the juice.

2. Add the rest of the ingredients for the ceviche to the bowl and mix gently to combine. Put the bowl in the fridge to rest for about an hour; not only will this allow the flavors to meld, but the acidity in the citrus will also take care of cooking the scallops. This ceviche will keep well in the fridge for up to 24 hours, so you can make it up to a full day in advance.

3. When ready to serve, cut the avocados in half, remove the pits, and place the halves on individual plates. Using a slotted spoon, fill each avocado half with the ceviche, dividing it evenly among the 4 halves. Top with chopped pistachios and a drizzle of olive oil.

Tip: Set your avocado boats on lemon rind wheels to keep them upright. To make the wheels, cut 4 relatively thick slices of lemon. Using a paring knife, cut around the inside of the rind to remove the lemon flesh and membrane, leaving you with a wheel of lemon rind.

NUTRITIONAL FACTS (per serving)

Calories: 207 | Total fat: 13.3 g | Total carbs: 13.6 g | Net carbs: 10.0 g | Protein: 12.1 g

plan ahead keto friendly

 make ahead

Makes 36 balls

SESAME SALMON BALLS WITH GINGER TAHINI DIPPING SAUCE

These cute little salmon balls are the perfect finger food for your next party. They are so delicious, no one will care that they are actually good for you! Plus, you can make the mixture and form the balls in advance and then cook them at the last minute, once your guests have arrived. Oh, and if you should have leftovers (which I doubt will ever happen), they reheat very well or can even be enjoyed cold.

For the salmon mixture

- 3 (6-ounce/170-g) cans wild-caught pink salmon, drained, or 1¼ pounds (570 g) cooked salmon
- ½ cup (60 g) almond flour
- 2 tablespoons coconut flour
- 2 tablespoons tapioca starch
- ¼ cup (15 g) chopped fresh parsley
- 2 green onions, chopped
- 2 cloves garlic, minced
- Grated zest of ½ lemon
- Juice of ½ lemon
- 2 tablespoons Dijon mustard
- 1 large egg
- 1 teaspoon red pepper flakes
- ½ teaspoon Himalayan salt
- ½ teaspoon freshly ground black pepper

For the dipping sauce

- ½ cup (120 ml) full-fat coconut milk
- ¼ cup (60 g) tahini
- 2 tablespoons apple cider vinegar
- 2 tablespoons raw honey
- 1 tablespoon toasted sesame oil
- Grated zest of ½ lemon
- Juice of ½ lemon
- ¼ cup (35 g) minced fresh ginger
- 1 clove garlic
- ½ teaspoon freshly ground black pepper
- ½ teaspoon red pepper flakes
- ¼ teaspoon Himalayan salt

- ½ cup (72 g) white sesame seeds
- 2 tablespoons black sesame seeds
- ¼ cup (55 g/60 ml) healthy cooking fat for the pan (see Notes)

1. Put all the ingredients for the salmon mixture in a large bowl and mix until evenly combined. Place in the refrigerator to chill for at least 2 hours.

2. While the salmon mixture is chilling, prepare the dipping sauce: Place all the ingredients in a small food processor and process until smooth and creamy. Put that too in the refrigerator to chill for a couple of hours.

3. Once the salmon mixture is fully chilled, spread the white and black sesame seeds on a plate. Roll or scoop the salmon mixture into 36 balls, roughly the size of Ping-Pong balls, then roll them in the sesame seeds to coat.

4. Heat the cooking fat in a large heavy skillet set over medium-high heat. Add the salmon balls and pan-fry, turning them often, until nice and golden all around, about 8 to 10 minutes total. You may have to work in 2 or 3 batches, depending on the size of your skillet. Make sure not to overcrowd the pan so that air can circulate freely between the balls, and don't be afraid to add more fat to the pan if you notice that the balls are beginning to stick.

5. Allow the balls to cool slightly before serving with the dipping sauce.

Equipment needed (optional):

1¼-inch (3.25-cm)-diameter spring-loaded ice cream scoop

Notes: I find that using a small spring-loaded ice cream scoop helps tremendously in getting the job of forming the salmon balls done faster and results in more evenly shaped balls. It's a small investment that's well worth the price, if you ask me!

The best choices of fat for pan-frying include lard, beef tallow, ghee, coconut oil, and avocado oil.

NUTRITIONAL FACTS (per salmon ball)

Calories: 38	Total fat: 1.8 g	Total carbs: 1.4 g	Net carbs: 1.4 g	Protein: 3.7 g

(per tablespoon of sauce)

Calories: 45	Total fat: 3.4 g	Total carbs: 3.4 g	Net carbs: 3.4 g	Protein: 0.8 g

under 30

 squeaky clean

 make ahead

 keto friendly

Makes 16 pieces

SMOKED SALMON DEVILED EGGS

Adding smoked salmon to this simple classic elevates it to the rank of "elegant and sophisticated." With a flavor this bold and a look this good, these eggs will no doubt steal the show at your next gathering. Oh, and they make for an amazing quick meal, too!

- 8 large hard-cooked eggs, cooled and peeled
- ¼ cup plus 2 tablespoons (75 g) Foolproof Mayonnaise (page 64)
- 1 tablespoon Dijon mustard
- ½ teaspoon smoked paprika
- Pinch of freshly ground black pepper
- 2 ounces (55 g) cold smoked salmon, such as Nova lox, chopped
- 1 teaspoon finely chopped fresh chives
- 2 tablespoons finely chopped raw pistachios

For garnish

- 2 or 3 slices cold smoked salmon, such as Nova lox, rolled up and sliced crosswise
- 5 or 6 raw pistachios, finely chopped
- A few fresh chives, cut into 1- to 2-inch (2.5- to 5-cm) lengths

1. Carefully cut the eggs in half and remove the yolks to a small mixing bowl.

2. To the bowl with the yolks, add the mayonnaise, mustard, paprika, and pepper and mix vigorously with a fork or small whisk until evenly combined and creamy. Throw in the smoked salmon, chives, and pistachios and mix gently until well incorporated.

3. Transfer the mixture to a pastry bag equipped with a medium round tip. You could also use a large resealable plastic bag with a hole cut in one corner.

4. Pipe the egg yolk mixture into the empty egg white halves and place them on a serving plate. Garnish with little rolls of smoked salmon, chopped pistachios, and fresh chive pieces.

5. These will keep for up to a few days in the refrigerator, provided that you cover them well with plastic wrap or store them in an airtight container to keep them from drying out.

NUTRITIONAL FACTS (per piece)

Calories: 76 | Total fat: 6.4 g | Total carbs: 0.5 g | Net carbs: 0.5 g | Protein: 4.5 g

under 30

plan ahead

 make ahead

egg-free

Makes 16 pieces

STUFFED DATES WRAPPED IN PROSCIUTTO

If you're a fan of everything sweet and savory, one taste of these dates will probably have you hooked for life. They're super easy to make, are equally good served warm or cold, and reheat very well in the microwave. Just pop them in for a minute or two, and they'll be as good as fresh. And in a pinch, you don't even need to go to the trouble of making the fancy stuffing. Just shove a piece of nut (any nut) in that cavity, or even cheese if you do dairy, and you'll still have yourself a very tasty bite. This is such a winning appetizer, you'll probably end up bringing it to every party you get invited to. The best part is, you can have fun, improvise, and make a new variety every time!

- 16 Medjool dates
- 8 slices prosciutto, cut in half lengthwise

For the stuffing

- ½ cup (70 g) raw cashew pieces, soaked for at least 8 hours
- 1 clove garlic
- 1 teaspoon Dijon mustard
- 1 teaspoon apple cider vinegar
- ¼ teaspoon smoked paprika
- ¼ teaspoon onion powder
- ¼ teaspoon Himalayan salt
- ¼ teaspoon ground white pepper
- Pinch of cayenne pepper
- ½ cup (52 g) chopped raw walnuts
- 1 tablespoon chopped fresh parsley

1. Preheat the oven to 375°F (190°C). Line a rimmed baking sheet with parchment paper.

2. Remove the pit from each of the dates by slitting the date across the top from one end to the other with a paring knife and carefully prying out the pit with the tip of your knife. It's important not to slice all the way through the date: You want to create a little pocket to contain the stuffing.

3. Place the soaked cashews in a fine-mesh sieve, rinse under cold running water, and then drain them really well. In a small food processor, process the nuts until creamy, then add the rest of the ingredients for the stuffing, except for the walnuts and parsley. Resume processing until well combined. Throw in the walnuts and parsley and pulse a few times until just incorporated; you want the walnuts to remain chunky.

4. Carefully stuff this mixture into the cavities of the dates with a small spoon or a pastry bag equipped with a large round tip.

5. Wrap a half slice of prosciutto around each date while trying to keep the seam neatly tucked underneath the date. Set the finished dates on the prepared baking sheet.

6. Bake for 12 to 15 minutes, until the prosciutto starts to color and gets slightly crispy. To get your prosciutto even crispier, set the oven to broil for the last minute or two. Remove from the oven and allow to cool for at least 15 minutes before serving.

7. These will keep in the refrigerator for 3 to 4 days and can be reheated slightly in the microwave or enjoyed straight out of the icebox.

NUTRITIONAL FACTS (per piece)

Calories: 135   Total fat: 5.5 g   Total carbs: 19.9 g   Net carbs: 17.8 g   Protein: 4.0 g

time intensive

squeaky clean

make ahead

egg-free

freezer friendly

Serves 8

SILKY-SMOOTH BEEF LIVER PÂTÉ

If you're not a fan of liver, try this recipe: It's an excellent way to get organ meat into your diet. While it is a little on the labor-intensive side to make, this silky-smooth pâté freezes very well, so you can make a batch, freeze it, and then enjoy a serving once or twice a week. I like to eat mine at breakfast, alongside a couple of pan-fried eggs. I usually enjoy it with a spoon, but if you prefer to spread yours on something, try apple slices; the two pair perfectly!

- 4 slices bacon, cut crosswise into ½-inch (1.25-cm) pieces
- 1 large onion, sliced
- 8 ounces (225 g) mushrooms, sliced
- 8 dried figs, chopped
- ¾ teaspoon Himalayan salt
- ½ teaspoon ground white pepper
- 2 pounds (910 g) beef liver
- 10 fresh sage leaves, finely chopped
- ¼ teaspoon freshly grated nutmeg
- ¼ teaspoon ground Ceylon cinnamon
- 2 tablespoons apple cider vinegar
- ¾ cup (180 ml) full-fat coconut milk
- ½ cup (120 ml) water
- ¼ cup (55 g) ghee
- ¼ cup (30 g) raw pistachios, chopped

1. Cook the bacon in a heavy skillet set over medium heat until crispy. Add the onion, mushrooms, figs, salt, and pepper and cook, stirring often, until the onion is soft and caramelized, 15 to 20 minutes.

2. Meanwhile, rinse the beef liver under cold running water; drain well, pat dry, and cut into fairly large chunks. Set aside.

3. When the onion mixture has taken on a nice golden color, add the liver, sage, nutmeg, cinnamon, and vinegar to the skillet and continue cooking just until the liver turns opaque. You do not want to overcook the liver.

4. Transfer this mixture to the bowl of a food processor and give it a few spins just to break everything down. Add the coconut milk, water, and ghee and start the motor again. This time, let it run until the mixture becomes as creamy as you think it's gonna get; for me that's 3 to 4 minutes.

5. Force the pâté through a fine-mesh sieve by swirling it around with a ladle. While this step is somewhat tedious, it is absolutely necessary if you want your pâté to be nice and smooth. You will probably find that a lot of the mixture gets left behind (about one-third, I would say), but by all means, don't let it go to waste. Though it's not really palatable to us humans, it makes an excellent treat for your furry friends (or your friends' furry friends!).

6. Fold in the chopped pistachios and divide the pâté among eight 6-ounce (180-ml) ramekins. Cover loosely with plastic wrap to prevent the tops from drying out and place in the refrigerator to set for at least 4 hours.

7. This pâté will keep in the refrigerator for about 3 to 4 days. It also freezes well: Just take it out of the fridge the night before and it'll be good to go by morning.

Note: *Serving size can greatly vary depending on what is left behind after straining; the nutritional facts below are approximations.*

NUTRITIONAL FACTS (per serving; see Note)

Calories: 500   Total fat: 10.0 g   Total carbs: 14.0 g   Net carbs: 12.2 g   Protein: 19.7 g

soups and salads

AVOCADO CUCUMBER GAZPACHO

Serves 2

The exotic flavor of this soup, slightly reminiscent of bananas, is without a doubt as intriguing as its color is eye-catching. As you might expect, it is extremely refreshing and speaks of beautiful days spent basking in the warm sun. Serve it as cold as you possibly can, and don't be afraid to make it in advance if you have to; its color will not degrade over time, even after spending a full day in the fridge.

- 1 ripe avocado
- 4 mini seedless cucumbers, cut into chunks
- 1 small white onion, chopped
- 1 cup (35 g) fresh spinach, roughly chopped
- 12 large fresh basil leaves, roughly chopped
- 1 cup (240 ml) full-fat coconut milk
- ½ cup (120 ml) water
- 2 tablespoons apple cider vinegar
- Juice of 1 lemon
- ½ teaspoon Himalayan salt
- ½ teaspoon freshly ground black pepper

For garnish

- Chopped fresh herbs, such as parsley, coriander, chives, tarragon, or fennel tops
- Chopped raw pistachios
- Extra-virgin olive oil

1. Place all the ingredients for the soup in a blender and process on the highest possible setting until reduced to a smooth puree.

2. Strain the soup through a fine-mesh sieve, then return it to the blender to give it another quick spin and make it even smoother and creamier.

3. Serve chilled, garnished with fresh herbs, chopped pistachios, and a drizzle of olive oil.

NUTRITIONAL FACTS (per serving)

| Calories: 376 | Total fat: 31.6 g | Total carbs: 19.4 g | Net carbs: 13.4 g | Protein: 7.9 g |

under 30

freezer friendly

plan ahead

squeaky clean

make ahead

egg-free

Serves 4

CREAM OF MUSHROOM SOUP

When winter sets in and it starts to get really cold out, I invariably begin to crave this soup. In fact, I can't think of another dish that's quite as soul-warming and comforting. This gluten- and dairy-free version will no doubt convince you that a good cream of mushroom soup need not be filled with loads of dairy and starch to fully satisfy.

- ¼ cup (55 g) plus 2 tablespoons ghee, divided
- 1 onion, finely chopped
- 2 cloves garlic, minced
- 2 celery ribs, chopped
- 1 small head cauliflower (1¼ pounds/570 g), roughly chopped
- 1½ teaspoons Himalayan salt
- 1 teaspoon garlic powder
- ½ teaspoon freshly ground black pepper
- ½ teaspoon ground white pepper
- ½ teaspoon onion powder
- ¼ teaspoon anise seeds
- 3 cups (710 ml) water
- 1 cup (240 ml) Brown Chicken Stock (page 76)
- ½ cup (70 g) raw cashew pieces, soaked for at least 8 hours, rinsed, and drained
- 1 teaspoon Dijon mustard
- 1 pound (455 g) mushrooms, chopped fairly finely, divided

1. Melt 2 tablespoons of the ghee in a large saucepan set over medium heat. Add the onion, garlic, and celery and cook for 1 to 2 minutes, just to soften up the veggies a little bit.

2. Add the cauliflower, salt, garlic powder, black pepper, white pepper, onion powder, and anise seeds and continue cooking for another minute or two.

3. Add the water, chicken stock, cashew pieces, remaining ¼ cup (55 g) of ghee, mustard, and half of the chopped mushrooms. Bring to a boil, then reduce the heat, cover loosely, and simmer until the cauliflower is fork-tender, about 5 to 7 minutes.

4. Ladle the mixture into a blender and process on high speed until super smooth and silky. You might have to work in several batches.

5. Return the soup to the pot and add the rest of the mushrooms (save a handful for garnish, if desired). Bring back to a boil, then reduce the heat and simmer until the mushrooms are fully cooked, 3 to 4 minutes.

6. Serve without delay.

NUTRITIONAL FACTS (per serving)

Calories: 353 · Total fat: 27.8 g · Total carbs: 22.1 g · Net carbs: 15.7 g · Protein: 10.2 g

plan ahead

squeaky clean

make ahead

egg-free

freezer friendly

nut-free

Serves 4

CREAMY CHICKEN SOUP

I don't know many people who don't appreciate a good bowl of piping-hot cream of chicken soup. This version is so hearty, so creamy, so dreamy, and so deliciously comforting—not to mention nutritious! I can already tell that it will become your go-to recipe for those days when you're feeling a bit under the weather, or when it's really cold outside and you need something vivifying to warm your bones.

For the soup base

- 1 tablespoon ghee
- ½ medium onion, chopped
- 1 celery rib, chopped
- 1 cup (140 g) cubed butternut squash
- 1 small red-skinned white sweet potato, diced
- ½ teaspoon Himalayan salt
- ½ teaspoon freshly ground black pepper
- ¼ teaspoon freshly grated nutmeg
- 2 cups (475 ml) Brown Chicken Stock (page 76)
- 2 cups (475 ml) water

For the cauliflower puree

- 1 tablespoon ghee
- ½ medium onion, finely chopped
- 1 clove garlic, minced
- ½ teaspoon Himalayan salt
- ½ teaspoon freshly ground black pepper
- 1 small head cauliflower (1¼ pounds/570 g), grated
- 2 tablespoons sesame seeds, toasted (see Tip, page 300)
- 1 tablespoon unseasoned rice vinegar
- 3 or 4 ladles soup base (from above)

- 2 cups (270 g) diced cooked chicken
- 1 cup (60 g) chopped baby spinach leaves

1. Make the soup base: Melt 1 tablespoon of ghee in a large saucepan set over medium heat. Add the onion, celery, squash, sweet potato, salt, pepper, and nutmeg and sweat for 3 to 4 minutes, until slightly softened.

2. Add the chicken stock and water and bring to a boil, then lower the heat and simmer until the squash is tender, 5 to 7 minutes.

3. Meanwhile, make the cauliflower puree: In a separate saucepan, melt 1 tablespoon of ghee over medium heat, then add the onion, garlic, salt, and pepper and sweat for a few minutes, until the onion is translucent.

4. Add the cauliflower, sesame seeds, and vinegar and continue cooking until the cauliflower is really soft and tender.

5. Transfer the cauliflower mixture to a blender; borrow 3 or 4 ladles of the soup and add that to the blender as well. Process on high speed until creamy, then pour this mixture into the soup.

6. Kill the heat, then add the cooked chicken and chopped spinach. Let it sit for a few minutes to warm the chicken and wilt the spinach, then give the soup a final stir and serve.

NUTRITIONAL FACTS (per serving)

Calories: 286   Total fat: 11.9 g   Total carbs: 17.9 g   Net carbs: 12.5 g   Protein: 28.5 g

plan ahead

 make ahead

 freezer friendly

 squeaky clean

 egg-free

nut-free

Serves 4 to 6

BRAISED BEEF AND CARAMELIZED ONION SOUP

French onion soup has been a longtime favorite in my household. My daughter is especially fond of it, and I've always taken great pleasure in making it for her on special occasions. Since going Paleo, though, I've had to lose the crouton and melted cheese that traditionally crown a bowl of French onion soup. To make up for that loss, I came up with the idea of adding leftover braised beef. Whoa! Talk about good! The tasty, tender morsels of meat make the soup so incredibly filling and satisfying; they'll make you forget all about the "missing" bread and cheese.

- 2 to 3 tablespoons healthy cooking fat
- 10 medium onions, sliced
- 4 cloves garlic, chopped
- 1 teaspoon Himalayan salt
- 1 teaspoon freshly ground black pepper
- 5 cups (1.2 L) Brown Bone Broth (page 74)
- 2 tablespoons Dijon mustard
- 2 tablespoons balsamic vinegar
- ½ teaspoon ground Ceylon cinnamon
- ½ teaspoon dried savory
- ¼ teaspoon freshly grated nutmeg
- 4 juniper berries
- 1 star anise
- 1 bay leaf
- ½ pound (225 g) leftover Easy Braised Beef (page 178)
- Fresh herbs of choice for garnish (optional)

1. Heat the cooking fat in a large stockpot set over medium heat. Add the onions, garlic, salt, and pepper and cook until the onions are super soft and take on a beautiful caramel color, 20 to 25 minutes. Stir often so the onions don't burn.

2. When the onions are ready, add the broth, mustard, vinegar, cinnamon, savory, nutmeg, juniper berries, star anise, and bay leaf. Bring to a boil, then cover, lower the heat, and simmer for 20 to 25 minutes to allow the flavors to meld.

3. Turn off the heat, add the leftover braised beef, and let the soup sit for a few minutes so the meat has a chance to warm up.

4. Remove the juniper berries, star anise, and bay leaf and serve. Garnish with fresh herbs, if desired.

NUTRITIONAL FACTS (per serving, based on 6 servings)

Calories: 172 | Total fat: 3.4 g | Total carbs: 24.2 g | Net carbs: 19.4 g | Protein: 11.3 g

time intensive

 make ahead

 plan ahead

 squeaky clean

Serves 4

For the meatballs

- 1 pound (455 g) lean ground pork
- 1 clove garlic, minced
- 1 large egg
- 2 green onions, finely chopped
- 2 tablespoons finely chopped fresh parsley
- 2 tablespoons Dijon mustard
- 1 teaspoon onion powder
- 1 teaspoon anise seeds
- ½ teaspoon Himalayan salt
- ½ teaspoon celery seeds
- ½ teaspoon red pepper flakes
- ¼ teaspoon ground white pepper

For the soup

- 1 tablespoon healthy cooking fat
- 1 small onion, chopped
- 2 cloves garlic, minced
- 1 teaspoon Himalayan salt
- 6 cups (1.4 L) Brown Bone Broth (page 74)
- 1 teaspoon freshly ground black pepper
- ¼ teaspoon freshly grated nutmeg
- 1 bay leaf
- 6 cups (10½ ounces/300 g) fresh spinach, chopped

For the pasta

- 1 cup (115 g) almond flour
- 1 tablespoon coconut flour
- 2 large eggs
- Pinch of Himalayan salt
- Freshly grated nutmeg

ITALIAN WEDDING SOUP

If you are a fan of Italian wedding soup, you will no doubt fall head over heels for this Paleo version. In fact, you might even like it better than the original! So much so that you might even want to…marry it?

1. Make the meatballs: Place all the ingredients for the meatballs in the bowl of a stand mixer equipped with the paddle attachment and mix on medium speed until very well combined and slightly airy. You can also knead it with your hands if you prefer, although this results in a coarser meatball.

2. Form the meat mixture into 60 mini meatballs, each about ¾ inch (2 cm) in diameter, and place them in the refrigerator to firm up for at least 2 hours.

3. Make the soup: Melt the cooking fat in a large stockpot set over medium heat, then add the onion, garlic, and salt and cook until the onion is fragrant and slightly translucent, about 5 minutes. Add the broth, pepper, nutmeg, and bay leaf and bring to a boil.

4. Add the meatballs one at a time, then bring the soup back to a simmer and cook until the meatballs are cooked all the way through, about 20 minutes.

5. Meanwhile, make the pasta: Bring about 4 cups (1 L) of salted water to a roaring boil. While you are waiting for the water to boil, place the ingredients for the pasta in a small mixing bowl and mix with a wooden spoon until well combined.

6. As soon as the water starts to boil, hold a box grater over the pot and, using a rubber spatula, force the pasta mixture through the largest holes of the grater into the boiling water. Repeat until you run out of "dough." Cook the pasta for 3 to 4 minutes, then drain and rinse well under cold running water.

7. Add the chopped spinach to the soup and let it cook for a few minutes, then gently stir in the pasta. Kill the heat but give the pasta a few minutes to heat through, then serve.

Tip: You can make the meatballs ahead of time and keep them in the refrigerator until you are ready to make the soup. You could even freeze them and use them straight from the freezer—just add a few minutes of cooking time for your soup.

NUTRITIONAL FACTS (per serving)

Calories: 344 · Total fat: 17.7 g · Total carbs: 16.4 g · Net carbs: 12.7 g · Protein: 30.4 g

under 30

squeaky clean

make ahead

egg-free

Serves 4 to 6

BRUSSELS SPROUTS AND SMOKED HAM SALAD

If you're looking for a salad that you can make ahead of time and will stay fresh for a very long time, this is it. In fact, it will taste and look just as good, if not better, on day five as it does on day one. The addition of chili pepper flakes confers an unexpected but tantalizing little kick to this salad. If you're not a fan of heat, feel free to leave them out.

For the salad

- 4 cups (1¼ pounds/570 g) Brussels sprouts, cut in half
- 2 large carrots, peeled and julienned
- ½ medium turnip, peeled and julienned
- ½ cup (70 g) chopped raw hazelnuts
- ½ pound (225 g) smoked ham, finely diced
- ½ cup (30 g) fresh parsley leaves, finely chopped

For the vinaigrette

- ¼ cup (60 ml) avocado oil
- 2 tablespoons Dijon mustard
- 2 tablespoons white wine vinegar
- Juice of 1 lemon
- 2 cloves garlic, minced
- 2 dried pili pili peppers or other dried chili peppers, crushed into flakes
- 2 tablespoons finely chopped fresh sage
- 1 tablespoon finely chopped fresh thyme
- ½ teaspoon Himalayan salt
- ½ teaspoon freshly ground black pepper

1. Place the Brussels sprouts in a steamer basket set over a pot of salted boiling water and cook for 3 to 4 minutes, until they are about three-quarters of the way cooked. Add the carrots and turnip to the basket and continue cooking for a minute or two, until the veggies are fully cooked but still retain a bit of crunch.

2. Plunge the vegetables into an ice water bath to stop the cooking process (don't be afraid to go heavy on the ice), then drain them really well. Transfer to a large mixing bowl.

3. Toast the hazelnuts in a dry skillet set over medium heat, then add them to the vegetables along with the ham and parsley.

4. In a separate bowl, place all the ingredients for the vinaigrette and whisk vigorously until slightly emulsified. Pour over the salad and mix to combine.

5. You can serve the salad immediately, but it will taste even better after it sits in the fridge for a couple of hours or, better yet, overnight. It will keep in the fridge for 4 to 5 days.

Tips: *I like to steam vegetables over salted water because the salt tends to penetrate the vegetables as they cook, which helps bring out their flavor.*

Don't skimp on the ice for the ice water bath. You want to use lots of it: The faster your vegetables get cold, the crunchier they will remain and the more vibrant their color will be. And COLD is really what you're after. That's the only way to stop the cooking. Warm or room temperature will not cut it.

NUTRITIONAL FACTS (per serving, based on 6 servings)

Calories: 193   Total fat: 9.3 g   Total carbs: 18.4 g   Net carbs: 11.2 g   Protein: 12.3 g

quick & easy

squeaky clean

make ahead

egg-free

THE BEST CARROT SALAD EVER

Serves 6

In all honesty (and with all modesty), this salad is perfect. Not only is it absolutely delicious, but it is also very easy and economical to make and comes together in mere minutes! Plus, it's one of those sturdy salads that you can make on the weekend and feast on throughout the week. It only seems to get better with each passing day. I know that it'll become a favorite of yours, too.

For the vinaigrette

- ¼ cup (60 ml) extra-virgin olive oil
- ¼ cup (60 ml) white balsamic vinegar
- 2 tablespoons Dijon mustard
- ½ teaspoon Himalayan salt
- ½ teaspoon freshly ground black pepper

For the salad

- 8 large carrots, grated
- ½ cup (72 g) raisins
- ½ cup (40 g) unsweetened shredded coconut
- ½ cup (25 g) fresh parsley leaves, chopped
- ¼ cup (32 g) raw pumpkin seeds
- ¼ cup (28 g) chopped raw pecans
- ¼ cup (28 g) chopped raw walnuts

1. In a bowl, vigorously whisk together all the ingredients for the vinaigrette until slightly emulsified.

2. Place all the ingredients for the salad in a large mixing bowl, followed by the vinaigrette. Mix until well combined.

3. You can serve this salad immediately, but if time permits, put it in the refrigerator for a few hours to allow the flavors to meld. It will keep well in an airtight container in the fridge for 5 to 6 days.

NUTRITIONAL FACTS (per serving)

Calories: 316   Total fat: 23.8 g   Total carbs: 24.2 g   Net carbs: 19.9 g   Protein: 5.3 g

under 30

 make ahead

egg-free

Serves 8

CRUNCHY BROCCOLI SALAD

This sturdy salad seems to get better when given the chance to mellow in the fridge for a wee while. However, after being in contact with moisture for more than a few hours, the cashews tend to go a little soft, so if you plan to make it farther in advance of serving it, you could replace them with harder nuts such as almonds or additional hazelnuts. Or you could simply add the nuts at the last minute, right before serving. But if, like me, you don't mind nuts that are on the softer, creamier side, go ahead and throw those cashews right in. Their buttery flavor certainly won't fail to please your taste buds.

For the salad

- 6 cups (1 kg) broccoli florets, finely chopped
- 1 cup (100 g) finely chopped red cabbage
- 1 cup (140 g) chopped raw hazelnuts
- 1 cup (120 g) sliced green olives
- 3 large carrots, diced
- 2 celery ribs, sliced
- ½ cup (70 g) raw cashew pieces
- ½ cup (75 g) dried apricots, chopped
- ¼ cup (36 g) raisins

For the vinaigrette

- 2 cloves garlic, minced
- ½ cup (120 ml) avocado oil or extra-virgin olive oil
- Juice of 2 limes (about ¼ cup/ 60 ml)
- 2 tablespoons Dijon mustard
- 2 tablespoons raw honey
- 1 tablespoon white balsamic vinegar
- 1 tablespoon chopped fresh rosemary
- 1 tablespoon chopped fresh thyme
- ½ teaspoon Himalayan salt
- ½ teaspoon freshly ground black pepper

1. In a large mixing bowl, combine all the ingredients for the salad and mix until well distributed.

2. In a small food processor, combine all the ingredients for the vinaigrette and process until smooth and creamy. Pour the vinaigrette into the bowl with the salad and toss until thoroughly combined.

3. You can serve the salad immediately, but it's better to refrigerate it for a few hours to allow the flavors to meld.

4. This salad will keep in an airtight container in the refrigerator for 5 to 6 days.

NUTRITIONAL FACTS (per serving)

Calories: 327 | Total fat: 23.9 g | Total carbs: 27.3 g | Net carbs: 22.0 g | Protein: 6.0 g

under 30

 egg-free

 make ahead

JULIENNED CARROT AND RUTABAGA SALAD

Serves 4 to 6

This salad is just as tasty as it is pretty, if not more so! Though getting the vegetables cut into fine julienne strips is a bit of a challenge, the extremely pleasant gustatory experience that you will be rewarded with makes all the effort very much worth your while.

For the salad

- 1 medium rutabaga (1¾ pounds/ 800 g)
- 2 large carrots
- ¼ cup (35 g) chopped hazelnuts
- ¼ cup (15 g) chopped fresh parsley

For the vinaigrette

- ¼ cup (60 ml) avocado oil
- 2 tablespoons apple cider vinegar
- 1 tablespoon Dijon mustard
- 1 tablespoon raw honey
- 1 tablespoon dried oregano leaves
- 2 cloves garlic, minced
- ½ teaspoon Himalayan salt
- ½ teaspoon freshly ground black pepper

1. Peel the rutabaga and carrots and cut them into fine julienne strips. I strongly recommend the use of a mandoline here.

2. Place the julienned vegetables in a steamer basket and steam them over a pot of salted boiling water until softened but still slightly crunchy, 3 to 4 minutes.

3. Immediately plunge the steamed vegetables into an ice water bath (really, add ice cubes to the water!) and gently move them around until they're completely chilled; transfer to a colander and let them drain for about 15 minutes.

4. Meanwhile, place all the ingredients for the vinaigrette in a large mixing bowl and whisk vigorously until slightly emulsified.

5. Toast the hazelnuts in a dry skillet set over medium heat; let cool completely.

6. Add the rutabaga, carrots, toasted hazelnuts, and parsley to the bowl with the vinaigrette, then toss until well combined and serve.

7. This salad can be made ahead of time and will keep in the refrigerator for 3 to 4 days.

NUTRITIONAL FACTS (per serving, based on 6 servings)
Calories: 185 | Total fat: 10.8 g | Total carbs: 17.2 g | Net carbs: 15.0 g | Protein: 0.5 g

under 30

 keto friendly

squeaky clean

Serves 4

GRILLED CAESAR SALAD

You could very well make this salad without grilling the lettuce, but there's something to be said for warm and slightly charred lettuce. If you have access to a grill, it's worth the extra effort...trust me! As for the cashew "Parmesan," I believe you will be pleasantly surprised by how closely it mimics the real thing. Personally, I think I like it even better!

For the "Parmesan"

- ¼ cup (30 g) raw cashew pieces
- 1 small clove garlic, finely chopped
- Pinch of Himalayan salt

- 2 large romaine lettuce hearts
- Olive oil from anchovies (if using), extra-virgin olive oil, or avocado oil for drizzling
- Himalayan salt and freshly ground black pepper
- ½ cup (120 ml) Creamy Caesar Dressing (page 58)
- 4 slices bacon, cooked until crispy and crumbled
- 4 anchovy fillets in olive oil, roughly chopped (optional)
- 1 tablespoon capers

1. Preheat a grill to high.

2. Make the "Parmesan": Place the cashew pieces, garlic, and salt in a small food processor and give them a few quick pulses until their texture resembles that of coarse sand. Set aside.

3. Cut the romaine lettuce hearts in half lengthwise and drizzle the cut side with some of the oil from the can of anchovies. (If you're not using anchovies, use extra-virgin olive oil or avocado oil.) Sprinkle lightly with salt and generously with freshly ground black pepper. Keep in mind that you are using a lot of salty ingredients, so you don't want to overdo things in the salt department.

4. Place the lettuce halves cut-side down on the hot grill. Close the lid and grill for 60 to 90 seconds, until they get nice grill marks and start to wilt. The lettuce should become only slightly warm; you do not want to cook it.

5. Chop the grilled lettuce and place it in a large mixing bowl. Add the dressing, bacon, anchovies (if using), and capers and toss gently until evenly combined.

6. Sprinkle with the "Parmesan" at the moment of serving.

NUTRITIONAL FACTS (per serving)

Calories: 333 · Total fat: 31.5 g · Total carbs: 5.8 g · Net carbs: 4.6 g · Protein: 9.6 g

CUCUMBER AND SWEET RED PEPPER SALAD

Serves 4

Refreshing, super crunchy, and a veritable explosion of flavors, this colorful summer salad will sit happily alongside your favorite grilled meats. Add some leftover cooked chicken, hard-cooked eggs, or smoked ham to turn it into a quick and complete meal!

- 7 mini seedless cucumbers, cut into bite-sized chunks
- 4 red bell peppers, seeded and roughly chopped
- 2 medium carrots, peeled and finely diced
- 8 radishes, sliced paper-thin
- ½ cup (36 g) Kalamata olives, pitted
- ¼ cup (15 g) fresh parsley leaves, finely chopped
- ¼ cup (28 g) roughly chopped raw walnuts
- ½ cup (120 ml) Classic Dijon Herb Dressing (page 56)

1. Place all the ingredients in a large salad bowl and mix until well combined.

2. Serve without delay, if possible. This salad will keep in the fridge for a couple of days, but expect the cucumbers to wilt a little bit and release some of their water.

NUTRITIONAL FACTS (per serving)

Calories: 267 — Total fat: 23.8 — Total carbs: 12.7 g — Net carbs: 7.8 g — Protein: 5.0 g

egg-free

 make ahead

nut-free

squeaky clean

Serves 4

SPICY MANGO CUCUMBER SALAD

Fresh, colorful, and perfectly balanced, this tropical salad makes a solid partner for grilled meat or fish. And may I suggest that you make a double batch? It can very well bear to spend a couple of days in the fridge, and I can guarantee that you will be more than happy to have leftovers!

- 1 large ripe mango, peeled, seeded, and cut into 1-inch (2.5-cm) cubes
- 4 mini seedless cucumbers, cut into bite-sized chunks
- 3 radishes, sliced paper-thin
- 1 small red onion, finely chopped
- ¼ cup (15 g) fresh parsley leaves, chopped
- 12 large fresh basil leaves, chopped
- 1 fresh bird's-eye chili pepper or small jalapeño pepper, finely chopped
- 2 tablespoons extra-virgin olive oil
- 2 tablespoons white balsamic vinegar
- ½ teaspoon Himalayan salt
- ½ teaspoon freshly ground black pepper

1. Place all the ingredients in a large bowl and mix until well combined.

2. You can serve this salad immediately, but if time permits, let it rest in the refrigerator for a couple of hours to allow the flavors to meld. It will keep in the fridge for 1 to 2 days.

NUTRITIONAL FACTS (per serving)

Calories: 120 | Total fat: 7.2 g | Total carbs: 13.3 g | Net carbs: 10.6 g | Protein: 1.8 g

under 30

squeaky clean

plan ahead

keto friendly

make ahead

egg-free

Serves 4 to 6

MARINATED MUSHROOM SALAD

Make-ahead salads do not get any better than this! Exploding with flavor, these marinated mushrooms greatly benefit from spending a day or even two in the fridge before being served—perfect for those occasions when you know you'll be pressed for time.

- 1½ pounds (680 g) button mushrooms
- ½ cup (70 g) raw almonds
- 1 medium carrot, sliced
- 2 medium celery ribs, sliced
- 2 red bell peppers, seeded and chopped
- 1 small white onion, chopped
- ½ cup (60 g) sliced green olives
- ½ cup (60 g) sliced black olives
- 2 tablespoons finely chopped fresh parsley

For the vinaigrette

- ¼ cup (60 ml) extra-virgin olive oil
- Juice of 1 lemon
- 2 tablespoons Dijon mustard
- 1 tablespoon apple cider vinegar
- 1 tablespoon granulated onion
- 1 tablespoon dried oregano leaves
- 1 clove garlic, minced
- ½ teaspoon Himalayan salt
- ½ teaspoon freshly ground black pepper

1. Bring 8 cups (2 L) of salted water to a roaring boil; add the mushrooms and cook for 3 minutes. Pour the mushrooms into a fine-mesh sieve and leave them to drain until completely cool.

2. Toast the almonds in a dry skillet set over medium heat; let cool completely.

3. Place the mushrooms, almonds, carrot, celery, bell peppers, onion, green and black olives, and parsley in a large mixing bowl and toss to combine.

4. In a separate bowl, combine all the ingredients for the vinaigrette and whisk vigorously until slightly emulsified. Pour over the salad and mix until well coated.

5. Cover and place in the refrigerator to marinate overnight before serving.

6. This salad will keep in the refrigerator for 3 to 4 days.

NUTRITIONAL FACTS (per serving, based on 6 servings)

Calories: 201 · Total fat: 15.5 g · Total carbs: 13.1 · Net carbs: 8.5 g · Protein: 6.6 g

quick & easy

squeaky clean

make ahead

egg-free

SHAVED FENNEL, ORANGE, AND PISTACHIO SALAD

Serves 4

I just can't get enough of this combination. So refreshing, it is one of my ultimate summer side salads. It goes well with just about everything, but shines particularly brightly next to grilled chicken (see my recipe on page 154).

- 2 large fennel bulbs
- 2 navel oranges
- 1 large endive
- 8 to 10 paper-thin slices red onion
- 1 clove garlic, minced
- ¼ cup (30 g) raw pistachios, roughly chopped
- 2 tablespoons finely chopped fresh parsley
- 2 tablespoons finely chopped fresh basil
- 2 tablespoons finely chopped fresh mint
- 2 tablespoons white wine vinegar
- 2 tablespoons extra-virgin olive oil
- 1 teaspoon Himalayan salt
- 1 teaspoon freshly ground black pepper

1. Remove the tops from the fennel bulbs and reserve for garnish, if desired. Slice the bulbs as thinly as possible. If you own a mandoline, now would be a good time to use it.

2. Remove the peel and pith from the oranges with a knife and cut the oranges into pretty wheels.

3. Cut the endive in half lengthwise and cut each half lengthwise into thin matchstick strips.

4. Place the shaved fennel, orange wheels, endive, and the rest of the ingredients in a large mixing bowl and toss gently until well combined. Serve immediately, garnished with the fennel tops, if desired.

5. This salad will keep well in the refrigerator for up to a day.

NUTRITIONAL FACTS (per serving)

Calories: 236 · Total fat: 14.5 g · Total carbs: 26.4 g · Net carbs: 17.0 g · Protein: 6.3 g

CHAPTER 4

eggs

time intensive | squeaky clean
 plan ahead | keto friendly
 make ahead | nut-free

Serves 4

BAKED EGGS WITH CREAMED SPINACH

Here's a dish that's delicious at any time of day, but is particularly brilliant for breakfast. You can make the creamed spinach ahead of time and simply reheat it when you're ready to eat. This way, you can have a delicious and highly nutritious breakfast on the table in less than 15 minutes.

For the creamed spinach

- 2 tablespoons bacon drippings or ghee
- ½ small onion, finely chopped
- 1 clove garlic, minced
- ½ teaspoon Himalayan salt
- ½ teaspoon freshly ground black pepper
- 1 small head cauliflower (1¼ pounds/570 g), cored and roughly chopped
- 1 cup (240 ml) Brown Chicken Stock (page 76)
- 1 cup (240 ml) full-fat coconut milk
- 1 tablespoon finely chopped preserved lemon (see Notes, page 70) or the grated zest and juice of 1 lemon
- ¼ cup (55 g) ghee
- 1 tablespoon Dijon mustard
- ¼ teaspoon freshly grated nutmeg
- ⅛ teaspoon ground Ceylon cinnamon
- 2 pounds (910 g) baby spinach leaves, roughly chopped

- 4 large eggs
- 1 tomato, seeded and diced
- Himalayan salt and freshly ground black pepper
- Chopped fresh parsley for garnish

1. Make the creamed spinach: Put the bacon drippings, onion, garlic, salt, and pepper in a medium saucepan. Cook over medium heat for 1 to 2 minutes, until fragrant and slightly softened.

2. Throw in the cauliflower florets and continue cooking for another minute or two.

3. Add the chicken stock, cover, and bring to a boil, then lower the heat and continue cooking until the cauliflower is tender, 5 to 7 minutes.

4. Kill the heat, then add the coconut milk, preserved lemon, ghee, mustard, nutmeg, and cinnamon and process with an immersion blender set on high speed until super smooth and silky. Set aside. (You can also use a countertop blender, but you will probably have to work in several batches.)

5. Place the spinach in a large microwave-safe bowl. You will probably have to work in 2 or 3 batches, unless you own a giant microwave and gargantuan mixing bowls. Cook on high, uncovered, for 4 to 5 minutes or until completely wilted, then set aside to cool.

6. When the spinach is cool enough to handle safely, squeeze as much water as you can out of it and gently mix the spinach into the creamy cauliflower sauce.

7. Place an oven rack in the middle position. Set the oven to broil.

8. Divide the creamed spinach among four 4-ounce (120-ml) au gratin dishes. Make a shallow well in the center of the creamed spinach and crack an egg right into it. Divide the diced tomato equally among the 4 dishes, sprinkle with salt and pepper, and then place under the broiler until the egg whites are completely opaque while the yolks remain slightly runny, 10 to 12 minutes. Garnish with fresh parsley and serve.

NUTRITIONAL FACTS (per serving)

Calories: 436 | Total fat: 35.9 g | Total carbs: 18.4 g | Net carbs: 10.0 g | Protein: 16.6 g

quick & easy

squeaky clean

make ahead

keto friendly

Serves 4

SIMPLE EGG SALAD

I used to love egg salad sandwiches, but really, what I truly liked about them was the egg salad! I may have kicked bread out of my life, but the egg salad sure got to stay. This dish couldn't be easier to make. I enjoy eating it right out of the bowl for breakfast, but I often use it to stuff a pitted avocado half, too. Try it!

- 8 large hard-cooked eggs, cooled and peeled
- ¼ cup (50 g) Foolproof Mayonnaise (page 64)
- ¼ cup (28 g) chopped raw walnuts
- 1 celery rib, finely chopped
- 2 tablespoons finely chopped fresh parsley
- ½ teaspoon freshly ground black pepper
- ¼ teaspoon Himalayan salt
- ¼ teaspoon celery salt
- ¼ teaspoon curry powder

1. Place all the ingredients in a large mixing bowl and mash them roughly with a fork or an egg masher until the ingredients are well combined and your desired consistency has been attained.

2. Serve as is or over your favorite green salad.

3. Keep leftovers refrigerated in an airtight container for up to 4 days.

NUTRITIONAL FACTS (per serving)

Calories: 254 | Total fat: 22.1 g | Total carbs: 2.5 g | Net carbs: 1.3 g | Protein: 13.4 g

time intensive

 squeaky clean

 plan ahead

CREAMY EGG AND SPINACH CASSEROLE

Serves 4

When I was a kid, my dad would sometimes make a dish similar to this one, which he would more often than not serve with the best homemade French fries I have ever had. I would literally jump for joy on those nights! To this day, I find a lot of comfort in this creamy egg dish. I still make it fairly often, although the fries are no longer a part of the ritual. I especially enjoy it in the morning: It makes for a very different but extremely comforting breakfast.

For the béchamel sauce

- 1 tablespoon extra-virgin olive oil
- 1 small onion, chopped
- 2 cloves garlic, minced
- ½ teaspoon Himalayan salt
- ½ teaspoon freshly ground black pepper
- 1 small head cauliflower (1¼ pounds/570 g), cored and roughly chopped
- 2 cups (475 ml) Brown Chicken Stock (page 76)
- ¼ cup (55 g) ghee
- 1 tablespoon Dijon mustard

For the casserole

- 1 pound (455 g) baby spinach leaves, roughly chopped
- 12 large hard-cooked eggs, cooled and peeled
- ¼ cup (30 g) raw cashew pieces

1. Preheat the oven to 375°F (190°C).

2. Make the béchamel sauce: Put the olive oil, onion, garlic, salt, and pepper in a medium saucepan. Cook over medium heat for 1 to 2 minutes, until fragrant and slightly softened.

3. Throw in the cauliflower florets and continue cooking for another minute or two.

4. Add the chicken stock, cover, and bring to a boil, then lower the heat and continue cooking until the cauliflower is tender, 5 to 7 minutes.

5. Ladle the cauliflower mixture into a blender; add the ghee and mustard and process on high speed until super smooth and silky. Set aside.

6. Prepare the rest of the casserole ingredients: Place the spinach in a large microwave-safe bowl. Microwave on high, uncovered, for 2 to 4 minutes or until completely wilted, then set aside to cool.

7. Slice the hard-cooked eggs and place them in a large mixing bowl. Reserve 1 cup (240 ml) of the béchamel sauce and pour the rest over the sliced eggs. Mix very gently until well combined, then transfer to a 2½-quart (2.35-L) baking dish.

8. Squeeze as much water as you can out of the spinach, then mix it with the reserved béchamel sauce. Gently spoon that over the egg mixture, then sprinkle with the cashew pieces.

9. Bake the casserole for 20 to 25 minutes, until it starts to bubble and the top turns golden brown. Allow to cool for about 10 minutes before serving.

NUTRITIONAL FACTS (per serving)

Calories: 493 · Total fat: 35.9 g · Total carbs: 19.4 g · Net carbs: 12.1 g · Protein: 26.8 g

time intensive

 squeaky clean

 make ahead

QUICHE FLORENTINE

While most people prefer to eat their quiche warm, I'm one of those weirdos who enjoys hers cold. No matter how you like to eat your quiche, this one will adapt perfectly!

Serves 6

For the crust

- 1 small head cauliflower (1 pound/455 g)
- 2 large eggs
- ¼ cup plus 2 tablespoons (45 g) coconut flour
- 2 tablespoons tapioca starch
- 1 tablespoon Dijon mustard
- 1 teaspoon finely chopped fresh parsley
- 1 teaspoon Herbes de Provence (page 49)
- ½ teaspoon garlic powder
- ¼ teaspoon Himalayan salt

For the filling

- 1 pound (455 g) baby spinach leaves
- 1 tablespoon healthy cooking fat
- 1 small leek, green and white parts, finely chopped
- ½ teaspoon Himalayan salt
- ½ teaspoon freshly ground black pepper
- 6 large eggs
- 1 cup (240 ml) full-fat coconut milk
- ¼ cup (55 g) ghee, melted
- 2 tablespoons Dijon mustard
- 1 tablespoon finely chopped fresh thyme
- ½ teaspoon baking soda
- ¼ teaspoon freshly grated nutmeg

For garnish

- 2 tablespoons chopped raw walnuts
- 1 tablespoon extra-virgin olive oil

1. Preheat the oven to 400°F (205°C) and generously grease a 9-inch (23-cm) deep-dish pie pan, preferably with lard or ghee.

2. Make the crust: Grate the cauliflower with a box grater or food processor, then place it in a microwave-safe bowl and cover loosely. Microwave for 4 to 6 minutes on high, until soft and tender. Let the cauliflower cool for a few minutes until it can be handled safely, then squeeze it as dry as you possibly can.

3. Put the cauliflower in a large mixing bowl along with the rest of the ingredients for the crust and mix gently with your fingers until well combined and doughlike.

4. Transfer the dough to the prepared pie pan and, with your fingers, press it against the bottom and sides to form a crust. Bake the crust for 10 minutes. Remove from the oven and set aside; leave the oven on.

5. Meanwhile, prepare the filling: Chop the spinach and place it in a large microwave-safe bowl. Microwave on high, uncovered, for 2 to 4 minutes or until completely wilted, then set aside to cool.

6. Heat the cooking fat in a skillet set over medium-high heat. Add the leek, salt, and pepper and cook for 3 to 5 minutes, until softened. Kill the heat and set the skillet aside to cool.

7. Put the eggs, coconut milk, ghee, mustard, thyme, baking soda, and nutmeg in a large mixing bowl and whisk vigorously until combined and slightly frothy.

8. Squeeze as much water as you can out of the spinach, then add it to the egg mixture along with the leek. Mix well and pour into the par-baked crust.

9. Lower the oven temperature to 375°F (190°C) and bake the quiche for 35 minutes, then turn off the heat, crack the door open, and leave the quiche in the oven for an additional 15 minutes or until completely set.

10. Remove the quiche from the oven and let it cool to slightly warmer than room temperature before serving. Garnish with chopped walnuts mixed with extra-virgin olive oil at the time of serving.

11. This quiche will keep in the refrigerator for up to 3 to 4 days and can be reheated slightly in the microwave or enjoyed straight out of the icebox.

NUTRITIONAL FACTS (per serving)

Calories: 404 · Total fat: 30.3 g · Total carbs: 19.9 g · Net carbs: 18.0 g · Protein: 15.0 g

quick
& easy

 keto
friendly

 squeaky
clean

 nut-
free

SMOKED HAM AND ASPARAGUS OMELETTE

Serves 1

One of my favorite things to have for breakfast! Omelettes simply start your day right and are so versatile; you can stuff them with pretty much anything you want or happen to have on hand. I have a real sweet spot for ham and asparagus, but I regularly substitute bacon and spinach and add a few sliced green onions to the deal. Feel free to experiment—the possibilities are endless!

- 2 tablespoons healthy cooking fat, divided
- 5 or 6 button mushrooms, sliced
- 5 or 6 asparagus spears
- 4½ ounces (128 g) smoked ham, cut ¼ inch (6 mm) thick and then into 2-inch (5-cm)-long matchsticks
- 2 large eggs
- 2 tablespoons full-fat coconut milk
- ¼ teaspoon baking soda
- ¼ teaspoon freshly ground black pepper, plus more for the mushrooms
- ⅛ teaspoon Himalayan salt, plus more for the mushrooms

1. Put 1 tablespoon of the cooking fat in a 10-inch (25-cm) nonstick skillet set over medium-high heat. Add the mushrooms, sprinkle with salt and pepper, and cook until golden, about 3 to 4 minutes; remove the mushrooms to a plate.

2. Place the asparagus and ham in the same skillet, cover loosely, and cook for about 2 minutes, moving things around a few times, until the asparagus is fork-tender and the ham is heated all the way through. Set aside with the mushrooms.

3. Wipe the skillet clean, add the remaining tablespoon of cooking fat, and place the pan back over the heat.

4. Combine the eggs, coconut milk, baking soda, pepper, and salt in a small mixing bowl and give it a good whisk, until slightly frothy.

5. Pour the mixture into the preheated skillet and swirl it around to spread it evenly over the entire surface of the pan. Let the omelette settle for a few seconds, then run a heat-resistant rubber spatula around the edge to break it up a little bit, and then start swirling again. You want some of the uncooked egg from the top to get under the omelette. Repeat this process 2 or 3 times until the top really starts to set. Remove from the heat and let the omelette sit, covered, for a few minutes until the top is almost completely set.

6. Arrange the asparagus, ham, and mushrooms in the center of the omelette, then fold both edges inward toward the center, covering the filling.

7. Gently slide the omelette onto a plate and serve.

NUTRITIONAL FACTS

Calories: 450 · Total fat: 26.2 g · Total carbs: 15.8 g · Net carbs: 9.9 g · Protein: 40.5 g

quick
& easy

 keto
friendly

 squeaky
clean

Serves 1

PORTOBELLO STUFFED WITH SCRAMBLED EGGS AND PROSCIUTTO

This simple and hearty little dish makes a fantastic lunch or light dinner, but I think it's especially brilliant at breakfast! Quick and easy enough to make even on a weekday, it sure will kick off your day with a smile.

- 2 teaspoons ghee, divided
- 1 large portobello mushroom cap
- Himalayan salt and freshly ground black pepper
- 2 large eggs, beaten
- ½ cup (15 g) baby arugula
- 4 slices prosciutto (see Notes)
- 1 teaspoon capers
- 3 raw Brazil nuts, finely chopped

For garnish
- 1 teaspoon balsamic vinegar pearls (see Notes)
- Drizzle of extra-virgin olive oil

1. Melt 1 teaspoon of the ghee in a small skillet set over medium heat. Cook the mushroom cap for about 1 minute per side, until slightly softened. Sprinkle with salt and pepper and remove to a serving plate.

2. Place the skillet back over the heat, melt the remaining teaspoon of ghee, and add the beaten eggs. Sprinkle with a generous pinch of salt and pepper and cook, stirring constantly with a rubber spatula, until the eggs turn completely opaque. Kill the heat and set the skillet aside.

3. Arrange the arugula over the mushroom cap and top with 2 slices of prosciutto. Add the scrambled eggs, followed by the rest of the prosciutto. Sprinkle the capers and Brazil nuts all over the top. Garnish with balsamic pearls and olive oil.

Notes : If you like, replace the prosciutto with cold smoked salmon, such as Nova lox.

Balsamic vinegar pearls are cute and elegant little beads of gelled balsamic vinegar that look just like caviar and sort of burst onto your palate as you bite into them, delivering a whole suite of complex, tangy, and sweet flavors to your taste buds. Look for them at your local gourmet food store or search for them online.

NUTRITIONAL FACTS

Calories: 335   Total fat: 31.0 g   Total carbs: 7.5 g   Net carbs: 5.1 g   Protein: 27.5 g

time intensive
 make ahead
 plan ahead
 squeaky clean

Serves 4

SPINACH AND CHICKEN OMELETTE LASAGNA

After you've had a taste of this omelette lasagna, I bet you'll never miss "real" lasagna again! This version is so much easier to make and way tastier, too. Oh, and you know how lasagna noodles get all deliciously crispy on the edges? Just wait until you bite into one of these.

For the sauce

- 1 pound (455 g) fresh spinach
- 2 tablespoons ghee
- 1 large onion, finely chopped
- 1 clove garlic, minced
- 1 teaspoon Himalayan salt, divided
- 1 teaspoon freshly ground black pepper, divided
- 1 small head cauliflower (1¼ pounds/570 g), cored and roughly chopped
- ½ cup (120 ml) Brown Chicken Stock (page 76)
- ½ cup (130 g) cashew cream or tahini (see Note)
- ¼ cup (55 g) ghee
- 1 tablespoon Dijon mustard
- 1 teaspoon chopped fresh thyme
- ¼ teaspoon freshly grated nutmeg
- 1½ cups (200 g) finely chopped cooked chicken

For the "noodles"

- 8 large eggs
- ½ cup (120 ml) full-fat coconut milk
- 2 tablespoons tapioca starch
- ½ teaspoon Himalayan salt
- ½ teaspoon freshly ground black pepper
- ⅓ cup (55 g) chopped raw hazelnuts
- Extra-virgin olive oil for drizzling (optional)

1. Make the sauce: Chop the spinach and place it in a large microwave-safe bowl. Microwave on high, uncovered, for 2 to 4 minutes or until completely wilted, then set aside to cool.

2. Melt the ghee in a small saucepan set over medium heat. Add the onion, garlic, ½ teaspoon of the salt, and ½ teaspoon of the pepper and cook for 1 to 2 minutes, until fragrant and slightly softened.

3. Add the cauliflower and continue cooking for a minute or two. Pour in the chicken stock, cover, and bring to a boil; lower the heat and continue cooking until the cauliflower is really tender, 5 to 7 minutes.

4. Ladle the cauliflower mixture into a blender; add the cashew cream, ghee, mustard, thyme, nutmeg, and remaining ½ teaspoon each of salt and pepper and process on high speed until super smooth and silky. Transfer the mixture to a large mixing bowl. Squeeze the spinach dry and stir it in, along with the cooked chicken. Set aside.

5. Make the noodles: Preheat the oven to 350°F (177°C). Grease and line a 21 by 15-inch (53.5 by 38-cm) rimmed baking sheet with parchment paper. Make sure that the paper adheres really well to the pan so the egg mixture doesn't get underneath.

6. Place all the ingredients for the "noodles" in a large mixing bowl and mix energetically with a whisk until frothy. Pour this mixture into the prepared baking sheet and bake for 12 to 15 minutes, until set. Remove from the oven and increase the oven temperature to 375°F (190°C). Allow the egg mixture to cool for about 5 minutes, then cut it crosswise into 8 strips.

7. Assemble the lasagna: Spread about one-third of the sauce at the bottom of a lasagna dish, then top with 4 "noodles." Repeat with another third of the sauce and 4 more noodles, then spread on the last of the sauce and sprinkle the chopped hazelnuts all over the top.

   Note: At this point, you can put the lasagna in the refrigerator for up to a few days and then bake it when you are ready to serve it. You may want to increase the cooking time by 8 to 10 minutes to make up for the fact that the dish will be completely chilled when it hits the oven.

8. Bake for 25 minutes, until the edges of the "noodles" turn golden and start to crisp up. If you want the top to get nice and golden brown, drizzle with a few tablespoons of olive oil about 5 minutes before the lasagna is due to come out of the oven. Allow to rest for at least 15 minutes before serving.

9. This dish will keep in the refrigerator for 3 to 4 days.

NUTRITIONAL FACTS (per serving)

Calories: 689   Total fat: 49.9 g   Total carbs: 28.1 g   Net carbs: 18.8 g   Protein: 38.4 g

Note: To make cashew cream, soak ½ cup (70 g) of raw cashew pieces overnight or for at least 8 hours, then drain and process them in a small food processor until smooth. Add a few tablespoons of water until you get a thick and creamy consistency.

CHAPTER 5

chicken

under 30

 plan ahead

 freezer friendly

squeaky clean

 keto friendly

 egg-free

nut-free

Serves 6

BASIC GRILLED CHICKEN

This recipe proves that making delicious grilled chicken doesn't have to be complicated or take a big chunk of your time. You won't believe how tender, juicy, and tasty it is. And the best part is, it's absolutely stupid easy to make: The brining does practically all of the work for you. I get the feeling that once you've tried it, it will become a staple for you.

For the brine

- 4 cups (scant 1 L) water
- 2 tablespoons Himalayan salt

- 6 large boneless, skinless chicken breasts (about 10 ounces/285 g each)

For the coating

- ¼ cup (60 ml) extra-virgin olive oil
- Grated zest of 1 lemon
- 1 tablespoon dried oregano leaves
- 2 cloves garlic, minced
- 1 teaspoon Himalayan salt
- 1 teaspoon freshly ground black pepper

For garnish (optional)

- Fresh herbs of choice
- Lemon slices

1. The night before you grill the chicken, dilute the salt in the water, then place the chicken in a nonreactive container with a tight-fitting lid and pour the salted water over it until it's completely covered. Leave the chicken in the brine overnight or for up to a few days.

2. When you are ready to grill the chicken, preheat a grill to high heat, remove the chicken from the brine, and pat it dry.

3. In a large bowl, mix together the ingredients for the coating. Add the chicken breasts to the bowl and toss them around until they are completely coated.

4. Place the chicken on the grill, lower the heat to medium, and close the lid. Cook for 10 minutes per side or until the meat is cooked through and no longer pink on the inside.

5. Remove the chicken to a clean plate and tent it loosely with aluminum foil. Allow to rest for 10 minutes before serving. Garnish with fresh herbs and lemon slices, if desired.

Tip: *You won't believe how tasty and juicy your chicken will be after it's had a chance to spend a day or two in this super simple brine. You could even freeze it in that solution and have it brine as it thaws.*

NUTRITIONAL FACTS (per serving)

Calories: 419 · Total fat: 16.0 g · Total carbs: 1.0 g · Net carbs: 1.0 g · Protein: 63.8 g

keto friendly

nut-free

egg-free

Serves 4

BUFFALO WINGS

Be forewarned! These wings are not for the faint of heart: They pack some serious heat. But their intense fire comes loaded with so much flavor that it renders the heat more than bearable, even for those whose taste buds are a tad delicate.

- 24 chicken wings (2¼ pounds/1 kg total)
- 1 cup (240 ml) Frank's RedHot Sauce
- ⅓ cup (75 g) ghee
- 2 cloves garlic, minced
- 2 tablespoons Sriracha (see Note)
- 1 teaspoon cayenne pepper
- 1 teaspoon ground chipotle pepper

Serving suggestions

- Assorted crudités
- Classic Creamy Coleslaw (page 258)
- Fiery Buffalo Mayo (page 66)

1. Preheat the oven to 475°F (245°C).

2. Place the chicken wings on a wire rack set over a rimmed baking sheet. Bake the wings for 30 to 35 minutes, turning them 3 or 4 times, until golden and crispy all around.

3. While the wings are in the oven, bring the hot sauce, ghee, and garlic to a boil, then reduce the heat and simmer for 5 to 6 minutes, whisking almost constantly, until the sauce has thickened and reduced by half. Stir in the Sriracha, cayenne pepper, and ground chipotle pepper; keep warm.

4. As soon as the wings are ready, transfer them to a large bowl and pour the sauce over them. Toss well until the wings are evenly coated.

5. Serve with crudités and coleslaw, and if you're really brave, try eating the wings with my Fiery Buffalo Mayo.

Note: *Make sure to read your labels! Choose a brand of Sriracha sauce that's free of refined sugar and nasty food preservatives. My favorite is Sky Valley from OrganicVille.*

NUTRITIONAL FACTS (per serving)

Calories: 695 · Total fat: 55.1 g · Total carbs: 4.6 g · Net carbs: 4.6 g · Protein: 42.6 g

Serves 3 or 4

CHICKEN FINGERS WITH SPICY HONEY DIJON DIPPING SAUCE

Here's a dish that's guaranteed to be a winner and please every member of your family. Seriously, who doesn't like chicken fingers? These guys are particularly juicy, especially if you choose to brine the meat overnight, and they come out of the oven nicely golden and crispy. The sweet and spicy dipping sauce takes them over the top. In fact, I strongly suggest that you double the recipe!

For the brine (optional)

- 2 cups (475 ml) water
- 1 tablespoon Himalayan salt

- 2 large boneless, skinless chicken breasts (about 10 ounces/285 g each)

For the dry coating

- 1 cup (120 g) finely ground almonds
- ½ cup (57 g) tapioca starch
- ¼ cup (30 g) finely ground toasted sesame seeds (see Tip, page 300)
- 1 teaspoon garlic powder
- 1 teaspoon dry mustard
- 1 teaspoon freshly ground black pepper
- ½ teaspoon Himalayan salt
- ½ teaspoon smoked paprika
- ½ teaspoon cayenne pepper
- ¼ teaspoon ground fennel seeds

For the wet coating

- 2 large eggs

- 2 to 3 tablespoons avocado oil

For the dipping sauce

- ⅓ cup (75 g) Foolproof Mayonnaise (page 64)
- 2 cloves garlic, minced
- 2 tablespoons raw honey, melted
- 2 tablespoons Dijon mustard
- ½ teaspoon red pepper flakes

1. If time permits, brine the chicken overnight in a solution made of 2 cups (475 ml) water and 1 tablespoon salt. While this step is optional, it creates much juicier and tastier chicken and requires very little effort on your part. Trust me, it's worth it.

2. Preheat the oven to 425°F (220°C) and line a rimmed baking sheet with parchment paper.

3. If you brined the chicken, take the breasts out of the brine and pat them really dry. Cut each breast into 6 relatively even strips.

4. In a shallow bowl, stir together the ingredients for the dry coating until evenly combined.

5. In a separate shallow bowl, beat the eggs.

6. Dip a chicken finger in the eggs, then roll it in the dry coating mixture until evenly coated on all sides. Place it on the prepared baking sheet and repeat this process with the remaining chicken fingers.

7. Drizzle the coated chicken fingers generously with the avocado oil, place the baking sheet in the oven, and bake until the crust gets golden brown and the chicken is cooked through, about 20 to 25 minutes, depending on size. Flip the chicken fingers after about 15 minutes of cooking.

8. While the chicken fingers are cooking, prepare the dipping sauce by combining the mayonnaise, garlic, honey, mustard, and red pepper flakes in a small bowl.

9. Allow the chicken fingers to cool on the baking sheet for a few minutes, then serve with the dipping sauce.

Tip: *These chicken fingers reheat marvelously well! Simply pan-fry them in a skillet set over medium heat, and use plenty of ghee!*

NUTRITIONAL FACTS (per 3 chicken strips)

Calories: 496	Total fat: 24.1 g	Total carbs: 26.0 g	Net carbs: 21.0 g	Protein: 44.8 g

(per 2 tablespoons of sauce)

Calories: 155	Total fat: 13.5 g	Total carbs: 9.9 g	Net carbs: 9.9 g	Protein: 0.9 g

under 30

plan ahead

make ahead

egg-free

nut-free

Serves 4 to 6

HONEY SESAME CHICKEN

I cannot even find the words to describe how much I adore this dish. Had it been on the menu at my favorite Asian restaurant, which I admittedly still visit at least once or twice a year, it definitely would have been on my list of "must-haves" there, and may even have caused me to go there more often! The good thing is, I can whip up this dish in no time, in the comfort of my own kitchen, and savor it without feeling even an ounce of guilt. I guarantee that you will love it just as much!

For the sauce

- ¼ cup (85 g) raw honey
- ¼ cup (75 g) Date Paste (page 82)
- ¼ cup (60 ml) coconut aminos
- ¼ cup (2¼ ounces/65 g) tomato paste
- ¼ cup (60 ml) unseasoned rice vinegar
- ¼ cup (60 ml) water
- 1 tablespoon toasted sesame oil
- 1 clove garlic, minced
- 2 tablespoons grated fresh ginger
- 2 tablespoons sesame seeds, toasted (see Tip, page 300)
- ½ teaspoon Himalayan salt

- ¼ cup (28 g) tapioca starch
- ½ teaspoon Himalayan salt
- ½ teaspoon freshly ground black pepper
- 2 pounds (910 g) boneless, skinless chicken thighs
- ¼ cup (52 g) coconut oil

For garnish

- 2 tablespoons sliced green onions

1. Make the sauce: Place all the ingredients for the sauce in a large bowl and mix well with a whisk until evenly combined. Set aside.

2. Put the tapioca starch, ½ teaspoon salt, and pepper in a large bowl and mix well. Cut the chicken thighs in half and add them to the bowl with the tapioca starch mixture. Toss gently with your fingers until all the pieces of chicken are evenly coated.

3. Melt the coconut oil in a large skillet set over high heat until it is really hot, about 2 minutes. Working in batches, add the pieces of chicken, leaving at least 1 or 2 inches (2.5 or 5 cm) between them so that air can circulate freely around them and they don't start boiling as opposed to browning. Cook the chicken for 3 to 5 minutes per side, until it is brown and crispy, then remove to a plate.

4. Once all the pieces of chicken have been browned, return them all to the pan, lower the heat to medium, and cook uncovered for 10 minutes, until the chicken is cooked through and the juices that come out are no longer pink.

5. Add the sauce to the pan and mix until the chicken is well coated. Reduce the heat to medium-low and simmer for about 5 minutes, until the sauce has thickened and is a little darker in color.

6. Serve immediately, garnished with sliced green onions.

7. This dish will keep in the refrigerator for up to 3 days and reheats very well in the microwave.

NUTRITIONAL FACTS (per serving, based on 6 servings)

Calories: 392 | Total fat: 19.0 g | Total carbs: 26.8 g | Net carbs: 25.5 g | Protein: 30.6 g

under 30

squeaky clean

egg-free

nut-free

Serves 2

SZECHUAN CHICKEN

I've always been a huge fan of Asian food, and since I began making my own, I much prefer homemade to takeout. Not only is it healthier, but it's often tastier, too, without necessitating the addition of flavor-boosting agents like MSG. Plus, it often ends up on my table much quicker than if I'd picked up the phone and ordered in.

For the sauce

- 1 clove garlic, minced
- ¼ cup (60 ml) coconut aminos
- 2 tablespoons unseasoned rice vinegar
- 2 tablespoons toasted sesame oil
- 2 tablespoons Date Paste (page 82) or raw honey
- 1 tablespoon fish sauce
- 1 teaspoon Chinese five-spice powder (see Notes)
- 1 teaspoon red pepper flakes
- 1 teaspoon ground Szechuan pepper (see Notes)
- ½ teaspoon Himalayan salt
- ½ teaspoon freshly ground black pepper
- 2 tablespoons tapioca starch

- 2 large boneless, skinless chicken breasts (about 10 ounces/285 g each)
- 2 tablespoons coconut oil
- ½ medium yellow onion, sliced
- 1½ cups (3½ ounces/100 g) mushrooms, sliced
- 1 cup (3½ ounces/100 g) sugar snap peas
- 1 orange bell pepper, seeded and julienned

For garnish

- 1 green onion, green part only, thinly sliced
- ½ teaspoon white sesame seeds, toasted (see Tip, page 300)
- ½ teaspoon black sesame seeds

1. Put all the ingredients for the sauce in a large bowl and mix with a whisk until well combined. Set aside.

2. Cut the chicken breasts into very thin strips and add them to the bowl with the sauce. Toss until the chicken is completely and evenly coated.

3. Make sure that all the vegetables are prepped and arranged on your work surface in such a way that you can quickly grab them as needed. The rest of the process will go very fast, so you need to have everything ready and within reach.

4. Heat a wok or large heavy skillet over scorching heat for about 2 minutes, then add the coconut oil and wait for it to melt completely.

5. Add the onion and mushrooms and sauté for about 30 seconds; throw in the sugar snap peas and bell pepper and continue cooking for 30 to 45 seconds, until the vegetables are slightly softened and fragrant.

6. Carefully add the meat and sauce and cook, stirring every 45 seconds or so, until the chicken is opaque and no longer pink, 4 to 5 minutes.

7. Serve immediately, garnished with sliced green onions and white and black sesame seeds.

Notes: Chinese five-spice powder is a spice mixture made of ground star anise, cinnamon, fennel seeds, cloves, and Sichuan pepper that is used extensively in Chinese cuisine. It is widely available, so you should be able to find it in the spice aisle of your favorite grocery store.

Szechuan pepper is a commonly used spice in Asian cuisine. It has a unique flavor that is not hot or pungent like that of black peppercorns or chili peppers. Instead, it has slight lemony overtones and creates a tingly numbness in the mouth that sets the stage for hot spices. You should be able to find it in the spice aisle of your favorite grocery store, but if you come back empty-handed, try your local ethnic food store or turn to Amazon, my favorite online source; they definitely carry it.

To make the chicken easier to slice, place it in the freezer for about an hour before slicing it.

NUTRITIONAL FACTS (per serving)

| Calories: 663 | Total fat: 33.3 g | Total carbs: 34.3 g | Net carbs: 30.7 g | Protein: 52.1 g |

under 30

squeaky clean

plan ahead

keto friendly

make ahead

egg-free

freezer friendly

Serves 4 to 6

- 1 to 2 tablespoons coconut oil for the pan
- 2 pounds (910 g) boneless, skinless chicken breasts, cut into 1-inch (2.5-cm) chunks
- 1 medium onion, chopped
- 2 cloves garlic, minced
- 4 red bell peppers, seeded and chopped
- 2 tablespoons grated fresh ginger
- 1 tablespoon garam masala (see Note)
- 1 teaspoon Ras el Hanout (page 48)
- 1 teaspoon ground coriander
- ½ teaspoon ground chipotle pepper
- ½ teaspoon fennel seeds
- ½ teaspoon ground Ceylon cinnamon
- 2 dried pili pili peppers or other dried chili peppers, crushed into flakes
- 1½ cups (350 ml) canned crushed tomatoes
- 1½ cups (350 ml) water, divided
- ½ cup (120 ml) full-fat coconut milk
- ¼ cup (65 g) All-Natural Toasted Almond Butter (page 288)
- ¼ cup (60 g) tahini
- 1 teaspoon pure vanilla extract, homemade (page 84) or store-bought
- 6 cups (10½ ounces/300 g) baby spinach leaves, chopped
- Handful of chopped fresh parsley for garnish (optional)

SPICY INDIAN CHICKEN STEW

While this is in no way a traditional Indian dish, its flavor profile has a very strong Indian influence. I feel I should warn you that it's fairly hot, though the addition of coconut milk and almond butter helps tone it down some; feel free to adjust the level of heat to your liking.

1. Melt the coconut oil in a large skillet set over medium-high heat, then add the chunks of chicken in a single layer, being mindful not to over-crowd the pan (you will probably have to work in batches). Cook until the chicken is nice and golden all around, 5 to 6 minutes total. Remove the cooked chicken to a bowl to catch the juices.

2. Return the skillet to the heat, lower the heat to medium, and add the onion. Cook for 3 to 4 minutes, until the onion starts to turn translucent, then add the garlic, bell peppers, ginger, and spices and continue cooking for another 2 minutes, until fragrant.

3. Stir in the crushed tomatoes and 1 cup (240 ml) of the water and return the chicken, with juices, to the pan. Cover and simmer on low for 15 minutes.

4. Put the coconut milk, remaining ½ cup (120 ml) of water, almond butter, tahini, and vanilla extract in a large mixing bowl or liquid measuring cup. Whisk until well combined, then add the mixture to the chicken and stir well.

5. Bring the stew back to a simmer, then throw in the chopped spinach in 3 or 4 batches. Continue cooking until the spinach is completely wilted, then serve, garnished with fresh parsley, if desired.

6. This dish will keep in the refrigerator for up to 3 days and reheats very well in the microwave.

Tip: For juicier and tastier chicken, brine the chicken breasts overnight in a solution made of 2 cups (475 ml) water and 1 tablespoon salt. This step requires very little effort on your part but is so totally worth it!

Note: Garam masala is a commonly used spice blend in Indian and South Asian cuisine. It has a unique, distinctive, and aromatic essence and typically includes ground black and white peppercorns, cloves, cinnamon, nutmeg, mace, black and green cardamom, bay leaves, and caraway. Garam masala is fairly widely available even in the Western Hemisphere, so you should be able to find it in the spice aisle of your favorite grocery store. However, if your local grocer leaves you stranded, try your local ethnic food store or look for it online. Amazon carries it.

NUTRITIONAL FACTS (per serving, based on 6 servings)

Calories: 419 · Total fat: 21.1 g · Total carbs: 17.7 g · Net carbs: 12.0 g · Protein: 39.4 g

under 30

 squeaky clean

 keto friendly

 egg-free

nut-free

Serves 6

CREAMY COCONUT CHICKEN STEW

The pili pili, also called piri piri, is an extremely hot little pepper that must be used very sparingly. In Creole, this chili pepper was nicknamed *z'ozio*, hence the name "bird pepper" or "bird tongue." Pili pili peppers are a staple of Caribbean cuisine, and they are so strong that it is highly advisable to split them and remove the seeds before adding the peppers to your dish. If you can't find pili pili peppers, don't sweat it; you can use regular dried red chili peppers instead. Only you might have to use a little more…or less, depending on how hot you like it!

- 2 tablespoons coconut oil, divided
- 1 ripe plantain, cut into thick half-moons
- ½ pound (225 g) mushrooms, sliced
- ½ teaspoon Himalayan salt
- 1 teaspoon freshly ground black pepper
- 1 large onion, sliced
- 2 pounds (910 g) boneless, skinless chicken breasts, cut into 3-inch (7.5-cm)-long strips
- 3 to 4 sweet bell peppers of assorted colors, seeded and sliced
- 1 tablespoon Ras el Hanout (page 48)
- 2 dried pili pili peppers or other dried chili peppers, crushed into flakes
- 1 cup (240 ml) full-fat coconut milk

1. Melt 1 tablespoon of the coconut oil in a skillet set over medium-high heat. Add the plantain slices and sauté for 2 to 3 minutes or until golden on both sides; remove to a bowl.

2. Add the remaining tablespoon of coconut oil to the skillet, then throw in the mushrooms, salt, and pepper. Cook until golden on both sides, then add the onion and continue cooking until the onion is really soft and starts to caramelize, 10 to 15 minutes; remove the mushroom and onion mixture to the bowl with the plantains.

3. Reduce the heat to medium, add the chicken strips to the skillet, and sprinkle with a little bit of salt and pepper. You're not really looking to brown the chicken, you just want to cook it until it turns opaque and is no longer pink. This should take about 8 to 10 minutes. Stir often so that all the pieces get to visit the bottom of the pan.

4. When the chicken is cooked through, toss in the bell peppers and give them 1 or 2 minutes to soften up a bit, then add the Ras el Hanout, pili pili pepper flakes, and coconut milk. Stir well, then gently toss in the reserved plantains, mushrooms, and onions.

5. Serve immediately.

NUTRITIONAL FACTS (per serving)

Calories: 344 · Total fat: 15.2 g · Total carbs: 16.7 g · Net carbs: 16.7 g · Protein: 34.6 g

time
intensive

egg-
free

squeaky
clean

nut-
free

keto
friendly

Serves 4

OLIVE AND LEMON ROAST CHICKEN

Though you can make this dish without butterflying the chicken first, the butterflying process results in a bird that is much more tender and juicy, since the entire underside gets to sit in its juices as it roasts. That's on top of being visually interesting—very well worth the extra effort, methinks! But if butchering meat isn't your forte, you could look for a pre-butterflied chicken at the meat counter or ask your butcher to butterfly the chicken for you.

- 1 whole chicken (5½ pounds/ 2.5 kg)
- 2 to 4 tablespoons ghee
- 1 lemon, sliced
- 4 sprigs fresh rosemary
- Himalayan salt and freshly ground black pepper
- 8 to 10 cloves garlic, smashed with the side of a knife
- ½ medium red onion, thinly sliced
- 20 large green olives
- 2 tablespoons capers
- 2 tablespoons olive or caper brine

Note: Nutritional facts are approximations and will vary greatly depending on the size of the chicken, the part of the chicken you eat, and whether you include the skin.

1. Preheat the oven to 325°F (163°C).

2. Butterfly the chicken: Place the chicken breast-side down and, as seen in figures 1 and 2 on page 170, use a pair of poultry shears to cut down one side of the backbone and through the ribs. Make an identical cut on the opposite side of the backbone to remove the backbone completely (don't chuck it; reserve it for stock).

3. Place the bird cut-side down and flatten the breastbone with the heel of your hand (see figures 3 and 4). You will have to apply a good amount of pressure to really flatten it. If you want, you can stop there, but for an even flatter-looking bird, you can remove the keel bone, too. This small triangular-shaped bone consists of hard bone at one end and fairly soft white cartilage at the other, and is located in the center of the breastbone. To remove the keel bone, flip the chicken back over and, using a sharp knife, slit the little piece of gristle at the wider end of the breastbone to expose the keel bone (see figure 5). Now pick up the bird, crack the membrane open, and loosen the keel bone by bending the bird back and outward (see figure 6). Then slide your fingers under the keel bone. It should come right off. Run your fingers under the skin and carefully detach it from the flesh (see figures 7, 8, and 9).

4. With your fingers, rub some ghee under the skin directly on the flesh, then insert a sprig of rosemary and a slice of lemon under the skin for each part of the chicken (both breasts and both legs; see figures 10 and 11). Pat the skin dry, rub a little bit of ghee all over the bird, and then sprinkle generously with salt and pepper.

5. Place the bird in a shallow baking dish; add the garlic, red onion, olives, capers, and olive or caper brine to the pan, around the chicken. Cover loosely with foil and roast for 1½ hours, basting every so often.

6. Remove the foil, baste one last time, and roast for 30 more minutes.

7. Remove from the oven, place the foil back over the chicken, and let it rest for about 20 minutes before carving.

NUTRITIONAL FACTS (per serving; see Note)

Calories: 547   Total fat: 33.6 g   Total carbs: 5.1 g   Net carbs: 4.0 g   Protein: 52.2 g

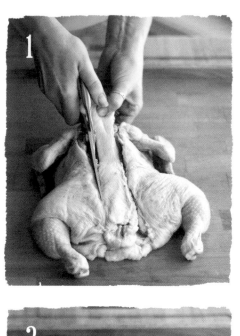

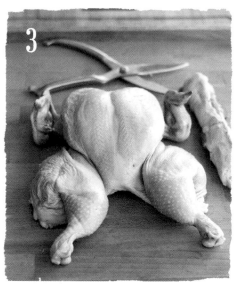

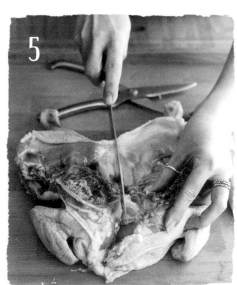

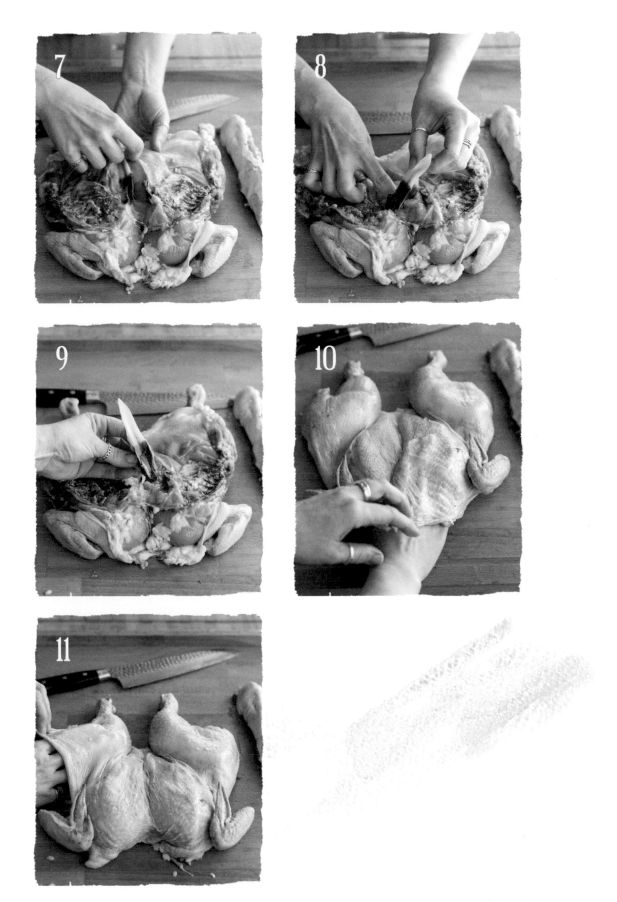

beef and lamb

under 30
 keto friendly
 squeaky clean
egg-free

ASIAN BEEF AND BROCCOLI

In the mood for a little Asian food? About to order in? Put the phone down right now. I swear, this dish is a million times better than take-out, and chances are it will be ready before the delivery guy could make it to your door.

Serves 4

- ¼ cup (21 g) sliced almonds

For the marinade

- ¼ cup (60 ml) coconut aminos
- 2 tablespoons unseasoned rice vinegar
- 2 tablespoons minced fresh ginger
- 1 tablespoon fish sauce
- 1 tablespoon toasted sesame oil
- 1 tablespoon tapioca starch
- 1 teaspoon Chinese five-spice powder (see Notes, page 162)
- 2 green onions, chopped
- 2 cloves garlic, minced
- 2 dried bird's-eye chili peppers, crushed into flakes (see Note)

- 1⅔ pounds (750 g) top round beef, cut into thin strips
- ½ teaspoon Himalayan salt
- ½ teaspoon freshly ground black pepper
- 2 tablespoons coconut oil, or more as needed
- 1 pound (455 g) broccoli florets

1. Toast the almonds in a dry skillet set over medium heat, stirring often, until they turn slightly golden and become fragrant, 3 to 5 minutes. Remove from the heat.

2. Place all the ingredients for the marinade in a large mixing bowl and mix with a whisk until well combined. Set aside.

3. Season the meat generously with the salt and pepper.

4. Place the coconut oil in a large wok or skillet set over scorching heat. When the pan is really hot, add the strips of beef in a single layer, being mindful not to overcrowd the pan (you will probably have to work in 2 or 3 batches, so add more oil to the pan as necessary), and cook until just browned with a little bit of pink still showing, 1 to 2 minutes; remove the cooked meat to the bowl that contains the marinade.

5. Add the broccoli to the wok or skillet. Cook for 2 to 3 minutes, until bright green and slightly softened, then add the reserved meat and marinade; continue cooking for about a minute until the sauce thickens. Stir in the toasted almonds and serve.

Note: If you can't find dried bird's-eye chili peppers, you can use a teaspoon of red pepper flakes instead.

NUTRITIONAL FACTS (per serving)

Calories: 476 · Total fat: 27.4 g · Total carbs: 14.0 g · Net carbs: 9.4 g · Protein: 47.1 g

under 30

squeaky clean

plan ahead

keto friendly

make ahead

Serves 4

BEEF TARTARE

A unique twist on a classic, this intriguing version of beef tartare packs a serious punch! Each bite will bring such a complexity of flavors and textures to your taste buds, you'll no doubt want to go back for more. Even if you're not a fan of raw meat, I suspect that this dish will make you a believer!

- 1½ pounds (680 g) top round beef
- 1 large egg yolk
- Juice of 1 lime
- 2 tablespoons Dijon mustard
- 2 tablespoons balsamic vinegar
- 2 tablespoons chopped red onion
- 6 dried apricots, finely chopped
- 2 tablespoons toasted hazelnuts, chopped
- 2 tablespoons chopped fresh parsley
- 1 tablespoon chopped fresh mint
- 1 tablespoon green peppercorns in brine, finely chopped
- 1 teaspoon red pepper flakes
- ½ teaspoon Himalayan salt
- ¼ teaspoon ground chipotle pepper

For serving
- Lettuce leaves
- Assorted crudités

1. Place the beef in the freezer for 30 minutes to 1 hour to firm up; this will make it much easier to cut.

2. Remove the beef from the freezer and slice it very thinly, then chop it into tiny pieces until its texture resembles that of coarsely ground beef. Place the meat in a large mixing bowl and set aside.

3. In a separate mixing bowl, whisk together the egg yolk, lime juice, mustard, and vinegar until well combined and slightly emulsified.

4. Add the rest of the ingredients and mix well, then pour the mixture over the chopped beef and mix gently until well incorporated.

5. Place a piece of plastic wrap directly over the beef so that no air comes into contact with the meat and, if time permits, place it in the refrigerator for 1 to 2 hours to allow the flavors to fully develop.

6. Divide among 4 individual (1-cup/240-ml) ramekins or mini cake pans and press well to form perfect patties.

7. Line 4 serving plates with lettuce leaves. Flip the tartare onto the lettuce leaves and serve immediately with crudités.

8. This tartare will keep in the fridge for up to 24 hours; however, since the meat may discolor a little bit, I recommend serving it to your guests no longer than 6 to 8 hours after making it.

NUTRITIONAL FACTS (per serving)

Calories: 387 · Total fat: 18.3 g · Total carbs: 8.7 g · Net carbs: 6.4 g · Protein: 06.6

time intensive

keto friendly

make ahead

egg-free

freezer friendly

nut-free

squeaky clean

Serves 8

- 3 tablespoons healthy cooking fat, or more as needed
- 1 (4½-pound/2-kg) beef blade roast
- ¼ cup plus 2 tablespoons (45 g) Chili Moka Steak Rub (page 48)
- 3 to 4 large yellow onions, sliced
- 4 cloves garlic, chopped
- 2 cups (475 ml) water

EASY BRAISED BEEF

When I think of comfort food, braised beef is one of the first things that comes to mind. To me, nothing is more comforting than meat so tender and juicy that it practically melts in your mouth. And this braised beef recipe is so easy to make; I take a lot of comfort in that simple fact, too! For the ultimate comfort food experience, serve this dish piping hot over a generous mound of Roasted Garlic Cauliflower Mash (page 278) with a side of Oven-Roasted Glazed Carrots (page 260).

1. Preheat the oven to 300°F (150°C).

2. In a large skillet that can handle serious heat, melt the cooking fat over very high heat.

3. While the pan is heating, pat the roast really dry and rub it generously on both sides with the steak rub. Place the roast in the hot pan and sear it on both sides until a beautiful golden crust forms, then transfer the meat to a 4-quart (3.8-L) or larger Dutch oven.

4. Scrape off and discard any burned bits from the skillet, then place the skillet back over medium heat. Add the onions, as well as more cooking fat, if needed. Cook the onions for 4 to 5 minutes or until they start to turn golden, then toss in the garlic and continue cooking for another minute. Transfer to the Dutch oven with the roast and add the water as well as any leftover spices that didn't get used to rub the meat.

5. Cover, place in the oven, and braise for 3 to 3½ hours, until the meat can easily be pulled apart with a fork. Remove from the oven and allow to cool for about 10 minutes before serving.

6. This dish will keep in the refrigerator for up to 3 to 4 days and reheats very well in the microwave or in a saucepan over low heat.

NUTRITIONAL FACTS (per serving)

Calories: 408 ; Total fat: 17.2 g ; Total carbs: 8.0 g ; Net carbs: 5.8 g ; Protein: 53.6 g

time intensive · keto friendly

plan ahead · egg-free

freezer friendly · nut-free

Serves a crowd or generates a lot of leftovers (which I'm sure you won't mind)

For the brine

- 8½ quarts (8 L) water
- ¾ cup (48 g) pickling spice
- 1 whole cinnamon stick
- ½ whole nutmeg (not grated)
- 10 to 12 whole cloves
- 2 cups (480 g) kosher salt
- 1⅓ cups (192 g) coconut sugar
- ½ cup (72 g) pink curing salt (Prague powder #1; see Notes)

- 1 (11- to 12-pound/5- to 5½-kg) beef brisket (see Notes)
- 2 small onions, quartered
- 5 or 6 cloves garlic, smashed with the side of a knife
- 3 or 4 celery ribs, cut in half
- 2 or 3 carrots, cut into large chunks

MONTREAL-STYLE CORNED BEEF

While making your own corned beef at home may seem like a lot of work, it basically takes care of itself, and the resulting meat is so delicious that no one will ever believe it's not from the local deli! Push the envelope a bit further and serve it with homemade sauerkraut, whole-grain mustard, and pickles, why don't you? Deli made healthy. Who would've thought?

1. Place all the ingredients for the brine in a large stockpot over medium-high heat, stirring occasionally, until the salt has completely dissolved.

2. Remove the brine from the heat and let it cool to room temperature, then place it in the refrigerator overnight or until completely chilled.

3. Once the brine is ready, remove all visible fat from the meat and place it in a food-grade container that's large enough to hold both the brisket and the brine. A large-capacity stainless-steel roasting pan is a perfect candidate for this task. Whatever you use, make sure that it will fit in your refrigerator, where it will have to sit undisturbed for the next 10 to 14 days! Since the meat has to cook for an entire day, this range is provided as a flexible window so that you can cook the meat when it best accommodates you. Make sure to leave the meat in the brine for at least 10 days, but not longer than 2 weeks.

4. Pour enough brine over the brisket to completely cover it, then place a heavy object such as a plate over the meat to ensure that it remains submerged for the entire curing time; transfer the whole rig to the fridge. Reserve the leftover brine. Check on the brisket daily to make sure that the meat is completely submerged at all times. This is absolutely imperative, as contact with the air will likely cause the meat to go bad. Top off with the leftover brine as needed.

5. After the meat is done curing, discard the brine, rinse the meat under cold running water, and place it back in the roasting pan. Add the onions, garlic, celery, and carrots and cover with cold water by about 1 inch (2.5 cm).

6. Seal completely with aluminum foil and place in a 250°F (120°C) oven for 9 to 10 hours, until fork-tender.

7. Take the brisket out of the oven and remove almost all of the cooking liquid (leave about ¼ inch/6 mm), then cover loosely with the foil and place back in the oven for another 30 minutes.

8. Remove the foil, raise the oven temperature to 350°F (177°C), and leave the brisket in for another 25 minutes, basting it from time to time.

9. Your brisket is done! Remove it from the oven and let it rest for 10 to 15 minutes, then transfer to a cutting board, slice across the grain, and serve.

NUTRITIONAL FACTS (per 5½-ounce/155-g serving)

Calories: 265 · Total fat: 19.6 g · Total carbs: 0.0 g · Net carbs: 0.0 g · Protein: 20.9 g

Notes: Pink curing salt, not to be confused with pink Himalayan salt, is a mixture of about 94 percent salt and 6 percent sodium nitrite. Curing salt helps preserve meat and prevent spoilage by inhibiting the growth of fungus or bacteria. It also ensures that the cured meat will keep its beautiful pink color. Without it, the meat would likely turn an unappetizing shade of gray. Its use is a bit controversial in the Paleo world; personally, I don't have a problem using it in such minimal doses. I'd much rather play it safe, you know. If you firmly oppose adding nitrites to your food, you could experiment with using celery juice powder (not to be confused with celery salt) instead, which plays pretty much the same role. Both Prague powder #1 and celery juice powder can be found online, but you could also try your local butcher shop.

I realize that this recipe calls for a humongous piece of meat, but because corned beef takes so long to make, you might as well make it worth your while and make a huge batch, especially since it freezes so well. Also, the meat shrinks quite a bit in the process, so you're left with about half the initial slab when all is said and done. If you still think that this is too much meat for you, or you don't have access to the proper oversized equipment, feel free to halve the recipe. Of course, you will also need to shave a couple of hours from the total cooking time.

under 30

 nut-free

Serves 4

CORNED BEEF AND SWEET POTATO HASH

It doesn't matter where you are when you eat this dish; it will make you feel like you're at a cottage on a chilly winter morning, sitting by the fire and staring out at the snow that's slowly making its way to the ground. It's what I call comfort food to the tenth power. If I could choose but one comforting dish to eat for the rest of my life, it would definitely be this one.

- 4 small red-skinned, white-fleshed sweet potatoes, skin on, finely diced
- ¼ cup (55 g) ghee
- ½ small onion, finely chopped
- ½ large green bell pepper, seeded and finely chopped
- 1 celery rib, finely chopped
- ½ teaspoon Himalayan salt
- ½ teaspoon freshly ground black pepper
- 1 pound (455 g) Montreal-Style Corned Beef (page 180), chopped (see Note)
- 4 large eggs, fried

1. Steam the sweet potatoes over a pot of salted boiling water until tender but still a tad crunchy, about 10 minutes. Let cool completely.

2. Melt the ghee in a cast-iron skillet set over medium-high heat. Add the sweet potatoes and cook until golden brown on all sides, about 5 minutes; remove to a plate.

3. Add the onion, bell pepper, celery, salt, and pepper and cook for about 1 minute, until just softened, then add the corned beef and continue cooking until heated through, about 1 more minute.

4. Stir in the reserved sweet potatoes and cook just long enough to heat them through. Serve each portion of hash topped with a fried egg.

Note: If you don't have any leftover corned beef on hand, try subbing smoked ham, Italian sausage, or even cooked chicken.

NUTRITIONAL FACTS (per serving)

| Calories: 599 | Total fat: 36.2 g | Total carbs: 38.5 g | Net carbs: 32.4 g | Protein: 29.1 g |

quick & easy

 keto friendly

 plan ahead

 egg-free

 squeaky clean

 nut-free

Serves 4

GRILLED BEEF LIVER

If you want to add more offal and organ meats to your diet but don't really consider yourself a fan of liver just yet, you should definitely try cooking it on a grill. Grilling it over intense high heat produces liver that's melt-in-your-mouth tender with a nice, crispy exterior, just like good liver should be. And the addition of seasoned oil brings out so much flavor, it'll make you forget that you're eating liver and not steak! Try pairing it with Grilled Endives (page 266).

- 4 (4-ounce/115-g) slices beef liver, about ¾ inch (2 cm) thick
- ½ cup (120 ml) fresh lime or lemon juice
- 2 tablespoons avocado oil
- Himalayan salt and freshly ground black pepper

For the seasoned oil
- 2 tablespoons avocado oil
- 1 tablespoon balsamic vinegar
- 1 tablespoon finely chopped fresh rosemary
- 1 teaspoon finely chopped fresh sage
- 1 teaspoon Dijon mustard
- ½ teaspoon Himalayan salt
- ½ teaspoon freshly ground black pepper
- ½ teaspoon freshly grated nutmeg
- ½ teaspoon red pepper flakes

1. The night before, rinse the liver really well under cold running water, then place it in a nonreactive container with a tight-fitting lid or in a resealable plastic bag. Add the lime or lemon juice and move the slices around so that they all get covered with the juice, then place the container in the fridge to marinate overnight.

2. When you are ready to cook the liver, preheat a grill to turbo-combusting, scorching-high heat.

3. Place all the ingredients for the seasoned oil in a small mixing bowl and whisk until well combined.

4. Remove the slices of liver from the juice and pat them really dry; rub them with avocado oil on both sides and then sprinkle generously with salt and pepper.

5. Place the liver on the scorching-hot grill and cook, covered and undisturbed, for 2 minutes. Flip and brush each slice with some of the seasoned oil. Close the lid and continue cooking for 2 minutes, then flip the slices again and brush the other side with the rest of the seasoned oil. Close the lid and continue cooking for another 2 minutes.

6. Remove the liver to a plate and tent loosely with aluminum foil. Allow to rest for 5 minutes before serving.

NUTRITIONAL FACTS (per serving)

Calories: 300 | Total fat: 18.8 g | Total carbs: 6.1 g | Net carbs: 5.4 g | Protein: 25.8 g

under 30

 squeaky clean

 plan ahead

 egg-free

 make ahead

Serves 4

GROUND BEEF BREAKFAST HASH

While I like to refer to this dish as breakfast hash, it can be enjoyed at any time of day. I like to call it that because I find it to be the perfect kind of meal for those who are looking to replace traditional breakfast fare, such as cereal, toast, or pancakes, with more nutrient-dense and satisfying foods like meat and veggies.

- 1 cup (140 g) cubed butternut squash
- 1 cup Brussels sprouts, cut in half
- 2 tablespoons coconut oil
- 1 medium onion, chopped
- 1 celery rib, chopped
- 1 pound (455 g) lean ground beef
- 1 teaspoon Himalayan salt
- 1 teaspoon freshly ground black pepper
- 1 tablespoon garam masala (see Note, page 164)
- ¼ cup (65 g) All-Natural Toasted Hazelnut Butter (page 292)
- ¼ cup (60 ml) full-fat coconut milk, plus more for serving (optional)
- ¼ cup (60 ml) water
- ¼ cup (36 g) raisins
- ¼ cup (21 g) unsweetened toasted coconut flakes
- ¼ cup (30 g) sliced green olives
- ¼ cup (30 g) chopped raw pistachios
- ⅓ pound (150 g) fresh spinach

1. Steam the squash and Brussels sprouts over a pot of salted boiling water for 6 to 8 minutes, until tender but still a tad crunchy. Let cool completely (you can rinse them under cold running water to help speed up the process).

2. Melt the coconut oil in a large skillet set over medium-high heat. Add the onion and celery and sweat for 2 to 3 minutes, until the onion is translucent and the celery is slightly softened.

3. Crank up the heat to high. Add the ground beef, salt, and pepper and cook until the beef is completely browned.

4. Stir in the garam masala, hazelnut butter, coconut milk, and water, then throw in the raisins, toasted coconut, olives, pistachios, and steamed squash and Brussels sprouts. Stir and continue cooking until heated through.

5. Kill the heat, add the spinach, and mix gently. Let sit for a few minutes, until the spinach is completely wilted, then serve. Spoon a little bit of coconut milk over the top, if desired.

6. This dish will keep in the refrigerator for up to 3 to 4 days and reheats very well in the microwave or in a nonstick skillet set over low heat.

NUTRITIONAL FACTS (per serving)

Calories: 470 | Total fat: 29.0 g | Total carbs: 23.1 g | Net carbs: 17.1 g | Protein: 28.0 g

quick
& easy

keto
friendly

plan
ahead

egg-
free

squeaky
clean

nut-
free

Serves 2

° 2 (9-ounce/255-g) skirt steaks

For the marinade

° Juice of 2 limes

° 2 teaspoons Ras el Hanout
(page 48)

° 1 teaspoon Himalayan salt

° 1 teaspoon freshly ground black
pepper

° 2 cloves garlic, minced

° 2 fresh bird's-eye chili peppers
or small jalapeño peppers, finely
chopped

MOROCCAN GRILLED SKIRT STEAK

Skirt steak loves intense heat but is very easy to overcook due to its thinness. It is best served rare to medium-rare; cook it for too long or over insufficient heat and it will turn into a tough, chewy mess. Give it the intense heat that it demands, and it'll thank you by becoming super tender and flavorful.

1. Place the meat in a nonreactive container with a tight-fitting lid or in a resealable plastic bag. Whisk together all the ingredients for the marinade and pour it right over the steaks. Move things around a bit to make sure that the meat is well coated, then place it in the fridge to rest for a minimum of 2 hours or up to 24 hours.

2. Preheat a grill to scorching-high heat.

3. Remove the steaks from the marinade and pat them dry, then place them on the scorching-hot grill. Cook for 1 to 2 minutes per side, depending on thickness and the desired level of doneness, turning the meat only once.

4. Tent the steaks loosely with aluminum foil and let them rest for 10 minutes, then slice across the grain into fairly thin strips before serving.

NUTRITIONAL FACTS (per serving)

Calories: 516 Total fat: 33.2 g Total carbs: 1.7 g Net carbs: 1.7 g Protein: 51.2 g

time intensive

squeaky clean

plan ahead

keto friendly

make ahead

egg-free

freezer friendly

Serves 6 to 8

MEATLOAF WITH SOUR CHERRY SAUCE

Incorporating pureed liver into ground beef is a brilliant way to sneak more organ meat into your diet. And if you hide it in a meatloaf as flavorful as this one, you can be sure that it will go totally unnoticed. There is so much meatiness, tanginess, and sweetness going on in this meatloaf, you won't be able to detect any "livery" flavor at all. In fact, this dish may well become a favorite of the entire family!

For the meatloaf

- 7 ounces (200 g) beef liver
- ¼ cup (60 ml) fresh lemon juice (optional; see Notes)
- 1 pound (455 g) lean ground beef
- 1 pound (455 g) lean ground pork
- 1 large onion, finely chopped
- 2 cloves garlic, minced
- 1 cup (140 g) fresh cherries, pitted and cut in half (see Notes)
- ½ cup (75 g) chopped raw almonds, toasted
- 2 tablespoons Dijon mustard
- 1 tablespoon finely chopped fresh rosemary
- 1 teaspoon Himalayan salt
- 1 teaspoon freshly ground black pepper
- ½ teaspoon ground Ceylon cinnamon
- ¼ teaspoon freshly grated nutmeg
- ¼ teaspoon ground cardamom

For the cherry sauce

- 2 cups (280 g) fresh cherries, pitted and cut in half (see Notes)
- ½ cup (120 ml) balsamic vinegar
- ½ cup (120 ml) Brown Chicken Stock (page 76)
- 1 tablespoon Dijon mustard
- 1 tablespoon finely chopped fresh rosemary
- ½ teaspoon Himalayan salt
- ¼ teaspoon ground Ceylon cinnamon
- ⅛ teaspoon ground cardamom

1. If marinating the liver, the night before making the meatloaf, place the liver and lemon juice in a nonreactive container with a tight-fitting lid or in a resealable plastic bag to marinate.

2. Preheat the oven to 375°F (190°C) and grease a 9 by 5-inch (23 by 12.75-cm) loaf pan.

3. Rinse the liver under cold running water, then puree it in the bowl of a food processor. Transfer the pureed liver to a large mixing bowl and add the rest of the ingredients for the meatloaf. Knead with your hands until well combined.

4. Place the meat mixture in the prepared loaf pan and bake for 1 hour, uncovered.

5. Meanwhile, place all the ingredients for the sauce in a medium saucepan. Bring to a boil, then lower the heat and simmer, uncovered, for 8 to 10 minutes or until thickened to your liking.

6. Finish the sauce by pureeing it roughly with an immersion blender. Don't puree it until it's completely smooth, though. You want the sauce to have a few chunks of fruit in it.

7. When the meatloaf is ready, let it cool for 5 to 10 minutes, then serve smothered in the cherry sauce.

8. This dish will keep in the refrigerator for up to 3 to 4 days and reheats very well in the microwave or in a covered skillet set over low heat.

Notes : *While not necessary, marinating the liver over-night in lemon or lime juice or even balsamic vinegar really changes its texture, making it much "creamier," and also helps tone down its slightly metallic flavor. I strongly recommend it.*

If you can't find fresh cherries, or if cherries aren't in season, use frozen: They will work just as well.

NUTRITIONAL FACTS (per serving, based on 8 servings)

Calories: 303   Total fat: 12.7 g   Total carbs: 13.1 g   Net carbs: 10.2 g   Protein: 32.6 g

plan ahead

 make ahead

squeaky clean

keto friendly

egg-free

nut-free

Makes 6 kebabs

SHISH KEBABS

Got company coming and don't know what to feed them? Why not throw some kebabs on the grill? These babies are fairly quick and easy to make, and you won't believe the amount of flavor they pack. A winning classic that's guaranteed to satisfy!

For the marinade

- ¼ cup (60 ml) extra-virgin olive oil
- Juice of 1 lemon
- 2 tablespoons balsamic vinegar
- 2 tablespoons coconut aminos
- 1 tablespoon Dijon mustard
- 1 clove garlic, minced
- 1 tablespoon finely chopped fresh thyme
- 1 teaspoon Himalayan salt
- 1 teaspoon freshly ground black pepper
- ½ teaspoon ground Ceylon cinnamon
- Pinch of ground clove

- 2 pounds (910 g) beef tenderloin, cut into 24 (2-inch/5-cm) chunks
- 2 small red onions
- 1 small white onion
- 1 red bell pepper
- 1 orange bell pepper
- 1 yellow bell pepper

Equipment needed:

6 skewers, about 12 inches (30 cm) long

1. Place all the ingredients for the marinade in a large mixing bowl and whisk until well combined.

2. Add the chunks of beef to the marinade and mix to coat them really well. Cover and place in the refrigerator for a couple of hours or, better yet, overnight.

3. If using wooden skewers, soak them in cold water for 30 minutes to 1 hour before you start building the kebabs.

4. Preheat a grill to scorching-high heat.

5. Cut the onions and bell peppers into chunks of roughly the same size as the chunks of meat.

6. Remove the beef from the marinade and thread onto 6 skewers, alternating between meat, onion, and bell pepper. Discard the marinade.

7. Grill the kebabs over scorching-high heat, turning them a few times, for about 5 to 8 minutes total, depending on the desired level of doneness.

8. Remove the kebabs from the grill, tent loosely with aluminum foil, and allow to rest for 5 minutes before serving.

Tip: Put together the skewers ahead of time and place them in the fridge for up to a full day. That way, most of the work will be done by dinnertime; all that'll be left to do is the grilling.

NUTRITIONAL FACTS (per kebab)

Calories: 343 · Total fat: 18.3 g · Total carbs: 8.4 g · Net carbs: 5.9 g · Protein: 34.5 g

under 30

plan ahead

squeaky clean

keto friendly

egg-free

nut-free

Serves 4

FILET MIGNON WITH BEURRE MAÎTRE D'HÔTEL

Steak made simple and elegant: That's what this dish is all about. The seasoned butter confers such a rich flavor to the meat, there's no point in adding much of anything else to it. A gentle kiss of the flame and a liberal amount of salt and pepper are all that are really needed here.

For the beurre maître d'hôtel

- ¼ cup (55 g) ghee
- 2 tablespoons finely chopped fresh parsley
- 1 clove garlic, minced
- 1 teaspoon fresh lemon juice
- Pinch of Himalayan salt and freshly ground black pepper

- 4 (½-pound/225-g) beef tenderloins
- Himalayan salt and coarsely ground black pepper

1. Mix together all the ingredients for the beurre maître d'hôtel and place the mixture on a piece of parchment paper. Roll it into the shape of a log and put it in the fridge to set, about 2 hours.

2. Thirty minutes before you are ready to cook the steaks, take them out of the refrigerator.

3. Preheat a grill to scorching-high heat.

4. Pat the steaks really dry and season them generously on all sides with salt and pepper.

5. Place the steaks on the hottest part of the grill and cook for about 2 minutes, then turn them 45 degrees and continue cooking for another 2 minutes. Flip the steaks and grill for an additional 2 to 4 minutes, depending on thickness and the desired level of doneness.

6. Remove the steaks from the grill, tent loosely with aluminum foil, and allow to rest for at least 5 minutes.

7. Meanwhile, take the beurre maître d'hôtel out of the refrigerator and slice it into ¼-inch (6-mm)-thick pucks.

8. Place one or two pucks of butter on each steak at the moment of serving.

NUTRITIONAL FACTS (per serving)

| Calories: 460 | Total fat: 27.2 g | Total carbs: 0.7 g | Net carbs: 0.7 g | Protein: 50.6 g |

time intensive

 squeaky clean

 plan ahead

 keto friendly

 freezer friendly

Serves 6

HEARTY MEATBALLS IN WILD MUSHROOM SAUCE

Meals just don't get much heartier than this one. With its generous quantity of wild mushrooms, pungent herbs, and toasted nuts, this dish of tender meatballs in a creamy sauce is a symphony of bold flavors and textures. Your palate will be so pleased, you'll want to make it time and time again.

For the meatballs

- 2 pounds (910 g) lean ground beef
- 2 green onions, finely chopped
- 1 clove garlic, minced
- ¼ cup (65 g) All-Natural Toasted Almond Butter (page 288)
- ¼ cup (35 g) finely ground toasted hazelnuts
- 2 large eggs
- 2 tablespoons Dijon mustard
- 1 teaspoon Himalayan salt
- 1 teaspoon freshly ground black pepper
- 1 teaspoon ground coriander
- 1 teaspoon dried chives
- 1 teaspoon finely chopped fresh rosemary
- ½ teaspoon baking soda

- 4 tablespoons lard or ghee, divided

For the sauce

- 4 cups (100 g) wild mushrooms of choice (see Note)
- 1 small onion, chopped
- ½ teaspoon Himalayan salt
- 4 cups (scant 1 L) Brown Bone Broth (page 74)
- 1 teaspoon chopped fresh sage
- 1 teaspoon chopped fresh rosemary
- ½ cup (120 ml) full-fat coconut milk
- 2 tablespoons apple cider vinegar
- ¼ cup (35 g) finely ground toasted hazelnuts
- 2 tablespoons tapioca starch
- 2 tablespoons water

1. Place all the ingredients for the meatballs in a large mixing bowl and knead well to fully combine. Form the mixture into approximately 50 meatballs that are slightly smaller than Ping-Pong balls.

2. Melt a tablespoon of the lard in a large, heavy skillet set over medium-high heat. When the pan is nice and hot, sear the meatballs in batches until golden all around, about 2 to 3 minutes total. Remove the seared meatballs to a shallow bowl while you work on the remaining batches.

3. When all the meatballs are seared, melt 2 tablespoons of the lard in the skillet. Cook the mushrooms until golden and softened, 3 to 5 minutes; then remove them to a separate bowl and set aside.

4. Add the remaining tablespoon of lard to the skillet, along with the onion and salt. Cook until the onion is translucent, then add the broth, sage, and rosemary. Bring to a boil, add the meatballs, and then lower the heat and simmer uncovered for about 20 minutes.

5. Meanwhile, in a small mixing bowl, combine the coconut milk, vinegar, ground hazelnuts, tapioca starch, and water and mix with a whisk until well combined.

6. Ladle 1½ to 2 cups (350 to 475 ml) of the simmering broth into the coconut milk mixture, whisking constantly to prevent the formation of lumps. Pour this thick gravy into the stew and mix gently with a spoon until evenly combined.

7. Stir in the mushrooms and serve.

Tip: Using a small spring-loaded ice cream scoop really helps in making evenly sized meatballs quickly and efficiently.

Note: I used a combination of maitake, chanterelles, oyster mushrooms, and blue foot mushrooms. Feel free to substitute your favorite varieties of wild mushrooms.

Grind the hazelnuts after they have been toasted using a coffee grinder or a mortar and pestle.

NUTRITIONAL FACTS (per serving)

| Calories: 591 | Total fat: 35.1 g | Total carbs: 13.8 g | Net carbs: 11.7 g | Protein: 54.4 g |

Serves 6 to 8

- 2 large eggplants (2 pounds/910 g each)
- ¼ cup (60 ml) extra-virgin olive oil
- Himalayan salt and freshly ground black pepper
- 1 to 2 tablespoons dried oregano leaves

For the "béchamel"

- 2 tablespoons ghee
- 1 small onion, chopped
- 2 cloves garlic, minced
- ½ teaspoon Himalayan salt
- ½ teaspoon freshly ground black pepper
- 1 large head cauliflower (2 pounds/910 g), cut into small florets
- 1 cup (240 ml) Brown Chicken Stock (page 76)
- 1 cup (240 g) tahini
- 1 tablespoon Dijon mustard
- ¼ teaspoon freshly grated nutmeg

For the meat layer

- 2 tablespoons ghee
- 1 small onion, chopped
- 2 celery ribs, chopped
- 2 cloves garlic, minced
- ½ teaspoon Himalayan salt
- 2 pounds (910 g) ground lamb
- ½ teaspoon freshly ground black pepper
- ½ teaspoon red pepper flakes
- 1½ cups (350 g) crushed tomatoes
- 2 tablespoons fish sauce
- 1 teaspoon Chai Spice (page 49)
- ¼ teaspoon freshly grated nutmeg

PALEO MOUSSAKA

While this is not your typical Greek moussaka, I believe that something has to be said for this hearty combination of creamy eggplant, spicy lamb, and silky "béchamel" sauce. If you are a fan of authentic moussaka and can't resist a good bowl of piping-hot shepherd's pie, the other dish that immediately comes to mind when I think of moussaka, then I think you will go gaga over this immensely comforting dish. I know I do!

1. Preheat the oven to 350°F (177°C).

2. Slice the eggplants into 1½-inch (4-cm)-thick rounds and place them on 2 rimmed baking sheets. Brush each slice with olive oil and sprinkle liberally with salt, pepper, and oregano. Bake for 25 to 30 minutes or until tender.

3. Meanwhile, make the "béchamel": Place the ghee, onion, garlic, salt and pepper in a medium saucepan. Cook over medium heat for 1 to 2 minutes, until fragrant and slightly softened. Throw in the cauliflower florets and continue cooking for about 5 minutes, until slightly golden. Add the chicken stock, cover, and bring to a boil; lower the heat and continue cooking until the cauliflower is tender, 5 to 7 minutes.

4. Ladle the cauliflower mixture into a blender. Add the tahini, mustard, and nutmeg and process on high speed until super smooth and silky. Set aside.

5. Make the meat layer: Melt the ghee in a heavy skillet (cast iron is preferred) set over medium-high heat. When the ghee is nice and hot, add the onion, celery, garlic, and salt and cook until the veggies are fragrant and softened, 2 to 3 minutes.

6. Add the lamb, black pepper, and red pepper flakes and cook until the meat is completely browned, about 10 minutes.

7. Add the crushed tomatoes, fish sauce, Chai Spice, and nutmeg and cook until all the water in the tomatoes has evaporated. Stir in 1 cup of the reserved "béchamel" and set aside.

8. Arrange the cooked eggplants in a 13 by 9-inch (33 by 23-cm) baking dish. Top with the meat mixture, followed by the "béchamel."

Note: At this point, you could put the moussaka in the refrigerator for up to a few days and bake it when you are ready to serve it. Because the dish will be completely chilled when it hits the oven, you may need to increase the cooking time by 10 minutes or so.

9. Bake for 30 minutes or until the top is lightly browned. Allow to rest for 20 to 25 minutes before serving.

10. This dish will keep in the refrigerator for up to 3 to 4 days and reheats really well in the microwave.

NUTRITIONAL FACTS (per serving, based on 8 servings)

| Calories: 558 | Total fat: 36.2 g | Total carbs: 27.3 g | Net carbs: 14.6 g | Protein: 33.5 g |

time intensive

keto friendly

plan ahead

egg-free

freezer friendly

nut-free

Serves 8

ORANGE ROSEMARY BRAISED LEG OF LAMB

If you've never experienced lamb cooked this way, I strongly suggest that you give it a try. This method not only infuses the meat with intense flavors, but also slowly cooks it to juicy, fork-tender, melt-in-your-mouth perfection while maintaining a very tasty and crispy exterior. It's so good, you may never want to cook lamb any other way again!

For the spice mixture

- ¼ cup (62 g) whole-grain mustard
- 2 tablespoons raw honey
- Grated zest of 2 oranges
- Leaves from 3 or 4 sprigs fresh rosemary, finely chopped
- 6 to 8 fresh sage leaves, finely chopped
- 4 cloves garlic, minced
- 1 teaspoon Himalayan salt
- 1 teaspoon freshly ground black pepper

- 1 (6-pound/2.75-kg) boneless leg of lamb
- Himalayan salt and freshly ground black pepper
- Juice of 2 oranges
- 3 or 4 sprigs fresh rosemary

1. Place the ingredients for the spice mixture in a small mixing bowl and stir until evenly combined; set aside.

2. Remove the netting from the leg of lamb and unroll it, then lay it flat on a cutting board. Trim off any large pieces of fat. Sprinkle with salt and pepper and, with your fingers, spread about three-quarters of the spice mixture all over the meat.

3. Roll the lamb back up and tie it up with a few pieces of butcher's twine, or put the netting back on if you can. Dab the rest of the spice mixture all over the roast and cover tightly with plastic wrap. Place in the refrigerator to rest for at least 4 hours or, better yet, overnight.

4. When you're ready to cook the lamb, preheat the oven to 325°F (163°C).

5. Put the lamb in a Dutch oven or roasting pan with a tight-fitting lid, then pour the orange juice into the bottom of the pan. Place a few sprigs of fresh rosemary around the meat.

6. Cook the lamb for 3½ to 4 hours, checking every hour or so to make sure that the liquid hasn't completely evaporated (and adding a little bit of water if it has), until the meat can easily be pulled apart with a fork.

NUTRITIONAL FACTS (per serving)

Calories: 414   Total fat: 14.0 g   Total carbs: 6.0 g   Net carbs: 5.3 g   Protein: 64.1 g

time intensive

freezer friendly

plan ahead

squeaky clean

make ahead

egg-free

Serves 8

- 1 (5-pound/2.3-kg) boneless leg of lamb
- ½ teaspoon Himalayan salt, plus more to season the meat
- 1 teaspoon freshly ground black pepper, plus more to season the meat
- 2 to 4 tablespoons lard or other healthy cooking fat, divided
- 1 large onion, chopped
- 2 cloves garlic, minced
- 2 cups (475 ml) Brown Bone Broth (page 74)
- ¼ cup (60 ml) apple cider vinegar
- 2 tablespoons Dijon mustard
- 2 tablespoons finely chopped fresh rosemary
- 1 teaspoon red pepper flakes
- 1 cup (150 g) dried apricots
- ½ cup (60 g) raw pistachios

For garnish (optional)
- Handful of chopped raw pistachios
- Handful of chopped fresh parsley

APRICOT PISTACHIO LAMB STEW

When my daughter tasted this dish, she said that it was bar none the best food ever to have crossed her lips, and probably the best recipe ever to have been created on the entire surface of this planet. And she said it with sincere enthusiasm, too. Hey, who am I to contradict her?

1. Preheat the oven to 300°F (150°C).

2. Trim off any excess fat from the lamb, then cut the meat into 2½- to 3-inch (6.5- to 7.5-cm) chunks and sprinkle generously with salt and pepper.

3. Melt 1 tablespoon of the lard in a heavy skillet set over high heat. Add the chunks of lamb in a single layer, making sure that the pieces do not touch, and cook until browned on all sides. Work in batches if you have to, and add more lard as needed. Remove the cooked pieces of meat to a 4-quart (3.8-L) or larger Dutch oven.

4. Once all the meat has been cooked, lower the heat to medium, add a little more lard to the pan if necessary, and then throw in the onion and garlic and cook, stirring often, until the onion is fragrant and translucent. Add the onion and garlic to the meat in the Dutch oven.

5. Deglaze the skillet with the bone broth, scraping the bottom really well to detach all the bits of flavor stuck to it; add all that to the Dutch oven.

6. In a small mixing bowl, whisk together the vinegar, mustard, rosemary, ½ teaspoon of salt, 1 teaspoon of black pepper, and red pepper flakes; pour that into the Dutch oven as well.

7. Cover, place in the preheated oven, and cook for 3 hours. After 3 hours, add the apricots and pistachios, mix them in very gently, and then continue cooking for another 30 minutes, until the meat is fork-tender.

8. Garnish with chopped pistachios and parsley, if desired.

Tip: *Serve this stew with a simple side of braised greens, Roasted Garlic Cauliflower Mash (page 278), or sautéed mushrooms.*

NUTRITIONAL FACTS (per serving)

Calories: 781 | Total fat: 51.4 g | Total carbs: 20.0 g | Net carbs: 17.2 g | Protein: 52.8 g

time intensive

squeaky clean

make ahead

egg-free

freezer friendly

nut-free

Serves 4

SHEPHERD'S PIE

Shepherd's pie is one of those timeless classics that needs no introduction—except when it's been completely reinvented. The presence of lamb in this dish just feels so natural, and the rusticity of the vegetables, combined with the delicate yet robust flavor of the cauliflower mash, complements the pungency of the meat to absolute perfection. Simply put, this dish is a perfect harmony of flavors and textures that will have you coming back for more.

For the cauli-mash layer

- 1 large head cauliflower (2 pounds/910 g), cut into florets
- ¼ cup (60 g) tahini
- 2 tablespoons ghee
- 1 clove garlic
- ¼ teaspoon Himalayan salt
- ¼ teaspoon freshly ground black pepper

For the veggie layer

- 1 tablespoon ghee
- ½ pound (225 g) mushrooms, sliced
- ½ teaspoon Himalayan salt
- ½ teaspoon freshly ground black pepper
- 1 large carrot, finely diced
- 2 large zucchinis, finely diced

For the meat layer

- 1 tablespoon ghee
- 1 large onion, chopped
- 2 cloves garlic, minced
- ½ teaspoon Himalayan salt
- 1 pound (455 g) ground lamb
- 1 tablespoon finely chopped fresh thyme
- 1 tablespoon finely chopped fresh rosemary
- ½ teaspoon freshly ground black pepper

- Extra-virgin olive oil for drizzling
- Fresh thyme leaves for garnish (optional)

1. Preheat the oven to 350°F (177°C).

2. Steam the cauliflower florets over a pot of salted boiling water until really tender, 8 to 10 minutes, then remove from the heat and let cool.

3. Meanwhile, make the veggie layer: Melt 1 tablespoon of ghee in a heavy, oven-safe skillet (cast iron is preferred) set over medium-high heat. When the skillet is nice and hot, add the mushrooms, sprinkle with the salt and pepper, and cook until golden. Add the carrot and continue cooking for about a minute, then throw in the zucchinis and cook for another 2 to 3 minutes, until slightly softened. Transfer to a bowl and place the skillet back over the heat to make the meat layer.

4. Add another tablespoon of ghee to the skillet, then add the onion, garlic, and salt. Cook until fragrant and softened, 2 to 3 minutes. Add the lamb, thyme, rosemary, and pepper and continue cooking until the meat is completely browned and cooked all the way through, 8 to 10 minutes.

5. Kill the heat and spread the cooked veggies evenly over the meat. Set aside.

6. Squeeze as much water as you possibly can out of the cauliflower, then transfer it, along with the rest of the ingredients for the cauli-mash layer, to the bowl of a food processor. Process until smooth and creamy, stopping to scrape the sides of the bowl as needed.

7. Spread the cauli-mash evenly over the vegetables, then drizzle with a little bit of olive oil. Bake for 30 minutes or until the top is golden.

8. Let rest for at least 10 to 15 minutes before serving. Drizzle with more olive oil and garnish with fresh thyme at the moment of serving, if desired.

NUTRITIONAL FACTS (per serving)

Calories: 451 | Total fat: 24.9 g | Total carbs: 28.7 g | Net carbs: 17.9 g | Protein: 33.9 g

squeaky clean

 egg-free

 keto friendly

 nut-free

Serves 6

CLASSIC LAMB ROAST

Don't be intimidated by lamb roast; it's actually super easy to make. Just keep in mind that this delicate and earthy meat is best served rare to medium-rare. Cooking it beyond 145°F (63°C) is not recommended; past this temperature, the meat has a tendency to dry out and become somewhat tough. Also, don't ever deprive it of its rest time. Follow these simple guidelines and you'll be rewarded with meat that is melt-in-your-mouth tender and juicy.

- 1 (3-pound/1.4-kg) boneless rolled lamb shoulder roast
- 5 or 6 sprigs fresh rosemary, broken into 1- to 1½-inch (2.5- to 4-cm) lengths
- 5 or 6 cloves garlic, peeled
- 2 tablespoons ghee
- 1 teaspoon Himalayan salt
- 1 teaspoon freshly ground black pepper

1. Preheat the oven to 325°F (163°C).

2. Pat the lamb dry, then use the tip of a sharp paring knife to make a series of little incisions all over the meat. Insert a garlic clove and/or piece of rosemary into each incision.

3. Rub the ghee all over the lamb, then sprinkle it with the salt and pepper.

4. Place the lamb in a ceramic baking dish and roast, uncovered, for 75 to 90 minutes or until the desired doneness is reached. A meat thermometer will register an internal temperature of around 120°F (50°C) for rare, 130°F (55°C) for medium-rare, or 140°F (60°C) for medium.

5. Take the lamb out of the oven and tent it loosely with aluminum foil. Let the meat rest for 15 to 20 minutes.

6. Transfer the meat to a cutting board, remove the twine, carve, and serve.

NUTRITIONAL FACTS (per serving)

Calories: 323 | Total fat: 14.2g | Total carbs: 1.1g | Net carbs: 1.1g | Protein: 46.3g

time intensive

plan ahead

make ahead

squeaky clean

egg-free

nut-free

GREEK-STYLE BRAISED LAMB

With its mixture of salty olives, creamy artichokes, melt-in-your-mouth-tender pieces of lamb, and just a hint of tangy lemon, this casserole has what it takes to bring the Mediterranean right to your kitchen table!

Serves 6

- 3 pounds (1.4 kg) lamb stew meat, cubed
- ½ teaspoon Himalayan salt
- ½ teaspoon freshly ground black pepper
- 2 to 3 tablespoons ghee, plus more if needed
- 2 large onions, chopped
- 3 cloves garlic, chopped
- 2 cups (475 ml) water

For the braising liquid

- 2 cups (475 ml) Brown Bone Broth (page 74)
- ½ preserved lemon, finely chopped (see Notes, page 70), or the grated zest and juice of 1 lemon
- 2 tablespoons dried oregano leaves
- 1 tablespoon dried savory leaves
- 1 teaspoon freshly ground black pepper
- 1 teaspoon ground Ceylon cinnamon
- ½ teaspoon Himalayan salt
- ½ teaspoon freshly grated nutmeg
- ½ teaspoon ground allspice

- 2 (14-ounce/400-g) cans quartered artichoke hearts
- 1 cup (160 g) pitted jumbo green olives
- ¼ cup (30 g) sliced Kalamata olives

1. Preheat the oven to 325°F (163°C).

2. Pat the lamb really dry, then sprinkle with the salt and pepper.

3. Melt 2 to 3 tablespoons of ghee in a heavy skillet set over high heat. Add the cubes of lamb in a single layer, making sure that the pieces do not touch, and cook until browned on all sides. Work in batches if you have to, and add more fat as needed. Remove the cooked pieces to a 4-quart (3.8-L) or larger Dutch oven.

4. Once all the meat has been cooked, lower the heat to medium, add a little more fat to the pan if necessary, and then throw in the onions and garlic. Cook, stirring often, until the onions are fragrant and translucent. Add the onions and garlic to the meat in the Dutch oven.

5. Deglaze the pan with the water, scraping the bottom really well to detach all the bits of flavor stuck to it, and add that to the Dutch oven.

6. In a small mixing bowl, whisk together all the ingredients for the braising liquid, then pour the mixture into the Dutch oven.

7. Cover, place in the preheated oven, and cook for 2½ hours, then add the artichoke hearts and olives and cook for another 30 to 45 minutes, until the meat is practically falling apart.

8. Remove from the oven, uncover, and allow to rest for 10 to 15 minutes before serving.

9. Leftovers can be kept in the fridge for up to 4 days and reheat well in the microwave or in a covered saucepan set over low heat.

NUTRITIONAL FACTS (per serving)

Calories: 443   Total fat: 20.1 g   Total carbs: 16.0 g   Net carbs: 10.1 g   Protein: 48.8 g

CHAPTER 7

pork

time intensive

 keto friendly

freezer friendly

egg-free

squeaky clean

nut-free

Serves 6 to 8

For the spice rub

- ¼ cup (52 g) coconut oil
- ¼ cup (60 ml) apple cider vinegar
- 2 tablespoons Dijon mustard
- 3 cloves garlic
- 2 dried figs
- 4 or 5 fresh sage leaves
- 1 sprig fresh rosemary
- 1 teaspoon freshly ground black pepper
- ½ teaspoon Himalayan salt
- ½ teaspoon smoked paprika

- 1 (4½-pound/2-kg) boneless pork loin
- 4 to 5 cloves garlic
- 2 or 3 sprigs fresh rosemary
- 2 or 3 sprigs fresh sage
- ¾ pound (340 g) bacon (10 to 12 strips)
- About ¼ cup (60 ml) water

BACON-WRAPPED PORK LOIN

Despite being fairly simple to make, this beautiful pork roast looks spectacular and is sure to wow your guests even before they've had a taste. And then, when they do get to taste it, they will deem you the star of the night!

1. Preheat the oven to 350°F (177°C).

2. Place all the ingredients for the spice rub in a small food processor and process until smooth and creamy.

3. Trim any visible fat from the pork loin. Spread the spice rub all over the pork and set aside.

4. Place the garlic cloves, rosemary, and sage in a 4-quart (3.8 L) Dutch oven.

5. On a work surface, weave a rectangular lattice with the bacon strips, then carefully lift and slide the lattice over the roast, covering the roast entirely. Hold the lattice in place by inserting a few toothpicks here and there.

6. Carefully transfer the roast to the Dutch oven over the herbs and garlic cloves, add about ¼ cup (60 ml) of water, and cover. Place in the oven and cook for 2½ hours, then remove the lid and continue cooking for an additional 15 minutes or so, just to crisp up the bacon.

NUTRITIONAL FACTS (per serving, based on 8 servings)

| Calories: 509 | Total fat: 28.8 g | Total carbs: 5.8 g | Net carbs: 4.5 g | Protein: 54.5 g |

time
intensive

 squeaky
clean

 plan
ahead

 keto
friendly

 freezer
friendly

egg-
free

Makes about 5 cups (1.12 kg)

CRETONS À LA QUÉBÉCOISE

Cretons are a real staple here in Québec. Typically they are spread on toast and served at breakfast alongside a couple of eggs, sausage, ham, and/or bacon. While I must admit that they are particularly delicious spread thick over a slice of warm, crunchy bread, I find them equally good when eaten by the forkful.

- 1 cup (120 g) raw cashew pieces, soaked for at least 8 hours
- 2 cups (475 ml) water
- 1 pound (455 g) lean ground pork
- 1 pound (455 g) lean ground beef
- 1½ cups (350 ml) Brown Bone Broth (page 74)
- 1 large onion, chopped
- ¼ cup (55 g) lard
- ¼ cup (15 g) fresh parsley leaves, chopped
- 3 tablespoons Salted Herbs (page 50; optional)
- 2 tablespoons ground Ceylon cinnamon
- 1 tablespoon Dijon mustard
- 1 tablespoon garlic powder
- 1 tablespoon dried savory
- 1 teaspoon Himalayan salt
- 1 teaspoon ground white pepper
- 1 teaspoon ginger powder
- 1 teaspoon freshly grated nutmeg
- ½ teaspoon ground clove
- ½ teaspoon ground coriander

1. Drain the cashew pieces and place them in a food processor along with the 2 cups (475 ml) of fresh water; process on high speed until reduced to a smooth puree.

2. Transfer the cashew puree to large stockpot set over medium-high heat along with the rest of the ingredients. If not using the salted herbs, add an additional tablespoon of salt.

3. With the help of a potato masher, mix until the meat is completely broken down and all the ingredients are well combined.

4. Bring to a boil, then reduce the heat to low, cover loosely, and simmer for about 1½ hours, stirring from time to time, until all the liquid has evaporated.

5. Transfer to individual (1-cup/240-ml) ramekins and refrigerate until completely set, preferably overnight.

NUTRITIONAL FACTS (per ½ cup/112 g serving)

Calories: 320 | Total fat: 22.3 g | Total carbs: 0.0 g | Net carbs: 0.0 g | Protein: 10.0 g

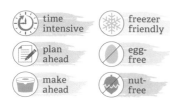

time intensive

freezer friendly

plan ahead

egg-free

make ahead

nut-free

Serves 4

MAPLE BALSAMIC PULLED PORK

The sweetness of maple syrup is nicely balanced by the tanginess of balsamic vinegar in this comforting pork dish. Try it for breakfast alongside a couple of fried eggs. Talk about starting your day in a tasty way!

- 1 small onion, chopped
- 2 cloves garlic, minced
- ¼ cup (60 ml) pure maple syrup (dark color or Canadian Medium)
- ¼ cup (60 ml) balsamic vinegar
- 2 tablespoons white wine vinegar
- 2 tablespoons Dijon mustard
- Juice of 1 lemon
- 1 tablespoon chopped fresh rosemary
- 1 teaspoon Himalayan salt
- 1 teaspoon freshly ground black pepper
- ½ teaspoon fennel seeds
- 2 pounds (910 g) boneless pork shoulder

1. Place all the ingredients except for the pork shoulder in a 3-quart (2-L) enameled Dutch oven and mix until well combined.

2. Remove the netting from the pork, if present, and place the meat in the Dutch oven. Move it around to make sure that it's entirely coated with the marinade, then cover and place in the refrigerator to marinate overnight.

3. Preheat the oven to 300°F (150°C), then cook the pork for 4 to 4½ hours, until the meat falls apart easily when pulled at with a fork.

4. Use 2 forks to pull the meat into strands and mix well until all the strands are nicely coated with the braising liquid. Return to the oven for 15 to 20 minutes to crisp up the meat.

5. Serve without delay.

NUTRITIONAL FACTS (per serving)

Calories: 598 • Total fat: 42.7 g • Total carbs: 17.0 g • Net carbs: 15.7 g • Protein: 34.9 g

under 30

keto friendly

make ahead

egg-free

freezer friendly

nut-free

squeaky clean

BREAKFAST SAUSAGE

These cute little breakfast sausage patties are the perfect complement to your morning eggs! Make them in advance and reheat them quickly and easily by throwing them right in the pan with your eggs as they cook. Way to get an awesome breakfast on the table in just minutes!

Makes 10 patties

- 1 pound (455 g) lean ground pork
- ½ red apple, shredded
- 1 clove garlic, minced
- 1 tablespoon Dijon mustard
- 2 tablespoons chopped fresh parsley
- 1 tablespoon chopped fresh sage
- 1 teaspoon onion powder
- ½ teaspoon Himalayan salt
- ½ teaspoon freshly ground black pepper
- ½ teaspoon fennel seeds
- ½ teaspoon red pepper flakes
- ¼ teaspoon ground white pepper
- ¼ teaspoon ground Ceylon cinnamon
- Healthy cooking fat for the pan

1. Place all the ingredients in a fairly large mixing bowl and knead by hand until very well combined; form into 10 small patties.

2. Melt the cooking fat in a heavy skillet set over medium heat. Add the sausage patties and cook until no longer pink in the middle, 3 to 4 minutes per side.

3. Serve alongside your favorite breakfast foods.

NUTRITIONAL FACTS (per patty)

| Calories: 81 | Total fat: 4.1 g | Total carbs: 2.6 g | Net carbs: 1.5 g | Protein: 9.9 g |

under 30

nut-free

egg-free

Serves 2

SPICY GINGER LEMON PORK STIR-FRY

Who needs takeout when you can make your own stir-fry? Especially when this version tastes just as good, if not better, than any dish that a restaurant could deliver to your door?

For the sauce

- Grated zest of 1 lemon
- Juice of 1 lemon
- ¼ cup (60 ml) unseasoned rice vinegar
- 2 tablespoons coconut aminos
- 2 tablespoons raw honey
- 2 tablespoons water
- 1 tablespoon fish sauce
- 1 teaspoon toasted sesame oil
- 1 teaspoon ginger powder
- 1 teaspoon Chinese five-spice powder (see Notes, page 162)
- 2 to 3 dried bird's-eye chili peppers, crushed into flakes, or ½ teaspoon red pepper flakes
- 2 tablespoons tapioca starch

- 1 (1-pound/455-g) pork loin, cut into thin strips
- Himalayan salt and freshly ground black pepper
- 2 tablespoons healthy cooking fat
- 1 large onion, sliced
- 2 cloves garlic, thinly sliced
- 1 (1½-ounce/40-g) piece fresh ginger, julienned
- ½ pound (225 g) snow peas

1. In a large mixing bowl, whisk together all the ingredients for the sauce until well combined. Set aside.

2. Pat the pork dry, then sprinkle liberally with salt and pepper.

3. Place the cooking fat in a large wok or skillet set over high heat. When the pan is scorching hot, add the pork strips and sauté until slightly browned with maybe a little bit of pink still showing, about 2 minutes; remove the cooked meat to the bowl with the sauce.

4. Return the wok or skillet to the heat, add the onion, garlic, and ginger, and sauté for 1 to 2 minutes, until the onion is slightly softened. Add the snow peas and continue sautéing for about a minute. Add the reserved meat and sauce and continue cooking for a minute or so, until the sauce thickens.

5. Serve real hot, with a side of cauliflower rice (page 256), if desired.

> Tip: Change it up! For example, use shrimp or chicken instead of pork, or opt for broccoli, baby bok choy, or chopped collards instead of snow peas.

NUTRITIONAL FACTS (per serving)

Calories: 503 | Total fat: 10.3 g | Total carbs: 43.6 g | Net carbs: 38.1 g | Protein: 52.6 g

plan ahead · keto friendly · make ahead · egg-free · squeaky clean · nut-free

Makes 6 souvlaki

PORK SOUVLAKI

These juicy, meaty sticks taste exactly like the ones I used to order from my former favorite local Greek restaurant. I say they're as authentic as authentic can be. Oh, and they happen to be super garlicky, too, so make sure that you don't have anywhere important to go after feasting on these bad boys.

For the marinade

- ¼ cup (60 ml) extra-virgin olive oil
- Grated zest of 1 lemon
- Juice of 1 lemon
- 5 cloves garlic, minced
- 2 tablespoons red wine vinegar
- 2 tablespoons za'atar spice blend (see Note)
- 1½ teaspoons Himalayan salt
- 1 teaspoon freshly ground black pepper

- 1 (1⅔-pound/750 g) pork loin, cut into 24 (1½-inch/4-cm) chunks
- Extra-virgin olive oil for drizzling
- Chopped fresh thyme or sage leaves for garnish

Equipment needed:

6 skewers, about 12 inches (30 cm) long

1. Place all the ingredients for the marinade in a large mixing bowl and whisk until well combined.

2. Add the pork to the bowl and mix to coat really well. Cover and place in the refrigerator to marinate for at least 4 hours or, better yet, overnight.

3. If using wooden skewers, soak them in cold water for 30 minutes to 1 hour before you start building the souvlaki.

4. Preheat a grill to high heat.

5. Remove the chunks of pork from the marinade and thread them onto 6 skewers. Discard any remaining marinade.

6. Lower the heat to medium-high and grill the souvlaki, turning them a few times, for 6 to 8 minutes total, depending on the desired level of doneness. (Six minutes will give you meat that is still a little pink in the middle; if you prefer pork well-done, leave the skewers on the grill for the full 8 minutes.)

7. Remove the souvlaki from the grill, tent loosely with aluminum foil, and allow to rest for 5 minutes.

8. Drizzle with extra-virgin olive oil and sprinkle with fresh thyme or sage at the moment of serving.

Note: Za'atar is a spice mix from the Middle East, generally made with ground dried thyme, oregano, marjoram, toasted sesame seeds, and salt. Sumac is sometimes added to the mix. Get it from your local ethnic food store or look for it online.

NUTRITIONAL FACTS (per souvlaki)

Calories: 227 · Total fat: 13.8 g · Total carbs: 1.7 g · Net carbs: 1.7 g · Protein: 23.9 g

time intensive
 squeaky clean
 plan ahead
 keto friendly
make ahead
egg-free
freezer friendly
nut-free

Serves 4

RAS EL HANOUT AND LIME PORK CARNITAS

I feel I should warn you: The explosive flavor that the lime and exotic spice mix confer to these crispy yet tender meat nuggets makes them extremely more-ish. Chances are they will disappear faster than you can say "pork carnitas." It might be a good idea to make a double batch!

For the marinade

○ Juice of 3 limes

○ 2 tablespoons Ras el Hanout (page 48)

○ 1 teaspoon Himalayan salt

○ ½ teaspoon freshly ground black pepper

○ 2¾ pounds (1.25 kg) boneless pork shoulder, cut into large chunks (about 3 inches/7.5 cm)

○ 2 small onions, sliced

○ ½ cup (120 ml) water

1. In a small bowl, mix together the ingredients for the marinade; set aside.

2. Place the meat in a resealable bag or nonreactive container with a tight-fitting lid, then add the marinade. Move the meat around to make sure that it's well coated, then place it in the refrigerator to marinate overnight.

3. Preheat the oven to 300°F (150°C).

4. Put the meat in a 3-quart (2-L) Dutch oven, then add the sliced onions and water. Bake, covered, for 3 hours.

5. Crank up the heat to 375°F (190°C), remove the lid, and continue cooking for another hour, turning the pieces of meat from time to time.

6. Drain the fat that has accumulated at the bottom of the Dutch oven and resume cooking for an additional 15 to 20 minutes, until the chunks of meat get really golden and crispy. Serve immediately.

NUTRITIONAL FACTS (per serving)

Calories: 446 Total fat: 25.4 g Total carbs: 3.4 g Net carbs: 2.6 g Protein: 47.9 g

time intensive

squeaky clean

plan ahead

egg-free

make ahead

nut-free

Serves 4

FIG AND PROSCIUTTO-WRAPPED PORK KEBABS

Melt-in-your-mouth pieces of pork tenderloin covered in a thin layer of sweet fig paste, tangy mustard, and aromatic fresh herbs and then wrapped up in crispy prosciutto: These elegant and luxurious kebabs are perfect for special occasions, or simply to treat yourself to something blissfully good!

For the fig paste

- 6 dried figs, coarsely chopped
- 2 tablespoons whole-grain mustard
- 1 tablespoon balsamic vinegar
- 1 teaspoon fresh thyme leaves
- Leaves from 3 sprigs fresh rosemary
- ½ teaspoon Himalayan salt
- ½ teaspoon freshly ground black pepper
- ½ teaspoon ground Ceylon cinnamon
- Pinch of ground clove
- 1 to 2 tablespoons water

- 12 slices prosciutto
- 2 small pork tenderloins (9½ ounces/270 g each)
- Whole-grain mustard for serving (optional)

Equipment needed:

4 skewers, about 12 inches (30 cm) long

1. Make the fig paste: Place the figs, mustard, vinegar, thyme, rosemary, salt, pepper, cinnamon, clove, and 1 tablespoon of water in a small food processor and process until the mixture turns into a thick paste. If you feel that a little more water is needed to get it to turn into a paste, add the second tablespoon of water. Be careful not to make the mixture too liquidy, though; it needs to maintain a thick consistency.

2. On a piece of parchment paper, lay 6 slices of the prosciutto vertically (with the short ends facing you), overlapping them slightly in order to form a kind of blanket in which you will wrap the pork tenderloins.

3. Spread half of the fig mixture very thinly over the prosciutto blanket, leaving about 1 inch (2.5 cm) at the top where the seam will be.

4. Place one of the pork tenderloins at the bottom of the prosciutto blanket and roll it as tightly as you can.

5. Repeat with the remaining prosciutto, fig paste, and tenderloin.

6. Wrap the rolls tightly in plastic wrap and place them in the fridge to rest for at least 4 hours or, better yet, overnight.

7. If using wooden skewers, soak them in cold water for 30 minutes to 1 hour before you start building your kebabs.

8. Preheat a grill to medium-high heat.

9. Carefully slice each pork tenderloin into 8 equal pieces (for a total of 16) and carefully thread them onto 4 skewers. Grill for 2 to 3 minutes per side, then remove from the grill and loosely tent with aluminum foil; allow to rest for 5 minutes before serving.

10. Serve with additional whole-grain mustard, if desired.

NUTRITIONAL FACTS (per serving)

Calories: 305 Total fat: 10.4 g Total carbs: 19.1 g Net carbs: 15.8 g Protein: 34.6 g

under 30

 egg-free

 make ahead

nut-free

squeaky clean

PORK SCALOPPINE ROLL-UPS

Whether you choose to serve them as an appetizer or as part of a main meal, these little meat rolls are guaranteed to add a bunch of color and flavor to your plate. They work great as party finger food, too, and leftovers make for a brilliant snack: Simply eat them cold, right out of the icebox!

Makes 6 rolls, 2 to 3 servings as part of a main meal or 6 servings as an appetizer

- 6 small pork scallops (10½ ounces/300 g total), pounded to ¼-inch (6-mm)-thick rectangles (see Note)
- Himalayan salt and freshly ground black pepper
- 18 thin asparagus spears
- 1 red bell pepper, seeded and julienned
- 1 yellow bell pepper, seeded and julienned
- 1 orange bell pepper, seeded and julienned
- Extra-virgin olive oil for drizzling

1. Preheat a grill to medium-high heat.

2. Lay the pork scallops on a cutting board and sprinkle them generously with salt and pepper. Divide the asparagus and bell peppers evenly among the scallops, arranging them nicely across the centers of the pieces of meat.

3. Roll the meat around the vegetables and tie each roll securely with butcher's twine. Sprinkle with more salt and pepper.

4. Grill, covered, for 2 to 3 minutes per side, turning once. Drizzle with extra-virgin olive oil and serve.

Note: *Pork scallops, also referred to as cutlets, are very thin pieces of lean, boneless meat. They are readily available at most meat counters, but if you can't find them, don't hesitate to ask your butcher to prepare them for you, or you can easily make your own: Start with a piece of pork loin or tenderloin, cut it into thin slices of approximately 2 ounces each, and then pound each piece with a meat mallet to an even, ¼-inch (6-mm)-thick rectangle. Voilà! Pork scallops ready for action.*

NUTRITIONAL FACTS (per roll-up)

Calories: 93 | Total fat: 2.0 g | Total carbs: 6.4 g | Net carbs: 3.6 g | Protein: 12.6 g

time intensive

plan ahead

make ahead

freezer friendly

squeaky clean

keto friendly

Makes two 9-inch (23-cm) deep-dish pies, serves 16 to 24

FRENCH CANADIAN MEAT PIE

Tourtière, a French Canadian meat pie, is a traditional part of Christmas celebrations here in Québec, but it is also enjoyed on many other occasions, especially during the harsh winter months, and throughout Canada as well. Some say the dish was named after the now-extinct passenger pigeons, called "tourtes," that were once part of the pies. Others believe that the name derives from the vessel in which the dish was originally cooked, a tourtière. There is no one correct filling for the pie; it varies greatly depending on the region, but the most commonly used meats include pork, beef, rabbit, and/or wild game.

In my household, Christmas just wouldn't be Christmas if tourtière wasn't on the menu. I started making this dish with my parents back when I was a little kid and then worked on perfecting the recipe over the years. Without a doubt, this Paleo version tops them all! This recipe is a labor of love; that's why I like to make two large pies so that I can savor the results of my toil for some time.

Ingredients for Part 1

- 1 to 2 tablespoons lard or other healthy cooking fat
- 3 tablespoons ground Ceylon cinnamon
- 1 tablespoon ground clove
- 1 tablespoon ginger powder
- 1 tablespoon freshly grated nutmeg
- 1 tablespoon Himalayan salt
- 1 tablespoon freshly ground black pepper
- 4 large pork shanks (about 3 pounds/1.4 kg total)
- 4 cups (scant 1 L) water
- 2 small onions, coarsely chopped
- ¼ cup (15 g) fresh parsley leaves
- 1 tablespoon dried savory
- 1 tablespoon dry mustard

Ingredients for Part 2

- 2 pounds (910 g) lean ground pork
- 2 pounds (910 g) lean ground beef
- 3 cups (710 ml) water
- 2 small red-skinned, white-fleshed sweet potatoes, peeled and finely diced

Ingredients for Part 3

- 1 recipe Paleo Pie Crust dough (page 78)
- Beaten egg and/or coconut milk for brushing the pie dough (optional)

NUTRITIONAL FACTS (per serving, based on 24 servings)

Calories: 431 | Total fat: 30.1 g | Total carbs: 17.1 g | Net carbs: 10.8 g | Protein: 21.5 g

Part 1

1. Preheat the oven to 350°F (177°C).

2. In a heavy skillet set over high heat, melt the lard.

3. While the pan is heating up, mix together the cinnamon, clove, ginger, nutmeg, salt, and pepper on a large plate. Pat the pork shanks dry, then dredge them in the spice mixture, making sure that all sides are well coated.

4. Place the shanks in the hot pan and sear them on all sides until a nice golden crust forms, about 3 to 4 minutes per side.

5. Transfer the shanks to a 4-quart (3.8-L) Dutch oven, add the 4 cups (scant 1 L) of water, onions, parsley, savory, and mustard as well as any leftover spice mixture that didn't get used to coat the pork shanks. Cover and place in the oven to cook slowly for about 2½ hours, until the meat is falling off the bones.

6. Remove the shanks from the Dutch oven and set aside to cool, but leave the cooking liquid in the pot.

Part 2

1. To the Dutch oven, add the ground pork, ground beef, and 3 cups (710 ml) of water. Mix well with a large spoon until the meat is completely broken down into what almost looks like a puree.

2. Pick the meat off the pork shanks and add it to the ground meat in the Dutch oven. Cover and place back in the oven for about 1½ hours, mixing well from time to time.

3. After 1½ hours, add the sweet potatoes. Return to the oven, uncovered, for another 20 to 25 minutes or until the cooking liquid has almost completely evaporated. Allow the meat mixture to cool for about an hour.

Part 3

1. Preheat the oven to 375°F (190°C). Grease 2 deep-dish pie plates with ghee. (Not only does the ghee prevent the crust from sticking to the pan, but it also confers a beautiful golden color to the pastry.)

2. Line the bottoms of the pie plates with the pie dough and divide the meat mixture between the pies. For better adherence, brush the edge of the pie dough with beaten egg, coconut milk, or a mixture of the two before placing the top layer. Cover each pie with the top crust, crimp the edges, and cut vents in the top with a sharp knife.

3. Bake the pies for 20 to 25 minutes, until the crust turns a nice golden color.

Tips: While most Québécois like to eat their tourtière smothered in ketchup, I tend to enjoy mine with cranberry sauce (see page 72 for my recipe). I dare you to give it a try; I bet you won't be sorry you did.

This recipe makes two large meat pies. If you wanted to, you could halve the recipe and make only one pie, but I think you'd regret it. Make two pies and freeze one, why don't you? You can freeze it either before or after baking it? If you choose to freeze it before baking, thaw the pie completely before putting it in the oven. You may have to add a few minutes to the cooking time to make up for the fact that it'll be cold when it hits the oven. If you freeze the pie after it's been baked, thaw the pie completely, then cover it loosely with foil and reheat it in a 350°F (175°C) oven for about 20 minutes, until the blade of a butter knife inserted in the center comes out warm. Or you could reheat it in the microwave, preferably in individual slices, but the crust might come out somewhat soft.

CHAPTER 8

fish and seafood

under 30

 egg-free

 squeaky clean

 nut-free

CURRIED COCONUT SHRIMP

It's hard to believe that such a simple dish can pack so much flavor and transport you so quickly to a land of pure exoticism!

Serves 2

- 1 tablespoon coconut oil
- 1 small onion, chopped
- 1 clove garlic, minced
- 1 teaspoon spicy/hot curry powder
- ½ teaspoon garam masala (see Note, page 164)
- ¼ teaspoon turmeric powder
- ¼ teaspoon Himalayan salt
- ¼ teaspoon freshly ground black pepper
- 1 pound (455 g) large shrimp (26 to 30 count), peeled and deveined
- 1 cup (240 ml) coconut water
- 2 tablespoons tapioca starch
- 2 tablespoons water
- ½ cup (120 ml) full-fat coconut milk
- ¼ cup (20 g) unsweetened shredded coconut, plus more for garnish (optional)

1. In a large skillet set over medium heat, melt the coconut oil, then add the onion and garlic and cook until softened, 3 to 4 minutes. Add the curry powder, garam masala, turmeric, salt, and pepper and cook, stirring, until fragrant, about 1 minute.

2. Throw in the shrimp and cook until they turn pink and are completely opaque, 4 to 5 minutes. Add the coconut water and mix well.

3. In a small bowl, dilute the tapioca starch in the water. Add this slurry to the skillet and mix well. Bring to a simmer and cook for about 1 minute, until the sauce thickens.

4. Stir in the coconut milk and shredded coconut and serve, garnished with extra shredded coconut, if desired.

NUTRITIONAL FACTS (per serving)

Calories: 469   Total fat: 22.9 g   Total carbs: 24.9   Net carbs: 23.0 g   Protein: 41.8 g

under 30

squeaky clean

make ahead

keto friendly

Makes 8 patties

FATTY FISH PATTIES

Here's the perfect way to add more fatty fish (and omega-3s) to your diet! Eating sardines and herring fillets out of the can is certainly an acquired taste, but these patties are so unbelievably tasty, creamy, and delicious that they'll make you forget about what went into them.

- 1 small head cauliflower (1 pound/455 g), cut into small florets
- 2 large eggs, beaten
- 2 to 3 tablespoons Frank's RedHot Sauce
- ¼ cup (30 g) almond flour
- 2 tablespoons coconut flour, plus more if needed
- 2 tablespoons tapioca starch
- ½ teaspoon baking soda
- ½ teaspoon Himalayan salt
- 2 (4.375-ounce/125-g) cans sardines in extra-virgin olive oil
- 2 (3¼-ounce /92-g) cans smoked herring fillets
- ½ small white onion, finely chopped
- 2 tablespoons chopped fresh parsley
- 2 tablespoons ghee for the pan

For serving
- Extra ghee or Foolproof Mayonnaise (page 64)
- Fresh parsley

1. Steam the cauliflower florets over a pot of salted boiling water until really tender, 8 to 10 minutes; let cool completely.

2. Squeeze the water out of the cauliflower until there's not a drop more to be squeezed out, then transfer it to the bowl of a food processor. Add the eggs, hot sauce, flours, tapioca starch, baking soda, and salt and process until completely combined and smooth.

3. Transfer the mixture to a large bowl and, without draining, add the sardines and herring fillets, followed by the chopped onion and parsley. Mix with a large spoon until the ingredients are well combined, then place in the refrigerator to chill for about an hour.

4. Very gently form the mixture into 8 equal patties; it will be fairly soft even after resting in the fridge. If you find that it's still too soft, add a few tablespoons of coconut flour and let it rest for a few more minutes before forming the patties.

   Make-ahead tip: Arrange the patties in a single layer on a large plate; cover well with plastic wrap and put them back in the fridge until you are ready to cook them, up to a full day.

5. Melt the ghee in a large skillet set over medium heat. Once the ghee is fully melted, gently add the patties and cook undisturbed until a nice golden crust forms, 4 to 5 minutes per side.

6. Serve piping hot topped with a little dollop of ghee or mayonnaise and fresh parsley.

7. These patties will keep in the refrigerator for up to 3 to 4 days and reheat very well in a nonstick skillet set over medium-low heat.

NUTRITIONAL FACTS (per patty)
Calories: 154   Total fat: 8.3 g   Total carbs: 8.0 g   Net carbs: 5.6 g   Protein: 12.8 g

LOBSTER MEAT CRUSTED SALMON FILLETS

Serves 4

Talk about turning a fairly ordinary meal into a celebratory feast for the eyes and the palate! As an added bonus, these fillets are super easy to make.

- ¼ cup (33 g) raw macadamia nuts, coarsely chopped
- ¼ cup (34 g) raw Brazil nuts, coarsely chopped
- 6 ounces (170 g) cooked lobster meat (see Note)
- ¼ cup (50 g) Foolproof Mayonnaise (page 64)
- 1 clove garlic, finely chopped
- 2 tablespoons fresh parsley leaves, chopped
- 2 tablespoons fresh lime juice
- 1 teaspoon Old Bay seasoning
- ¼ teaspoon Himalayan salt
- ¼ teaspoon freshly ground black pepper
- 4 (8-ounce/225-g) wild-caught salmon fillets

1. Preheat the oven to 375°F (190°C). Line a rimmed baking sheet with parchment paper.

2. Place the nuts and lobster meat in a small food processor and pulse a few times until the mixture is well combined and the lobster meat is nicely shredded (or chop the meat very finely with a knife); set aside.

3. In a separate bowl, mix together the mayonnaise, garlic, parsley, lime juice, Old Bay seasoning, salt, and pepper. Add the lobster mixture and mix well.

4. Spread this mixture thickly and evenly on top of the salmon fillets. Place the fillets on the prepared baking sheet, cover loosely with another piece of parchment paper, and sprinkle the top of the paper with a little bit of water.

5. Bake for 15 to 20 minutes, depending on thickness of the fillets and the desired level of doneness. If you like salmon slightly pink in the middle, 15 minutes should do the trick; if you prefer it to be cooked all the way through, give it the extra 5 minutes of cooking time.

6. Remove the top piece of parchment paper and set the oven to broil. Leave the fish under the broiler for 3 to 4 minutes, until the top turns golden brown.

Note: *If you can't find lobster meat, you can substitute cooked shrimp, scampi, or crab meat.*

NUTRITIONAL FACTS (per serving)

Calories: 576 | Total fat: 37.4 g | Total carbs: 3.1 g | Net carbs: 1.4 g | Protein: 57.8 g

under 30

squeaky clean

plan ahead

egg-free

SCALLOP, FENNEL, AND STRAWBERRY SALAD

Serves 2

This spectacular salad could easily warrant a spot on the menu of a fancy restaurant. Don't let its elegant looks fool you, though; it comes together very quickly and easily!

For the salad

- 1 large fennel bulb
- 18 medium strawberries, hulled
- 3 tablespoons healthy cooking fat, such as lard, tallow, ghee, or coconut oil
- 6 large scallops, patted very dry
- ¼ cup (30 g) chopped raw pistachios

For the vinaigrette

- 6 large strawberries, hulled
- Strawberry trimmings (from above)
- ¼ cup (60 ml) balsamic vinegar
- 2 tablespoons coconut aminos
- 1 tablespoon Date Paste (page 82)
- ½ teaspoon freshly ground black pepper
- ¼ teaspoon Himalayan salt
- ¼ teaspoon freshly grated nutmeg

For garnish

- Chopped fresh chives
- Balsamic vinegar pearls (optional; see Note)

1. Remove the top from the fennel bulb and slice it as thinly as possible; I strongly recommended the use of a mandoline here. Set aside.

2. Cut each of the strawberries for the salad lengthwise into 4 heart-shaped slices. Remove the little rounded edges of the outer slices and reserve them for the vinaigrette.

3. In a small food processor, combine all the ingredients for the vinaigrette, including the reserved strawberry trimmings, and process until smooth and creamy. Set aside.

4. Melt the cooking fat in a heavy skillet (cast iron is preferred) set over very high heat. When the fat is nice and hot, add the scallops one at a time, making sure that they do not touch. Leave the scallops undisturbed until a nice golden crust forms, which should take about 1 minute, then flip them and let them cook undisturbed until a nice crust forms on the other side.

5. Remove the scallops from the pan and slice each one in half crosswise (you want thinner, round scallops, not semicircles).

6. Divide the fennel between 2 serving plates; top with the strawberry slices, then the scallops, and finally the chopped pistachios. Drizzle with the vinaigrette and garnish with chopped fresh chives and balsamic vinegar pearls, if using.

Notes: *Balsamic vinegar pearls are cute and elegant little beads of gelled balsamic vinegar that look just like caviar and sort of burst onto your palate as you bite into them, delivering a whole suite of complex, tangy, and sweet flavors to your taste buds. Look for them at your local gourmet food store or search for them online.*

NUTRITIONAL FACTS (per serving)

Calories: 298 | Total fat: 8.1 g | Total carbs: 36.0 g | Net carbs: 28.4 | Protein: 21.2 g

quick & easy

plan ahead

make ahead

keto friendly

egg-free

nut-free

squeaky clean

Serves 4

ORANGE GINGER SALMON TATAKI

Tataki is a Japanese technique of preparing meat or fish. The meat or fish is seared very briefly over a hot flame or in a pan before being marinated in vinegar and then sliced thinly before serving. The key to success is to cook the meat or fish over extremely high heat for a very short time. You need to sear the exterior really quickly while keeping the interior raw.

For the tataki

- 2 to 3 tablespoons avocado oil
- 1 (1¼-pound/570-g) salmon fillet from the thickest part of the fish, skin removed
- Generous sprinkle of Himalayan salt

For the marinade

- 2 green onions, thinly sliced
- 2 tablespoons unseasoned rice vinegar
- 2 tablespoons coconut aminos
- 2 tablespoons minced fresh ginger
- 1 tablespoon toasted sesame oil
- 1 teaspoon fish sauce
- Grated zest of 1 orange
- Juice of 1 orange
- 2 cloves garlic, minced
- 3 dried bird's-eye chili peppers or 1 teaspoon red pepper flakes

- 2 tablespoons white sesame seeds, toasted (see Tip, page 300)
- 1 tablespoon black sesame seeds

1. In a medium skillet that can handle serious heat, heat the avocado oil over blazing-high heat.

2. Meanwhile, trim the salmon fillet, if necessary, to get it as evenly shaped as possible. You're looking for a rectangle of relatively even thickness. Sprinkle both sides of the fillet generously with salt.

3. When the pan is nice and hot, sear the fillet very briefly, 20 to 25 seconds per side, or just long enough to get a little bit of a golden crust.

4. Remove the salmon to a dish just large enough to accommodate it plus about 1 cup (240 ml) of liquid, and let it rest for a few minutes.

5. Combine all the ingredients for the marinade in a small mixing bowl, then pour it over the salmon. Cover with plastic wrap and refrigerate for at least 4 hours or, better yet, overnight.

6. Combine the sesame seeds in a shallow bowl. Gently remove the fish from the marinade, let it drip for a few seconds, and then roll it in the sesame seeds until it's completely coated.

7. Slice the salmon as thinly as you can and serve with the leftover marinade for dipping.

Tip: *Don't worry about the marinade being contaminated with bacteria; it was used to marinate cooked fish, so it's totally safe to eat!*

NUTRITIONAL FACTS (per serving)

Calories: 333 · Total fat: 19.1 g · Total carbs: 7.6 g · Net carbs: 5.8 g · Protein: 31.3 g

quick
& easy

keto
friendly

squeaky
clean

Serves 1

EASY TUNA SALAD FOR ONE

Whenever I get kinda stuck without a plan and start scratching my head, going from fridge to pantry to fridge and wondering what to eat, there's a very good chance that I'll wind up making this salad, because it comes together in mere minutes, is incredibly filling and nutritious, won't dirty the entire kitchen, and tastes absolutely incredible. All things that I love and appreciate; I bet you will, too!

For the salad

- 1 (6-ounce/170-g) can wild-caught albacore tuna, drained
- 1 large broccoli floret, chopped
- ¼ orange bell pepper, chopped
- ¼ red apple, diced
- 3 raw Brazil nuts, chopped
- 2 tablespoons Foolproof Mayonnaise (page 64)
- 2 tablespoons sliced green olives
- 1 tablespoon minced fresh ginger
- 1 tablespoon fresh lime juice
- 1 teaspoon raisins
- ¼ teaspoon Himalayan salt
- ¼ teaspoon freshly ground black pepper

For serving / garnish

- 2 cups (75 g) mixed greens
- Apple slices
- Small handful of chopped raw nuts (optional)
- Lime slices (optional)

1. Place all the ingredients for the salad in a large mixing bowl and toss gently until evenly combined.
2. Serve the salad over mixed greens with apple slices on the side, garnished with chopped nuts and a few slices of lime, if desired.

NUTRITIONAL FACTS

| Calories: 573 | Total fat: 44.8 g | Total carbs: 20.9 g | Net carbs: 15.3 g | Protein: 45.5 g |

quick & easy

 egg-free

 squeaky clean

 nut-free

 keto friendly

Serves 4

PAN-SEARED SCALLOPS WITH BALSAMIC REDUCTION

Scallops are often considered synonymous with fancy and elegant meals. As such, people tend to serve them when they have valued guests at their dinner table, and with good reason. Scallops are so tender, so pretty, and so naturally tasty, you don't need to add much at all to them to turn them into a spectacular dish. Here, the sweet tanginess of balsamic vinegar and the tart saltiness of capers complement the delicate flavor of these sea muscles to absolute perfection.

- 1 cup (240 ml) balsamic vinegar
- 12 jumbo dry scallops (about 1¾ ounces/50 g each)
- Pinch of Himalayan salt
- Pinch of freshly ground black pepper
- 4 tablespoons ghee, divided
- 2 tablespoons capers
- 1 tablespoon grated lemon zest
- Juice of 1 lemon
- Generous handful of fresh microgreens
- 1 teaspoon finely chopped fresh parsley

1. In a skillet or small saucepan, bring the balsamic vinegar to a boil over high heat, then reduce the heat and let the vinegar simmer until it becomes thick and syrupy and a little less than a ¼ cup (60 ml) remains in the pan, which should take 3 to 4 minutes. Remove from the heat and allow to cool while you work on the scallops. Better yet, place the reduced vinegar in the refrigerator to chill for a couple of hours so it gets even thicker.

2. Remove the foot from each scallop, if present. (The foot is small piece of tissue on the side of the scallop that feels tougher than the rest of the scallop. It can easily be torn off with your fingers.) Pat the scallops really dry, then sprinkle both sides with a pinch of salt and pepper.

3. Heat a heavy skillet (cast iron is preferred) over very high heat for about 2 minutes. When the pan is scorching hot, add 2 tablespoons of the ghee and allow it to melt until it completely coats the pan.

4. Place the scallops in the pan, leaving at least 1 or 2 inches (2.5 or 5 cm) between them so that air can circulate freely around them and they don't start boiling as opposed to browning; work in batches if you have to. Let the scallops cook, undisturbed, for 1 to 1½ minutes or until a beautiful golden crust forms. (Searing scallops tends to generate smoke, and lots of it. Expect your smoke detector to go off!) Flip the scallops with tongs and cook for an additional minute, until a crust forms on the other side, then remove them to a plate.

5. Add the remaining 2 tablespoons of ghee to the skillet, followed by the capers and lemon zest. Let that fry for about 30 seconds or until the capers have "popped" and appear crispy. Add the lemon juice and continue cooking until the liquid has almost completely evaporated. Remove from the heat.

6. Spoon or drizzle some of the reduced balsamic vinegar onto 4 individual plates, arrange the scallops on top, 3 per plate, and then garnish with some of the fried capers and lemon sauce. Add a little handful of microgreens and a bit of chopped parsley to each plate, then serve without delay.

NUTRITIONAL FACTS (per serving)

Calories: 250   Total fat: 14.0 g   Total carbs: 4.6 g   Net carbs: 4.0 g   Protein: 25.7 g

Tips: *Most people think that getting a nice golden crust on a scallop is darn near impossible. Nothing could be further from the truth; in fact, it's extremely easy. There are, however, a few simple rules that you must obey in order for it to work:*

1. *Make sure that your scallops are EXTREMELY dry before you add them to the pan; a good way to achieve that is to place them on a paper towel and leave them to dry uncovered in the refrigerator overnight.*

2. *Always cook the scallops over scorching heat.*

3. *Give the scallops ample room to breathe as they cook, leaving a good inch or two (2.5 or 5 cm) of space between them.*

4. *Resist the urge to move the scallops around as they cook. Let that caramelization happen. Touch them only when they are ready to flip.*

under 30

 egg-free

 squeaky clean

nut-free

Serves 4

TUNA AND PINK GRAPEFRUIT TARTARE WITH SWEET POTATO STRAWS

The combination of soft, delicate raw fish, tangy grapefruit, a subtle hint of ginger, and the slightest kick of heat from the jalapeño pepper makes this dish incredibly refreshing. Top it with a handful of deliciously hot and crunchy sweet potato straws, and you'll find yourself in culinary heaven!

For the tuna tartare

- 1 pound (455 g) fresh tuna, cut into very fine dice
- 1 pink grapefruit, cut into supremes (see Note) and finely diced
- 1 small jalapeño pepper, seeded and finely chopped
- ¼ cup (15 g) fresh cilantro leaves, finely chopped
- 2 tablespoons finely chopped green onion (green part only)
- 2 tablespoons white sesame seeds, toasted (see Tip, page 300)
- 1 tablespoon black sesame seeds
- 1 tablespoon grated fresh ginger
- 1 tablespoon coconut aminos
- 1 tablespoon avocado oil
- ½ teaspoon toasted sesame oil
- ½ teaspoon Himalayan salt

For the sweet potato straws

- 1 medium red-skinned, white-fleshed sweet potato (about 12 ounces/340 g), skin on
- ¼ cup (52 g) coconut oil for the pan
- Pinch of Himalayan salt

For garnish

- ¼ cup (15 g) microgreens
- Pinch of black sesame seeds
- Pinch of toasted white sesame seeds

1. Place all the ingredients for the tuna tartare in a large mixing bowl and toss delicately until evenly combined. Put the mixture in the refrigerator or over a large bowl filled with ice.

2. Using a mandoline equipped with the ⅛-inch (3-mm) julienne cutter, cut the sweet potato into thin straws and set aside.

3. Heat the coconut oil in a large skillet set over high heat for about 2 minutes. Add a handful of sweet potato straws and fry, moving them around with a large spoon until they get nice and golden. Remove the fried potatoes to a bowl lined with paper towels to absorb the excess oil. Sprinkle lightly with salt as soon as they come out of the hot oil. Repeat with the remaining sweet potato straws.

4. Place a 3-inch (7.5-cm) round cookie cutter on a serving plate and spoon one-quarter of the fish mixture into it. Pack the fish down lightly with a spoon and remove the ring. Repeat with the remaining 3 servings.

5. Top each portion of fish with a small handful of microgreens and a small handful of sweet potato straws. Sprinkle with a little bit of black and toasted white sesame seeds and serve without delay with the rest of the sweet potato straws.

Note: To supreme the grapefruit, begin by removing the top and bottom of the fruit with a sharp knife. Then carefully remove the skin and pith from the flesh, beginning at the top and following the curves all the way down. Next, working over a bowl to catch the juice, carefully remove each section of the fruit by inserting the blade of the knife between the flesh and the membrane on both sides. The wedges should come out easily, leaving only the membranes intact.

NUTRITIONAL FACTS (per serving)

Calories: 389 | Total fat: 19.5 g | Total carbs: 24.5 g | Net carbs: 19.8 g | Protein: 30.1 g

CHAPTER 9

sides

under 30

freezer friendly

make ahead

squeaky clean

Makes 6 fritters

- 1 medium head cauliflower (1¾ pounds/800 g)
- 1 shallot, very thinly sliced
- 1 clove garlic, minced
- 2 large eggs, beaten
- ¼ cup (30 g) almond flour
- 2 tablespoons tapioca starch
- 2 tablespoons coconut flour
- ½ teaspoon baking soda
- ½ teaspoon Himalayan salt
- ½ teaspoon freshly ground black pepper
- ¼ teaspoon ground white pepper
- ¼ teaspoon freshly grated nutmeg
- 2 tablespoons ghee for the pan, plus more for serving
- Chopped fresh parsley for garnish

CAULIFLOWER FRITTERS

Who needs potatoes? Crispy and perfectly golden on the outside, creamy and buttery on the inside, these fritters will simply blow your mind.

1. Cut the cauliflower into florets and steam them over a pot of salted boiling water until really tender, 8 to 10 minutes; let cool completely.

2. Squeeze the water out of the cauliflower until there's not a drop more to be squeezed out, then transfer it to a large mixing bowl.

3. Add the rest of the ingredients, except for the ghee and parsley, and mix by hand until well combined. Form into 6 equal patties.

4. Melt the ghee in a large skillet set over medium heat. Once the ghee is fully melted, gently add the patties and cook undisturbed until a nice golden crust forms, 3 to 4 minutes per side.

5. Serve piping hot with a little dollop of ghee and chopped parsley for garnish.

6. These fritters will keep well in the fridge for 3 to 4 days, so you can make them ahead and reheat them quickly in a nonstick skillet over medium heat. Use a good amount of healthy cooking fat and they'll be just as good as when freshly made.

Tip: *Instead of steaming the cauliflower florets, you could grate the cauliflower and cook it in the microwave for 5 to 6 minutes. That will save you a little time, but you'll still have to squeeze the water out of it!*

NUTRITIONAL FACTS (per fritter)

Calories: 81 · Total fat: 2.6 g · Total carbs: 10.5 g · Net carbs: 6.2 g · Protein: 5.3 g

under 30

squeaky clean

plan ahead

keto friendly

make ahead

egg-free

Serves 4 to 6

BASIC CAULI-RICE

Cauliflower rice is found all over the Paleo realm, and there are probably as many versions of it as there are people making it. While nothing will ever be able to truly replace sticky rice for me, when the craving for rice strikes, cauli-rice is often an acceptable substitute. In this version, chopped almonds provide a little crunch that helps fool my brain and taste buds, granting them the satisfaction they're after.

- 1 large head cauliflower (2 pounds/910 g)
- ½ cup (70 g) raw almonds, chopped
- 1 tablespoon ghee
- 1 medium onion, finely chopped
- ¾ teaspoon Himalayan salt
- ½ teaspoon freshly ground black pepper
- ½ cup (120 ml) Brown Bone Broth (page 74) or Brown Chicken Stock (page 76)
- 1 tablespoon unseasoned rice vinegar
- 1 green onion, finely chopped
- Chopped fresh parsley for garnish

1. Cut the cauliflower into small florets and place them in the bowl of your food processor. Give them a few quick pulses (for me it takes 10 to 15) until their texture resembles that of rice.

2. Toast the almonds in a large dry skillet set over medium heat; when golden and fragrant, remove to a plate.

3. Add the ghee, onion, salt, and pepper to the skillet and cook until the onion is fragrant and slightly translucent, about 5 minutes.

4. Add the riced cauliflower to the pan, followed by the broth and vinegar. Mix well and continue cooking for an additional 4 to 5 minutes, until the cauliflower is cooked but still somewhat firm and the cooking liquid is completely absorbed.

5. Mix in the toasted almonds and chopped green onion. Serve piping hot, garnished with chopped parsley.

6. Keep the rice in the refrigerator for up to 5 days; it reheats very well in the microwave.

NUTRITIONAL FACTS (per serving, based on 6 servings)

Calories: 114   Total fat: 6.3 g   Total carbs: 11.7 g   Net carbs: 6.5 g   Protein: 4.9 g

quick
& easy

 squeaky
clean

 make
ahead

 keto
friendly

Serves 8

CLASSIC CREAMY COLESLAW

Coleslaw is one of those things that you could probably find in my fridge at any given time. I find that slaw goes well with just about everything, from pan-fried eggs to pulled pork to grilled beef to roasted chicken, and is equally good at breakfast, lunch, and dinner. I like to make a huge batch on the weekend to last me throughout the week. I also like to play with the ingredients—sometimes. Don't be afraid to change things up and make this one your own!

- ¼ cup (33 g) raw sunflower seeds, toasted
- ½ medium head cabbage (about 2¼ pounds/1 kg), shredded
- 1 cup (200 g) Foolproof Mayonnaise (page 64)
- 2 large carrots, finely grated
- ¼ cup (15 g) fresh parsley leaves, chopped
- ¼ cup (28 g) chopped raw walnuts
- ¼ cup (60 ml) white wine vinegar
- 1 teaspoon ginger powder
- 1 teaspoon ground Ceylon cinnamon
- 1 teaspoon Himalayan salt
- ½ teaspoon ground allspice
- ½ teaspoon ground white pepper
- ¼ teaspoon cayenne pepper

1. Toast the sunflower seeds in a small skillet over medium-low heat, until the seeds turn lightly golden and become fragrant, about 5 minutes.

2. Place all the ingredients in a large mixing bowl. Mix well with your hands, taking care to massage the slaw for a minute or two to soften the cabbage and get it to release some of its water.

3. The slaw can be eaten immediately but will be much better after it rests in the fridge for a couple of hours, or even overnight.

4. This slaw will keep in an airtight container in the refrigerator for 4 to 5 days.

NUTRITIONAL FACTS (per serving)

Calories: 220   Total fat: 20.0 g   Total carbs: 10.2 g   Net carbs: 8.1 g   Protein: 9.4 g

under 30

 egg-free

 nut-free

OVEN-ROASTED GLAZED CARROTS

Serves 6

Carrots have never been among my favorite vegetables. In fact, I've always found them to be kind of boring. That is, until I discovered glazed carrots. Prepared this way, they are everything but boring! I'm always amazed at how a few carefully chosen ingredients and a little bit of roasting action can totally turn a simple, all-too-common vegetable into a spectacular side dish. Do yourself a favor and whip up a batch tonight!

- 10 to 12 large carrots
- 2 tablespoons avocado oil
- 2 tablespoons raw honey
- 2 tablespoons white balsamic vinegar
- 1 tablespoon Dijon mustard
- 1 tablespoon fresh thyme, finely chopped
- 1 tablespoon fresh oregano leaves, finely chopped
- 2 cloves garlic, minced
- 1 teaspoon Himalayan salt
- 1 teaspoon freshly ground black pepper
- Chopped fresh parsley for garnish

1. Preheat the oven to 425°F (220°C). Line a rimmed baking sheet with parchment paper.

2. Peel the carrots, slice them on the diagonal, and place them in a large mixing bowl.

3. In a separate bowl, mix together the avocado oil, honey, vinegar, mustard, thyme, oregano, garlic, salt, and pepper until very well combined, then pour over the carrots and mix to coat evenly.

4. Spread the mixture in a single layer on the prepared baking sheet. Roast for 20 to 25 minutes, turning once or twice, until the carrots are tender and have taken on a nice golden color.

5. Sprinkle with chopped parsley and serve immediately.

NUTRITIONAL FACTS (per serving)

Calories: 129 · Total fat: 4.9 g · Total carbs: 21.4 g · Net carbs: 17.2 g · Protein: 1.5 g

quick & easy keto friendly

squeaky clean egg-free

Serves 4

GRILLED AVOCADO

If you've never tried grilled avocado, you don't know what you're missing. It's amazing how just a few minutes on the grill completely transforms them: You won't believe how creamy they get! And if you don't have access to an outdoor grill, a cast-iron grill pan works just as well. Seriously, treat yourself and grill some avocados today!

- 2 large ripe avocados
- 2 tablespoons avocado oil
- 1 lime wedge
- Himalayan salt and freshly ground black pepper

For garnish
- Chopped raw pistachios
- Chopped fresh chives
- White balsamic vinegar

1. Preheat a grill to medium-high heat.

2. Cut the avocados in half and remove the pits. Drizzle the cut surfaces with the avocado oil, squirt some lime juice on them, and then season generously with salt and pepper.

3. Place the avocados on the grill, flesh-side down, and close the lid. Cook for 2 to 3 minutes, until the fruits bear nice char marks and have gotten deliciously warm and creamy.

4. Serve garnished with chopped pistachios, chopped chives, and a splash of white balsamic vinegar.

NUTRITIONAL FACTS (per serving)

Calories: 186   Total fat: 18.3 g   Total carbs: 7.6 g   Net carbs: 5.1 g   Protein: 2.5 g

under 30

egg-free

squeaky clean

nut-free

Serves 4

GRILLED CAULIFLOWER

Talk about an original and tasty way to serve cauliflower. This is an awesome summertime alternative to oven-roasted cauliflower. Perhaps too good an alternative, even: It'll definitely have you wishing that summer never goes away.

- 1 medium head cauliflower (1¾ pounds/800 g)
- ¼ cup (60 ml) avocado oil
- 2 tablespoons Montreal Steak Spice (page 48)
- Chopped fresh parsley for garnish
- Extra-virgin olive oil for garnish (optional)

1. Preheat a grill to high heat.

2. Remove the large outer leaves from the cauliflower, leaving the core intact. Cut two roughly 3-inch (7.5-cm)-thick slices from the center of the head. Hold onto the larger pieces that were cut loose.

3. Coat the cauliflower slices and the larger florets that came loose generously with the avocado oil and then sprinkle liberally with the steak spice.

4. Throw the cauliflower on the grill, lower the heat to medium, and close the lid. Grill for 5 minutes, turn the slices a quarter turn, and continue grilling for another 5 minutes. Flip the slices and florets over and repeat the process, cooking for 5 minutes, turning a quarter turn, and then cooking for an additional 5 minutes.

5. Transfer to a plate, garnish with chopped parsley and a drizzle of extra-virgin olive oil, if desired, and serve immediately.

NUTRITIONAL FACTS (per serving)

Calories: 174 · Total fat: 14.2 g · Total carbs: 11.1 g · Net carbs: 6.4 g · Protein: 4.0 g

quick & easy

 egg-free

squeaky clean

 nut-free

 keto friendly

Serves 4 to 8

For the marinade

- ½ cup (120 ml) extra-virgin olive oil
- ¼ cup (60 ml) fresh lemon juice
- 2 tablespoons Dijon mustard
- 2 large cloves garlic, minced
- 1 tablespoon dried oregano leaves
- 1 tablespoon dried chives
- 1 teaspoon granulated onion
- 1 teaspoon Himalayan salt
- 1 teaspoon freshly ground black pepper
- ¼ teaspoon red pepper flakes

- 8 large endives
- Chopped fresh parsley for garnish

GRILLED ENDIVES

You won't believe the amount of flavor that these grilled endives deliver! Plus, they're so quick and easy to make, they're bound to find their way onto your table regularly during grilling season. And for those days when grilling is not an option, a cast-iron grill pan makes a very decent substitute.

1. Preheat a grill to medium-high heat.

2. Place all the ingredients for the marinade in a large mixing bowl and whisk vigorously until evenly combined and slightly emulsified.

3. Cut the endives in half lengthwise. Trim off the ends, if necessary, but make sure to remove just enough to get rid of what needs to go. It's important that the core stays intact so your endives do not fall apart.

4. One by one, gently rub the endive halves with a few tablespoons of the marinade, making sure that it gets in between the leaves and the exterior gets generously coated.

5. Place the endives on the hot grill, cut-side down, and close the lid. Lower the heat to medium and cook for about 2 minutes, then flip and cook for an additional 2 minutes.

6. Transfer to a plate, garnish with chopped parsley, and serve immediately.

NUTRITIONAL FACTS (per serving, based on 8 servings)

Calories: 67   Total fat: 6.4 g   Total carbs: 2.4 g   Net carbs: 0.6 g   Protein: 0.8 g

under 30

keto friendly

plan ahead

egg-free

squeaky clean

nut-free

Makes 12 skewers

SKEWERED GRILLED VEGGIES

Talk about presenting grilled veggies to your guests and family members in a manner that's elegant and sophisticated, yet super simple and convenient. And did I mention how tasty these veggies are? They are so full of flavor that they may well end up stealing the show!

For the marinade

- ¼ cup (60 ml) avocado oil
- Juice of ½ lemon
- 1 tablespoon Dijon mustard
- 1 tablespoon finely chopped fresh thyme
- 1 tablespoon finely chopped fresh sage
- 1 teaspoon Himalayan salt
- 1 teaspoon freshly ground black pepper

- 24 button mushrooms, stems cut short
- 6 medium zucchinis, cut into 1-inch (2.5 cm)-thick rounds
- 3 long red bell peppers, seeded and cut into 1-inch (2.5 cm)-thick slices

Equipment needed:

12 skewers, about 12 inches (30 cm) long

1. If using wooden skewers, soak them in cold water for 30 minutes to 1 hour before grilling.

2. Preheat a grill to medium-high heat.

3. Make the marinade by vigorously whisking together all the ingredients until evenly combined and slightly emulsified.

4. Place the vegetables in a large mixing bowl and pour the marinade over them. Gently mix with your hands until all the veggies are well coated.

5. Skewer the vegetables, alternating between mushrooms, zucchini, and red bell pepper.

6. Place the skewers on the hot grill and cook for 8 to 10 minutes, turning 3 or 4 times to create nice grill marks.

NUTRITIONAL FACTS (per skewer)

Calories: 41　　Total fat: 1.0 g　　Total carbs: 6.8 g　　Net carbs: 4.4 g　　Protein: 2.8 g

quick & easy
 keto friendly
 make ahead
 egg-free
 squeaky clean
 nut-free

Serves 6

KALESLAW

Here's a salad that you'll want to add to your plate on a regular basis, if only for its vibrant colors. Honestly, though, its intriguing flavor profile and nutrient density are just two more reasons to make this slaw a part of your weekly rotation. That and the fact that it tastes and looks just as good after spending five days in the fridge as it does when you just finish making it. A definite winner!

For the vinaigrette

- ¼ cup (60 ml) extra-virgin olive oil
- ¼ cup (60 ml) unseasoned rice vinegar
- 2 tablespoons toasted sesame oil
- 1 tablespoon fish sauce
- 1 tablespoon grated fresh ginger
- 1 teaspoon freshly ground black pepper
- ½ teaspoon Chinese five-spice powder (see Notes, page 162)
- ½ teaspoon Himalayan salt

- ½ medium head red cabbage, shaved paper-thin
- 10 to 12 large kale leaves, stems removed and chopped
- 1 large carrot, peeled and julienned
- 3 tablespoons sesame seeds, toasted (see Tip, page 300)
- 2 fresh bird's-eye chili peppers, finely chopped, or ½ teaspoon red pepper flakes
- 2 green onions, finely chopped

1. Make the vinaigrette by vigorously whisking together all the ingredients until evenly combined and slightly emulsified.

2. In a large mixing bowl, combine the cabbage, kale, and carrot. Add the vinaigrette and mix well with your hands, massaging the vegetables to bruise them a little bit and to get them to release some of their moisture.

3. Add the sesame seeds, chili peppers, and green onions and continue mixing, more gently this time, until all the ingredients are evenly combined.

4. Serve immediately, or give the salad a couple of hours in the fridge to allow the flavors to meld. Store any leftovers in an airtight container in the refrigerator for up to a week.

NUTRITIONAL FACTS (per serving)

Calories: 194 · Total fat: 15.4 g · Total carbs: 12.3 g · Net carbs: 9.0 g · Protein: 3.1 g

quick & easy

 make ahead

 squeaky clean

egg-free

LEMONY BRUSSELS SPROUTS ALMANDINE

Serves 6

Here's a simple side dish that goes well with just about anything. To save time, steam and cool your Brussels sprouts on the weekend and store them in the fridge until you are ready to whip this up. And if Brussels sprouts aren't your thing, replace them with broccoli or even cauliflower!

- 2 pounds (910 g) Brussels sprouts
- ¼ cup (55 g) ghee
- ½ cup (42 g) sliced almonds
- ½ teaspoon Himalayan salt
- Grated zest of 1 lemon
- 2 tablespoons fresh lemon juice
- ½ teaspoon freshly ground black pepper

1. Clean the Brussels sprouts, trim off their bases, and cut them in half. Place them in a steamer basket and steam over a pot of salted boiling water until they turn a beautiful, vibrant green, 2 to 3 minutes.

2. Immediately plunge the steamed Brussels sprouts in an ice water bath and move them around gently until they're completely chilled, then transfer them to a colander and leave them to drain and dry. At this point, you can put the Brussels sprouts in the refrigerator until you are ready to assemble the dish for serving.

3. Melt the ghee in a large skillet set over medium heat. Add the sliced almonds and salt and cook until golden and fragrant, about 1 minute.

4. Lower the heat to medium-low, add the Brussels sprouts, lemon zest, lemon juice, and pepper and continue cooking until heated through, about 3 to 5 minutes.

5. This dish will keep in the refrigerator for up to 3 to 4 days and reheats very well in the microwave or in a nonstick skillet set over medium heat.

Tip: Don't skimp on the ice for your ice water bath. You want to use LOTS of it: The faster your Brussels sprouts get cold, the crunchier and greener they will remain. And cold is really what you're after. That's the only way to stop the cooking. Warm or room temperature will not cut it.

NUTRITIONAL FACTS (per serving)

Calories: 188 : Total fat: 13.0 g : Total carbs: 15.7 g : Net carbs: 9.0 g : Protein: 6.9 g

OVEN-ROASTED VEGETABLES

Serves 4 to 6

This is a classic side dish, and one that you should know by heart. In fact, this is the kind of recipe that you don't need to follow verbatim. You can make many additions and/or substitutions, depending on the mood of the moment or the content of your fridge, and still get amazing results. A true must-have in your culinary repertoire!

- 2 cups (10 ounces/285 g) Brussels sprouts, cut in half
- 1 large sweet potato, cut into 1-inch (2.5-cm) chunks
- ½ medium turnip, peeled and cut into 1-inch (2.5-cm) chunks
- 1 medium onion, sliced
- ¼ cup (52 g) coconut oil, melted
- 3 tablespoons Dijon mustard
- 1 tablespoon finely chopped fresh rosemary
- 1 tablespoon finely chopped fresh thyme
- 1 teaspoon Himalayan salt
- 1 teaspoon freshly ground black pepper

1. Preheat the oven to 475°F (245°C) and line a rimmed baking sheet with parchment paper.

2. In a large mixing bowl, combine all the ingredients and toss until the veggies are evenly coated.

3. Transfer the vegetables to the prepared baking sheet and roast for 15 to 18 minutes, until golden and fork-tender, stirring once or twice during cooking.

4. Serve with your favorite protein!

NUTRITIONAL FACTS (per serving, based on 6 servings)

| Calories: 156 | Total fat: 9.8 g | Total carbs: 16.6 g | Net carbs: 11.8 g | Protein: 3.2 g |

make ahead
 freezer friendly
 egg-free
 nut-free

Serves 6 to 8

RUSTIC ACORN SQUASH MASH

If you're not a fan of squash, I swear this mash will make you a believer. Roasting the squash, as opposed to boiling or steaming it, gives it such a rich, buttery, and nutty flavor; your taste buds will be begging for more. And if you're already a fan of squash, you will want to eat nothing but this for the rest of your life. This recipe does make a fairly large batch, but I bet you will be more than happy to have leftovers. Try reheating the mash in a hot skillet with coconut oil. Oh my word! Just drop it in the hot fat, cover the pan, and leave it be for a few minutes, and it will get all nice and crusty and caramelized for you. Scrumptious!

- 2 tablespoons avocado oil
- 1 tablespoon raw honey
- 2 acorn squash, cut in half and seeded
- 1 teaspoon freshly ground black pepper
- ½ teaspoon Himalayan salt
- 1 tablespoon fresh thyme leaves, chopped
- 5 or 6 fresh sage leaves, chopped
- ¼ cup (60 ml) water
- 2 tablespoons ghee

1. Preheat the oven to 375°F (190°C).

2. Dribble the avocado oil and honey over the squash halves, then sprinkle with the pepper, salt, and fresh herbs.

3. Place the squash cut-side down in a rimmed roasting pan. Add the water to the pan and place in the oven, uncovered. Bake for 40 to 45 minutes or until the squash is soft to the touch and can easily be scooped out with a spoon. You might want to check on it from time to time to make sure that it isn't burning. If you feel that more water is needed, add a little bit, but never more than ¼ cup (60 ml) at a time. You want the flesh to caramelize nicely, and for that to happen, the pan must remain fairly dry.

4. Remove the squash from the oven, carefully turn it over, and let it cool for a few minutes, until it can be handled safely.

5. Scoop out the flesh with a spoon and place it in a large mixing bowl. Add the ghee and mash very loosely with a fork or potato masher.

NUTRITIONAL FACTS (per serving, based on 8 servings)

Calories: 110 · Total fat: 6.8 g · Total carbs: 13.6 g · Net carbs: 11.9 g · Protein: 0.9 g

under 30

 plan ahead

 make ahead

 squeaky clean

 keto friendly

nut-free

Serves 4 to 6

ROASTED GARLIC CAULIFLOWER MASH

For most of my life, I was a hardcore fan of mashed potatoes. They were one of my favorite foods, and I had to have them at least once a week. And no one was to be trusted with my sacrosanct mashed potatoes: I was the one in charge of making them! Well, let me tell you, those days are gone. One taste of this cauli-mash and I never looked back. It's just so much creamier, lighter, and tastier! I bet one bite is all it will take to convince you, too…if you aren't already a convert.

- 2 medium heads cauliflower (about 3 pounds/1.4 kg total), cut into small florets
- 1 head Roasted Garlic (page 52)
- ¼ cup (50 g) Foolproof Mayonnaise (page 64)
- ¼ cup (55 g) ghee, plus more for serving
- ½ teaspoon Himalayan salt
- ¼ teaspoon ground white pepper
- Generous fresh grating of nutmeg
- Chopped fresh parsley for serving

1. Cut the cauliflower into small florets and steam them over a pot of salted boiling water until really tender, 8 to 10 minutes. Remove from the heat and let cool slightly.

2. Squeeze as much water out of the cauliflower as you possibly can, then transfer it to the bowl of a food processor.

3. Squeeze the roasted garlic from the cloves into the bowl of the food processor, then add the mayo, ghee, salt, pepper, and nutmeg and process until creamy. Stop to scrape the sides of the bowl as needed.

4. Serve with a little dollop of ghee and chopped parsley.

NUTRITIONAL FACTS (per serving, based on 6 servings)

Calories: 238   Total fat: 19.3 g   Total carbs: 15.4 g   Net carbs: 9.0 g   Protein: 5.5 g

quick & easy

 keto friendly

squeaky clean

egg-free

ZUCCHINI CARPACCIO WITH WALNUT PESTO

Serves 4

This salad is best served as soon as it's made, as the salt will draw moisture out of the zucchinis, causing them to release water. You could, however, make the pesto and slice the zucchinis ahead of time and then assemble the salad when you are ready to eat it. To change it up a bit, cut the zucchinis into fine julienne strips instead of ribbons. And if you eat dairy, try crumbling a little bit of soft unripened (fresh) goat cheese on top. Oh my, the goodness of it all!

- 6 medium zucchinis

For the pesto

- ½ cup (52 g) raw walnuts
- ½ cup (30 g) fresh parsley leaves, chopped
- ¼ cup (30 g) pitted Kalamata olives
- ¼ cup (60 ml) extra-virgin olive oil
- Juice of 1 lemon
- 1 clove garlic, minced
- 1 teaspoon Himalayan salt
- 1 teaspoon freshly ground black pepper

For garnish (optional)

- 1 tablespoon chopped raw walnuts
- 1 tablespoon sliced Kalamata olives

1. Slice the zucchinis into paper-thin ribbons and place them in a large mixing bowl. I strongly recommend the use of a mandoline here; those ribbons need to be really thin.

2. Place all the ingredients for the pesto in the bowl of a small food processor and process until well combined and pastelike in consistency.

3. Add the pesto to the bowl with the zucchini ribbons and toss gently with your hands, making sure that all the slices get separated and well coated in pesto.

4. Garnish with chopped walnuts and sliced Kalamata olives, if desired, and serve immediately.

NUTRITIONAL FACTS (per serving)

Calories: 275   Total fat: 24.1 g   Total carbs: 12.9 g   Net carbs: 7.5 g   Protein: 6.5 g

CHAPTER 10

nut butters

An entire chapter devoted to nut butters? I realize that you may be skeptical because, if you're like most people, when you think of nut butter, toast immediately comes to mind. You may be at a bit of a loss as to what to do with these nutty concoctions when bread isn't a part of your regular diet anymore.

But there are so many more uses for nut butters. When I'm not using them as part of a recipe, I like to enjoy my nut butters on the occasional Paleo muffin or pancake, or with a few slices of fruit, such as pear, apple, banana, and particularly avocado! Mostly, though, I like to eat them straight out of the jar, by the spoonful, especially the fancy varieties that I come up with. They are such a tasty treat; I bet you will find yourself doing the same!

Have you ever tried filling the pitted hole of an avocado with nut butter? It's a killer combo! My personal faves for this purpose include toasted almond, roasted cashew, and smoked almond butter. AH-MA-ZING!

The Basics of Nut Butter Making

Any nut, raw or toasted, can be turned into creamy nut butter. All you need is a powerful food processor or high-speed blender, such as a Blendtec or Vitamix, and a little bit of patience.

The process couldn't be easier: Simply add the nuts to the food processor or blender and spin them on the highest possible setting until they turn into creamy butter. Of course, you will have to stop the motor and scrape the sides of the bowl a few times during the process. And this process will take more or less time depending on the variety of nuts you are using. Some nuts have a higher fat content than others, and the higher their fat content, the faster the nuts will start releasing their oil and turn into butter. Processing times can vary greatly; you're looking at anywhere between five and thirty minutes. Also, the fattier the nut, the thinner the final product

NUT (per 30 grams)	FAT in grams	PROTEIN in grams	FIBER in grams
Macadamia nuts	21.5	2	2.5
Pecans	20.5	2.5	2.5
Pine nuts	19.5	4	1
Brazil nuts	19	4	2
Walnuts	18.5	4.5	2
Hazelnuts	17	4	2.5
Almonds	14	6	3.5
Sunflower seeds	14	6.5	3
Pistachios	13	6	3
Cashews	12.5	5	1

will be. Nut butters made from raw nuts tend to be much firmer in consistency than their toasted counterparts due to their higher moisture content.

To give you an idea of what to expect, I've compiled a little chart of the fat contents for different varieties of nuts and seeds. I also threw in protein and fiber contents, just for fun. As you can see, nuts are a much greater source of fat than they are of protein.

THINGS I'VE LEARNED
ALONG THE WAY

Use a Decent Amount of Nuts

To make 1 cup of nut butter, you will need approximately double that amount of nuts. However, I recommend working with a minimum of 3 to 4 cups of nuts, depending on the size of your food processor; just make sure that you fill the bowl at least halfway, and preferably three-quarters of the way. If you use too few nuts, the blades will simply send them flying against the sides of the bowl, so you'll have to constantly stop and scrape to get the nuts to go down into the blade's path. Using a good amount of nuts will ensure that they stay at the bottom of the bowl. You'll still need to stop and scrape, but much less often.

Add More Fat to Speed Things Up

Adding extra oil or fat right from the start will help speed up the process, but it often results in a thinner nut butter. Sometimes this is desirable, and sometimes not so much. After experimenting with different fats, I've decided that my favorite one to add is ghee. Not only does it not affect the final texture of the nut butter, since it is naturally smooth and creamy at room temperature, but it also gives the final product a deliciously rich and buttery flavor. Coconut oil is equally delicious in those concoctions that are on the sweeter side.

Add Sweeteners and Natural Flavorings at the End

It's best to add sweeteners, such as maple syrup, honey, and date paste, or natural flavorings, such as pure vanilla extract and essential oils, at the very end of the process, and then process for a short time—just long enough to incorporate them. These ingredients contain a certain amount of water, and it's a well-known fact that oil and water do not mix.

These additions will invariably cause your nut butter to change drastically in texture, usually making it much firmer, and may even cause it to separate if you process it for too long after adding the sweetener. (Don't worry, there is a fix for separated butters, which I've outlined below.)

Though I just mentioned adding vanilla extract at the very end of the process, I think you are better off avoiding it and using a dry form of vanilla instead. Vanilla extract will change the consistency of your nut butter and may even cause it to separate. Why risk it when there is such an easy alternative? To solve the issue, I started using whole vanilla beans or vanilla powder as opposed to vanilla extract. Vanilla beans can be added whole, too: no need to scrape the seeds or anything. Simply chop one up finely and add it at the very beginning of the process. It'll get pulverized into thousands of highly fragrant, minuscule black specks as the nuts are turned into butter. Vanilla powder can be added anytime during the process.

What About Salt?

The addition of salt is of utmost importance, as it really brings out the flavor of the nuts and adds immeasurable depth to the final product. Do not—I repeat, do not—leave it out!

If Your Nut Butter Separates, Add Water

Common sense would have you think that you could bring a separated butter back to a smooth consistency by letting it spin for an extended period, but nothing could be further from the truth. Once the butter is broken, the more you spin, the more the oil is drawn out, and you end up with a soupy, crumbly mixture.

The only way to save your nut butter when it breaks is to add water to it. Yep, you read that right! Add a little bit of warm water, a tablespoon at a time, and run the motor for fifteen to twenty seconds after each addition, until your nut butter becomes smooth and creamy again.

Prevention Is Key—Keep 'Em Dry!

Never use soaked nuts to make nut butter. It simply won't work. If you feel more comfortable soaking your nuts before consuming them, it's imperative that you dehydrate them again before attempting to turn them into creamy butter. You can do that in a dehydrator or in a low-temperature oven.

Also, do not add any ingredients that are likely to contain water until the very end of the process, be as brief as you can when incorporating them (running the machine the bare minimum of time, until just mixed in), and be prepared for the worst if you decide to start experimenting.

Oh, and one more thing: Make sure that your tools are nice and dry. There's nothing worse than a few drops of water left at the bottom of your food processor ruining an entire batch of dreamy nut butter!

Let Your Nut Butter Rest

Most freshly made nut butters will be fairly warm, if not downright hot, as they come out of the food processor. It's best to let them rest for twenty-four hours before consuming them. This allows the flavors to meld and fully develop. It also allows the nut butter to return to its rightful consistency.

No one says that you can't lick the bowl and spatula, though....

Where to Store Your Nut Butter

This is a matter of personal preference. Some people like to keep their nut butters in the refrigerator to prevent them from turning rancid. I like to keep mine in the pantry, where their texture remains much smoother and their flavor really gets to shine. When they're made from nothing but plain nuts, shredded coconut, salt, and dry spices, nut butters are totally shelf stable and can be kept safely in the pantry for up to a few months.

There are a few exceptions, however. Fancy varieties that contain perishable ingredients, such as pumpkin puree, date paste, or bacon, and nut butters that are high in moisture, like those that contain a fair amount of dried fruit or have been saved from the grave by having water added to them, are best kept in the fridge and consumed within three to four weeks.

In Time, Natural Separation Will Occur

When left to stand for a while, some natural nut butters have a tendency to separate, resulting in oil rising to the surface. It might be a good idea to give these nut butters a good stir from time to time to reincorporate the oil. I'm sure you won't mind doing that, though...after all, that spoon will need to be licked clean afterwards!

under 30

 keto friendly

 make ahead

 egg-free

 squeaky clean

Makes about 2 cups (525 g)

- 4 cups (560 g) raw almonds
- ½ teaspoon Himalayan salt
- 1 vanilla bean, chopped

ALL-NATURAL TOASTED ALMOND BUTTER

This is my go-to nut butter, the one I can never be without, the one I use in a whole bunch of recipes. Making your own costs so much less than buying the ready-made stuff, and it tastes so much better, too! While the addition of vanilla is entirely optional, it gives this already delicious spread a nice hint of sweetness. Oh, and don't bother scraping the vanilla seeds. Just throw the whole bean in there—it'll get pulverized anyway.

1. Preheat the oven to 350°F.

2. Spread the almonds in a single layer on a rimmed baking sheet and toast in the oven for 12 to 15 minutes or until fragrant. Move the nuts around a few times as they toast.

3. Let the nuts cool for about 10 minutes, until they can be handled safely, then add them, along with the salt and chopped vanilla bean, to the bowl of a food processor.

4. Process for about 15 minutes, stopping to scrape the sides of the bowl from time to time, until the nut butter is very smooth and creamy and almost liquid in consistency. It will return to a firmer consistency once it's had a chance to rest and cool down.

5. Transfer the nut butter to an airtight glass container and store in a cool, dark, dry place, where it will keep for up to a few months.

Tip: If you don't need to keep your almond butter neutral-tasting—that is, you're not planning on using it in all kinds of recipes—try adding a generous pinch of ground cinnamon. It's absolutely delicious!

NUTRITIONAL FACTS (per tablespoon)

Calories: 86 | Total fat: 7.4 g | Total carbs: 3.2 g | Net carbs: 1.3 g | Protein: 3.1 g

under 30

 keto friendly

 make ahead

 egg-free

 squeaky clean

Makes about 2½ cups (650 g)

- ¼ cup (55 g) ghee
- 1 teaspoon Himalayan salt
- 4 cups (600 g) raw cashew pieces
- 1 vanilla bean, chopped

ALL-NATURAL TOASTED CASHEW BUTTER

Missing your good ol' peanut butter? Not anymore! Once you've had a taste of this nut butter, I promise you will forget that peanut butter ever existed. You won't believe how creamy and buttery and heavenly it is. Plus, your house will be filled with the most intoxicating aroma every time you make a batch. Be careful; this may very well become your new addiction.

1. In a large skillet set over medium heat, melt the ghee and salt, then add the cashew pieces and toast, stirring almost constantly, until the cashews turn golden and fill the house with an intoxicating fragrance, about 5 minutes total.

2. Turn off the heat and let the nuts cool for 10 to 15 minutes or until they can be handled safely. Then place them in the bowl of your food processor along with the chopped vanilla bean.

3. Process for a total of 10 to 15 minutes, stopping to break up the lumps and scrape down the sides of the bowl as necessary. You will need to stop often in the beginning, but as the nuts begin to release their oil, the butter will become a lot looser, and you won't need to scrape quite as frequently.

4. When your cashew butter has reached the desired smoothness, transfer it to an airtight glass container and store in a cool, dark, dry place, where it will keep for up to a few months.

NUTRITIONAL FACTS (per tablespoon)

Calories: 112	Total fat: 9.5 g	Total carbs: 5.6 g	Net carbs: 5.1 g	Protein: 2.6 g

under 30

keto friendly

make ahead

egg-free

squeaky clean

Makes about 2½ cups (650 g)

- 5 cups (700 g) raw hazelnuts
- ½ teaspoon Himalayan salt
- 1 vanilla bean, chopped

ALL-NATURAL TOASTED HAZELNUT BUTTER

Toasted hazelnut butter is probably the most fragrant of all the nut butters, and as such, I love to use it in all kinds of baked goods. Not only does it add a ton of flavor, but its fairly runny consistency makes it super easy to combine with other ingredients. Of course, it also goes great with (Paleo) breads.

1. Preheat the oven to 350°F (177°C).

2. Spread the hazelnuts in a single layer on a rimmed baking sheet and toast in the oven for 15 to 20 minutes, until their skins darken and the nuts become highly fragrant. Move the nuts around a few times as they toast.

3. Let the nuts cool for about 10 minutes, until they can be handled safely, then place them in a clean tea towel and close it up into a little bundle. Hold that package in one hand and, with the other hand, wiggle the nuts around so they grind against each other. Do that for a good minute or two, and when you open up your little bundle, the hazelnuts will be totally skinless. Carefully pick out the nuts, leaving the skins behind.

4. Put the hazelnuts along with the salt and chopped vanilla bean in the bowl of a food processor and process for 5 to 8 minutes, until smooth, creamy, and fairly liquid in consistency. You will probably have to stop once or twice to scrape the sides of the bowl.

5. Transfer the nut butter to an airtight glass container and store in a cool, dark, dry place, where it will keep for up to a few months.

NUTRITIONAL FACTS (per tablespoon)

| Calories: 74 | Total fat: 7.1 g | Total carbs: 2.0 g | Net carbs: 0.9 g | Protein: 1.8 g |

make ahead

 egg-free

 squeaky clean

 nut-free

 keto friendly

Makes about 3 cups (780 g)

- 6 cups (800 g) unsalted raw sunflower seeds
- ½ teaspoon Himalayan salt
- 1 vanilla bean, finely chopped

ALL-NATURAL TOASTED SUNFLOWER SEED BUTTER

Of all these butters, sunflower seed butter is probably the one that will test your patience the most. The seeds take forever to start to release their oil and give the impression that they will eventually turn into a creamy butter. By all means, keep going and resist the urge to add oil to it. You'll be rewarded with the most luscious, thick nut butter you've ever tasted! Imagine the concentration of flavor that you get when chewing on a great big handful of toasted sunflower seeds, but in a creamy form. Oh yeah! That's what I'm talking about.

1. Preheat the oven to 350°F (177°C).

2. Spread the sunflower seeds on a rimmed baking sheet and toast them in the oven for about 20 minutes, moving them around often, until golden and fragrant. Be careful not to take the seeds too far. Sunflower seeds are very delicate and will burn fairly easily. You want them to be a very light golden color, no darker.

3. Let the seeds cool for a few minutes, until they can be handled safely, then transfer them to the bowl of a food processor along with the salt and chopped vanilla bean.

4. Process for 25 to 30 minutes, stopping as often as necessary to break up the clumps and scrape down the sides of the bowl. You may find that you have to do this fairly often in the beginning, and you may get discouraged and think that there's no way this lump of cement will ever turn into creamy butter, but do not despair. I guarantee you that it will.

5. After about 20 minutes, the seeds should start to release some of their oil, and the butter will finally relax and become creamy. After this point, let the processor run for 5 to 10 minutes until the butter is really smooth.

6. Transfer the seed butter to one or two airtight glass containers and store in a cool, dark, dry place, where it will keep for up to a few months.

Tip: Try using sunflower seed butter instead of tahini in recipes that call for tahini.

NUTRITIONAL FACTS (per tablespoon)

Calories: 100 | Total fat: 8.5 g | Total carbs: 3.5 g | Net carbs: 2.0 g | Protein: 3.5 g

make ahead

squeaky clean

keto friendly

egg-free

nut-free

Makes about 2 cups (525 g)

COCONUT BUTTER

Coconut butter is one concoction that I can't bear to be without. Not only is it heavenly eaten straight from the jar, but it also makes for a fantastic garnish on countless dishes, and I use it as a base ingredient in many of my culinary creations.

Since the ready-made stuff tends to cost an arm and a leg, I learned to make my own. I even came up with a few different methods, one building upon the other. Method 1 is the easiest and least time-consuming of the three, but it creates the least smooth product. Method 2 involves the additional step of straining out the coarser bits of coconut, resulting in a smoother product that is equivalent to store-bought coconut butter. Method 3, shown in the photo, has you whip the smooth coconut butter that was created using Method 2, resulting in the smoothest, creamiest, and lightest product possible. Feel free to try them all and decide for yourself which one you like best.

- 6 cups (480 g) unsweetened shredded coconut
- ½ cup (104 g) coconut oil
- ¼ teaspoon Himalayan salt
- 1 teaspoon pure vanilla extract, homemade (page 84) or store-bought

Method 1: Basic Coconut Butter

(This results in a butter that is creamy but remains a tad gritty.)

1. Place the shredded coconut, coconut oil, and salt in the bowl of a food processor and process for 8 to 12 minutes, until you have a very soupy mixture. You will have to stop and scrape the sides of the bowl a few times, but not all that often.

2. Add the vanilla extract and give the butter (or "coconut soup") another quick spin just to incorporate the vanilla.

3. Pour the butter into an airtight glass container and store in a cool, dark, dry place, where it will keep for several months. This coconut butter will need at least 24 hours to cool down, set, and get back to its proper consistency.

Method 2: Smooth and Silky Coconut Butter

The name says it all. This version is smooth and creamy. This method results in a coconut butter that is in every way identical to the product you find in stores, only it won't cost you a pretty penny. Store-bought coconut butter is sometimes called coconut manna.

1. Continuing from Method 1, opposite (expect for the jarring step), force the coconut butter through a fine-mesh sieve by pushing it down with a ladle or rubber spatula.

2. When the butter is just too thick and coarse to go through the sieve anymore, place whatever's left in the sieve back in the food processor and process it for a few more minutes until it becomes very soupy again.

3. Force that coconut butter through the fine-mesh sieve. Repeat this process one or two more times, until you're left with only a few tablespoons of the coarser stuff (see Note).

4. Pour the smooth butter into an airtight glass container and store in a cool, dark, dry place, where it will keep for several months. This coconut butter will need at least 24 hours to cool down, set, and get back to its proper consistency.

If you have a high-speed blender...

Should you be so fortunate as to own one of those fancy high-speed blenders, such as a Blendtec or Vitamix, you will not need to force your coconut butter through a fine-mesh sieve to achieve the silky-smooth result described above. The simple act of processing the ingredients on high speed for a long enough time (usually about 5 minutes) will give you a smooth, lump-free coconut butter.

Note: *By all means, do not discard the coarser butter; keep it in a separate jar and use it as a garnish on pancakes, muffins, omelettes, scrambled eggs, salads, or even fish—let your imagination run wild!*

Method 3: Whipped Coconut Butter

Now we are going to kick things up a notch. This version, pictured opposite, is smooth, creamy, light, and airy, just like frosting!

1. Instead of jarring your silky-smooth, sieved butter from Method 2, transfer it to a large mixing bowl and place it in the refrigerator for about 30 minutes, until it starts to solidify around the edges while remaining fairly soft in the center.

2. Take the butter out of the refrigerator and break it up with a spoon, then beat it with a hand mixer, starting on low speed and moving up to high, until it is well combined, soft, and creamy.

3. Return the butter to the refrigerator for 10 to 15 minutes to firm up, then beat it again on high speed for about 30 seconds to 1 minute, until fluffy.

4. Send your butter for one last 10-minute trip to the refrigerator and then give it a final 30-second whip.

5. Transfer the whipped butter to an airtight glass container and store in a cool, dark, dry place, where it will keep for several months. Unlike the other two versions, this coconut butter doesn't need time to set and can be enjoyed right away.

Things I've learned along the way about coconut butter

- *During the warmer months, coconut butter may refuse to firm up or suddenly go really soft on you. If that happens, simply place it in the fridge for about 30 minutes, then give it a good stir. This should bring it back to a nice spoonable consistency.*

- *Likewise, when it's really cold out, your coconut butter may have a tendency to become way too firm. In that case, place the jar in the microwave for a few seconds at a time (no more than 3 to 5) to soften it up a bit, then give it a good stir.*

- *Adding coconut oil to your butter not only makes it creamier and softer, but also helps the process happen a lot faster.*

- *You might be tempted to make a smaller batch, but trust me, using a lot of coconut makes the job much easier. If you use too little, all you will accomplish is to send it flying off to the sides of the bowl of your food processor as soon as the blades start spinning, which will have you constantly stopping the motor to scrape down the bowl. At that rate, you'll get nowhere fast.*

- *Read labels: Make sure that your shredded coconut is free of additives, namely sulfites and sulfates, which are very commonly added as preservatives.*

- *A pinch of cinnamon does wonders for coconut butter.*

NUTRITIONAL FACTS (per tablespoon)

| Calories: 48 | Total fat: 5.3 g | Total carbs: 0.8 g | Net carbs: 0.2 g | Protein: 0.2 g |

quick & easy

plan ahead

make ahead

squeaky clean

keto friendly

egg-free

nut-free

A TASTE OF INDIA SEED BUTTER

If you're into the exotic and highly aromatic flavors of Indian food, then you are truly in for a treat with this deliciously unique butter! Just one bite will have you hooked for life.

Makes about 1¼ cups (390 g)

- 1 cup (260 g) All-Natural Toasted Sunflower Seed Butter (page 294)
- ½ cup (75 g) sesame seeds, toasted (see Tip)
- ¼ cup (23 g) unsweetened finely shredded "macaroon" coconut
- 1 teaspoon garam masala (see Note, page 164)
- 1 teaspoon ground cumin
- ½ teaspoon curry powder
- ¼ teaspoon Himalayan salt
- ¼ teaspoon cayenne pepper
- ⅛ teaspoon vanilla powder

1. Place all the ingredients in a large mixing bowl and mix with a wooden spoon or rubber spatula until well combined.

2. Transfer the nut butter to an airtight glass container and store in a cool, dark, dry place, where it will keep for up to a few months.

Tip: To toast your own sesame seeds, simply lay them in a dry skillet set over medium heat and toss them regularly until they turn lightly golden in color and become highly fragrant, 4 to 5 minutes.

NUTRITIONAL FACTS (per tablespoon)

| Calories: 75 | Total fat: 6.2 g | Total carbs: 3.4 g | Net carbs: 3.4 g | Protein: 2.3 g |

Makes about 2½ cups (475 g)

APPLE CRUMBLE NUT BUTTER

This nut butter is not what I would call spreadable. In fact, I think the name "crumble" suits it very well. Not only does it taste much like the dessert in question, but its texture is surprisingly similar to that of a crumble topping. Chances are you'll end up eating this nut butter by the spoonful or sprinkling it over yummy treats such as pancakes or waffles. Be forewarned, though: This stuff tastes so buttery, so rich, and so insanely good that once you pick up that spoon, you'll have a very hard time putting it down. This treat will seriously test your self-control!

For the apple crumble

- 1 cup (85 g) diced dried apples
- ⅓ cup (38 g) chopped raw pecans
- ¼ cup (60 ml) pure maple syrup (dark color or Canadian Medium)
- 2 tablespoons ground Ceylon cinnamon
- ¼ teaspoon freshly grated nutmeg

For the nut butter base

- 1 cup (120 g) raw cashew pieces
- ¾ cup (105 g) Smooth and Silky Coconut Butter (page 297) or store-bought coconut butter
- ¼ cup (55 g) ghee
- ½ teaspoon Himalayan salt

1. Place the dried apples, pecans, maple syrup, cinnamon, and nutmeg in a medium bowl. Mix well and let sit on the counter for at least 4 hours or up to a full day, until the apples and nuts have absorbed pretty much all of the syrup.

2. To make the nut butter base, place the cashews, coconut butter, ghee, and salt in the bowl of a food processor and process on high speed for 8 to 10 minutes, until smooth and creamy, scraping the sides of the bowl as necessary.

3. Once the nut butter base has reached your desired consistency, throw in the apple crumble mixture and pulse a few times until just mixed in.

4. Transfer the nut butter to an airtight glass container and store in a cool, dark, dry place. It will keep in the pantry for up to 2 weeks or in the refrigerator for up to a few months.

NUTRITIONAL FACTS (per tablespoon)

Calories: 83 | Total fat: 6.6 g | Total carbs: 5.5 g | Net carbs: 4.4 g | Protein: 1.0 g

under 30

 egg-free

 make ahead

Makes about 1¼ cups (440 g)

BAKLAVA NUT BUTTER

The lyrics to Def Leppard's "Pour Some Sugar on Me" come to mind every time I have a spoonful of this glorious nut butter, for sticky and sweet is exactly what it is. If, like me, you're a big fan of baklava and really miss sinking your teeth into those heavenly pastries, this jarred version will definitely satisfy the craving and help fill the void!

For the candied pistachios
- ½ cup (60 g) raw pistachios
- 1 tablespoon raw honey
- Himalayan salt

For the nut butter base
- 3 tablespoons ghee, divided
- ¼ cup (85 g) raw honey
- 1 tablespoon orange blossom water
- ¼ teaspoon ground cardamom
- ½ teaspoon Himalayan salt, divided
- 1 cup (105 g) raw walnuts
- 1 cup (125 g) raw pistachios
- ¼ teaspoon vanilla powder
- Pinch of ground Ceylon cinnamon

1. Make the candied pistachios: In a small skillet set over medium-high heat, place the pistachios along with the tablespoon of honey and a pinch of salt. Heat until the honey thickens and sticks to the nuts, 1 to 2 minutes. Sprinkle with salt and set aside to cool.

2. Make the nut butter base: In a large skillet set over medium-high heat, bring 1 tablespoon of the ghee, ¼ cup (85 g) honey, orange blossom water, cardamom, and ¼ teaspoon of the salt to a boil. Once the mixture starts bubbling vigorously, add the walnuts and 1 cup (125 g) of pistachios and cook, stirring frequently, until the syrup becomes really thick and sticks to the nuts, 4 to 5 minutes.

3. Kill the heat and let the nuts cool completely, until they have hardened and can be handled safely. If you want to speed up the cooling process, spread the nuts in a single layer on a rimmed baking sheet.

4. Once cool, place the nuts in the bowl of a food processor and process until smooth, which should take no more than 4 to 5 minutes. Stop the motor to scrape the sides of the bowl a few times.

5. Add the remaining 2 tablespoons of ghee, remaining ¼ teaspoon of salt, vanilla powder, and cinnamon and resume processing until fully incorporated, then pulse in the candied pistachios just until mixed in.

6. Transfer the nut butter to an airtight glass container and allow to rest and settle, ideally until the next day. This nut butter will keep in the pantry for up to 2 weeks or in the refrigerator for up to a few months.

NUTRITIONAL FACTS (per tablespoon)

| Calories: 137 | Total fat: 10.8 g | Total carbs: 7.7 g | Net carbs: 6.4 g | Protein: 3.3 g |

plan ahead

egg-free

make ahead

Makes about 2½ cups (740 g)

CHAI NUT CLUSTERS AND DATE SWIRL NUT BUTTER

Sweet and deliciously spicy, fudgy, and intriguingly crunchy, this nut butter is way too addictive. Better keep it out of sight! Keep half the batch in the pantry and store the other half in the fridge to enjoy two completely different but equally blissful gustatory experiences.

For the nut clusters

- 1 cup (140 g) mixed raw nuts (almonds, Brazil nuts, hazelnuts, cashews)
- 2 tablespoons pure maple syrup (dark color or Canadian Medium)
- 1 teaspoon Chai Spice (page 49)
- ¼ teaspoon Himalayan salt

For the nut butter base

- 1 cup (140 g) raw cashews
- ½ cup (50 g) raw pecans
- ½ cup (70 g) raw almonds
- ½ cup (104 g) coconut oil
- 2 cups (160 g) unsweetened shredded coconut
- 1 tablespoon pure vanilla extract, homemade (page 84) or store-bought
- ½ teaspoon Himalayan salt

For the swirl

- ¼ cup (75 g) Date Paste (page 82)

1. Make the nut clusters: Place the mixed nuts in the bowl of a food processor and give them a few quick pulses until their texture resembles that of small gravel.

2. Transfer the nuts to a small nonstick skillet and toast over medium heat until slightly fragrant, 30 to 45 seconds. Add the maple syrup, Chai Spice, and salt, then stir until the syrup is hot and bubbly and small clusters begin to form.

3. Remove to a plate and allow to cool completely, stirring gently with your fingers from time to time to help little clusters form.

4. Meanwhile, make the nut butter base: Place the cashews, pecans, almonds, and coconut oil in the bowl of the food processor (no need to wash it) and process for 8 to 10 minutes, until smooth and creamy.

5. Add the shredded coconut, vanilla extract, and salt and resume processing until smooth, about 5 more minutes.

6. Transfer to a mixing bowl and place in the refrigerator to set for about an hour, until it resembles soft cookie dough. You might want to give the butter a stir from time to time to help it set evenly.

7. Once the base butter has reached the right consistency, gently mix in the nut clusters with a rubber spatula.

8. Drop dollops of the date paste over the top of the nut butter and barely mix them in with your rubber spatula; you want to create some kind of a swirl.

9. Transfer the nut butter to an airtight glass container and store in a cool, dark, dry place. Although it does get somewhat firm, this nut butter is also excellent refrigerated. It will keep in the pantry for up to 2 weeks or in the refrigerator for up to a few months.

NUTRITIONAL FACTS (per tablespoon)

Calories: 120 · Total fat: 11.3 g · Total carbs: 5.4 g · Net carbs: 3.8 g · Protein: 1.9 g

plan ahead

 make ahead

 egg-free

Makes about 3 cups (775 g)

CINNAMON ROLL NUT BUTTER

Intoxicatingly sweet and cinnamon-y, this nut butter is best served at breakfast or as a snack with apple slices or slathered thick over a warm Apple Cinnamon Spice Muffin (page 336). Of course, a good ol' spoon dip works just as well!

For the chunks

- ⅓ cup (48 g) raisins, chopped
- ⅓ cup (35 g) chopped raw walnuts
- ¼ cup (60 ml) pure maple syrup (dark color or Canadian Medium)
- 1 teaspoon ground Ceylon cinnamon
- ¼ teaspoon Himalayan salt

For the nut butter base

- 1 cup (140 g) raw cashews
- 1 cup (140 g) raw macadamia nuts
- 1 cup (140 g) Smooth and Silky Coconut Butter (page 297) or store-bought coconut butter
- 1 vanilla bean, chopped
- 1 teaspoon ground Ceylon cinnamon
- ½ teaspoon Himalayan salt

For the swirl

- ¼ cup (75 g) Date Paste (page 82)
- ¼ cup (55 g) ghee, melted
- ¼ cup (60 ml) pure maple syrup (dark color or Canadian Medium)
- 3 tablespoons ground Ceylon cinnamon

1. In a medium bowl, combine all the ingredients for the chunks. Let sit on the counter for at least 4 hours or up to a full day, until the raisins and nuts have absorbed pretty much all of the syrup.

2. Make the nut butter base: Place the cashews, macadamia nuts, coconut butter, chopped vanilla bean, cinnamon, and salt in the bowl of a food processor and process on high speed for 8 to 10 minutes, until smooth and creamy, scraping the sides of the bowl as necessary.

3. Transfer the nut butter to a mixing bowl and place in the refrigerator to set for about 2 hours, until it resembles soft cookie dough. You might want to give the butter a stir from time to time to help it set evenly.

4. Meanwhile, make the swirl: Place the date paste, ghee, maple syrup, and cinnamon in the bowl of the food processor (no need to wash it) and process until smooth. Set aside.

5. Once the base butter has reached the desired consistency, gently mix in the raisin and nut chunks with a rubber spatula.

6. Drop spoonfuls of the swirl mixture over the top of the nut butter and barely mix it in with your rubber spatula, creating little swirls as you go.

7. Transfer the nut butter to one or two airtight glass containers and store in a cool, dark, dry place. It will keep in the pantry for up to 2 weeks or in the refrigerator for up to a few months.

NUTRITIONAL FACTS (per tablespoon)

| Calories: 98 | Total fat: 8.0 g | Total carbs: 6.7 g | Net carbs: 5.1 g | Protein: 1.3 g |

under 30

egg-free

make ahead

DARK CHOCOLATE HAZELNUT SPREAD

Makes about 3 cups (780 g)

Growing up and even well into adulthood, I always had a major thing for Nutella; if there was a jar in the pantry, I could often be caught heading for it, spoon in hand! Had there been a jar of this homemade version sitting right next to the store-bought stuff, though, you can be sure that I'd have reached for this one instead. This healthier version has so much more to offer in the flavor department: You get to distinguish the rich, slightly smoky flavor of toasted hazelnuts as well as the deep, intense aroma of dark chocolate.

- ½ cup (35 g) coconut sugar
- 2½ cups (425 g) raw hazelnuts, toasted, skins removed (see Notes)
- 1 cup (140 g) raw almonds
- ½ cup (110 g) ghee
- ¼ cup (52 g) coconut oil
- ½ teaspoon Himalayan salt
- ¾ cup (67 g) cacao powder
- 1 teaspoon pure vanilla extract, homemade (page 84) or store-bought

1. Melt the coconut sugar in a large skillet set over medium heat, stirring gently from time to time. This will take anywhere from 5 to 10 minutes, depending on the heat of your stove and the thickness of your pan.

2. Once the coconut sugar has completely melted, add the toasted hazelnuts and raw almonds. Stir to coat, then transfer to a rimmed baking sheet lined with parchment paper. Spread the nuts in a single layer and let cool completely.

3. Put the cooled nuts, ghee, coconut oil, and salt in the bowl of a food processor and process for 8 to 10 minutes, until smooth and creamy, stopping to scrape the sides of the bowl as needed.

4. Add the cacao powder and resume processing until it's completely incorporated. Add the vanilla extract and give your nut butter a final spin just to mix in the vanilla.

5. Transfer the spread to one or two airtight glass containers and store in a cool, dark, dry place. This spread will keep in the pantry for several weeks or in the refrigerator for up to a few months.

Notes: Refer to the Toasted Hazelnut Butter recipe on page 292 for instructions on toasting the hazelnuts and removing their skins.

While waiting for the coconut sugar to melt, you may start thinking that it will never happen, but trust me, it will. By all means resist the urge to add water. Just keep stirring gently and the sugar will eventually turn to liquid. Don't go jacking up the heat, either; you'll only end up burning the sugar. Just be patient…it will melt!

NUTRITIONAL FACTS (per tablespoon)

Calories: 89 | Total fat: 7.7 g | Total carbs: 4.5 g | Net carbs: 3.3 g | Protein: 1.9 g

under 30

 make ahead

egg-free

TOASTED BUTTER PECAN SPREAD

Makes about 2 cups (485 g)

This spread is excellent eaten straight from the jar or laid on thick over your favorite cupcake.

- 3 cups (300 g) raw pecans
- ½ cup (110 g) ghee
- ½ teaspoon Himalayan salt
- ¼ teaspoon Chai Spice (page 49)
- ¼ teaspoon vanilla powder
- ¼ cup (85 g) raw honey

1. Preheat the oven to 350°F (177°C).

2. Spread the pecans in a single layer on a rimmed baking sheet and toast in the oven for 10 to 12 minutes, until fragrant. Remove from the oven and let cool for about 10 minutes, until the nuts can be handled safely.

3. Reserve 1 cup of pecans and place the rest in the bowl of a food processor. Process for 6 to 8 minutes, until smooth and creamy.

4. Add the ghee, salt, Chai Spice, and vanilla powder and process until completely incorporated. Add the honey and resume processing until combined; add the reserved pecans and pulse a few times just to break them down into smaller pieces.

5. Transfer to an airtight glass container and let sit for 24 hours to allow the flavors to meld, then store in the refrigerator, where it will keep for up to a few months.

NUTRITIONAL FACTS (per tablespoon)

Calories: 112 | Total fat: 11.0 g | Total carbs: 3.7 g | Net carbs: 2.5 g | Protein: 1.2 g

time intensive
squeaky clean
plan ahead
keto friendly
make ahead
egg-free

Makes about 2 cups (525 g)

- 4 cups (560 g) raw almonds, divided
- ½ teaspoon Himalayan salt
- 5 or 6 drops all-natural liquid smoke (optional)

Equipment needed:

5 cups hickory wood chips

Tip: Even though this recipe calls for only 2 cups (250 g) of smoked almonds, I strongly suggest that you double or even triple the batch, since the amount of wood chips needed and the overall smoking time will remain the same. Smoked almonds will keep at room temperature in an airtight container for several months, and they make an awesome snack. Plus, the next time you feel the urge to whip up a batch of this delicious butter, you won't have to go through the process of smoking the almonds.

CRUNCHY SMOKED ALMOND BUTTER

This recipe should come with a serious warning: Once you've tasted smoked almond butter, you may never want to eat it any other way. Try filling the pitted hole of an avocado with it. As weird as it may sound, I predict that it will become your next go-to snack!

1. Soak 4 cups of the wood chips in water for at least an hour prior to smoking the almonds.

2. Preheat a grill to 200°F (95°C). If using a gas grill, lighting a single element on the lowest setting should do the trick.

3. Make 4 wood chip pouches. For each pouch, cut out a 12 by 24-inch (30.5 by 61-cm) piece of heavy-duty aluminum foil and place about a cup of wet wood chips at one end. Add a handful of dry chips, then fold the foil over the wood chips. Fold all 4 edges toward the center at least twice, then poke holes in the top of the pouch with a fork.

4. Lift the grill grate that's above the lit element or charcoal and place a pouch directly on the heat source. Close the lid and wait until smoke starts to come out of the pouch.

5. Place 2 cups of the almonds in a single layer on a large cooling rack (make sure that the grid is fine enough for the almonds not to fall through; if not, place a sheet of foil on the rack and pierce small holes all over it) and place the whole rig on the unlit side of the grill; close the lid.

6. Smoke the almonds for about 4 hours, replacing the pouch with a fresh one every hour or so. If necessary, crank up the heat under the new pouch until smoke starts to come out, then bring the heat back down to low. Leave the lid open while you do that so as not to generate too much heat inside the grill. Try to keep the heat as stable as possible, at around 200°F (95°C). Note that it's not necessary to get huge amounts of smoke in order to get good flavor from it. However, if you feel you aren't getting enough, you can add more dry chips to your foil pouches or place an aluminum container with a handful of dry chips next to your smoldering foil pouch.

7. When the almonds are done smoking, let them cool for 5 to 10 minutes.

8. Put the remaining 2 cups (280 g) of raw almonds plus 1 cup (125 g) of the smoked almonds in the bowl of a food processor. Process for about 15 minutes, stopping to scrape the sides of the bowl from time to time, until the butter is very smooth and creamy. Add the salt and liquid smoke, if you'd like an even stronger smoke flavor, and process until well incorporated.

9. Add the remaining 1 cup (125 g) of smoked almonds and pulse just until the almonds are broken into crunchy little pieces.

10. Transfer the almond butter to an airtight glass container and store in a cool, dark, dry place, where it will keep for up to a few months.

NUTRITIONAL FACTS (per tablespoon)

| Calories: 86 | Total fat: 7.4 g | Total carbs: 3.2 g | Net carbs: 1.3 g | Protein: 3.1 g |

under 30

make ahead

egg-free

MAPLE CHAI CANDIED NUT SPREAD

Makes about 1½ cups (345 g)

An impeccable blend of sweet chai spices and maple flavor in a smooth, perfectly spreadable nut butter...words alone cannot describe what a blissful experience this butter will provide to your taste buds. You'll probably end up spreading it on just about everything. It's particularly good on a warm muffin or a thick slice of toasted banana bread (see my recipe on page 338).

- ¼ cup (60 ml) pure maple syrup (dark color or Canadian Medium)
- 4 tablespoons ghee, divided
- 1 teaspoon Chai Spice (page 49)
- ½ teaspoon Himalayan salt
- ½ cup (70 g) raw almonds
- ½ cup (52 g) raw walnuts
- ½ cup (50 g) raw pecans
- ¼ cup (34 g) raw Brazil nuts
- ¼ cup (33 g) raw macadamia nuts

1. In a medium saucepan set over high heat, bring the maple syrup to a boil and let it boil vigorously for 1 to 2 minutes. Add 2 tablespoons of the ghee, the Chai Spice, and salt and boil, stirring, for an additional 30 seconds or until well combined. Stir in the nuts and continue cooking for another minute or two or until there is no more syrup at the bottom of the pan.

2. Transfer the candied nuts to a piece of parchment paper and spread them lightly. Set aside to cool and harden for about 15 minutes.

3. Put the cooled candied nuts and the remaining 2 tablespoons of ghee in the bowl of a food processor and process for 3 to 5 minutes, until smooth but slightly grainy.

4. Transfer the spread to an airtight glass container and store in a cool, dark, dry place, where it will keep for up to a few months.

NUTRITIONAL FACTS (per tablespoon)

| Calories: 103 | Total fat: 17.2 g | Total carbs: 5.2 g | Net carbs: 3.3 g | Protein: 3.5 g |

under 30

egg-free

make ahead

Makes about 2 cups (535 g)

° **3 cups (315 g) raw walnuts**

For the candied walnuts

° **¼ cup (60 ml) pure maple syrup (dark color or Canadian Medium)**

° **1 teaspoon pure vanilla extract, homemade (page 84) or store-bought**

° **¼ teaspoon Himalayan salt**

° **1 cup (105 g) raw walnuts, chopped**

° **¼ cup (55 g) ghee**

° **½ teaspoon Himalayan salt**

° **2 tablespoons pure maple syrup (dark color or Canadian Medium)**

MAPLE WALNUT SPREAD

Made with just enough pure maple syrup to give it the perfect amount of sweetness and some mildly intoxicating notes, this delicious spread is an experience you won't soon forget (and will probably want to repeat time and time again).

1. Preheat the oven to 350°F (177°C).

2. Spread the 3 cups of walnuts in a single layer on a rimmed baking sheet and toast in the oven for about 10 minutes, until fragrant. Let cool for about 10 minutes, until they can be handled safely.

3. Meanwhile, make the candied walnuts: In a saucepan, bring the ¼ cup (60 ml) of maple syrup, vanilla extract, and ¼ teaspoon of salt to a roaring boil. Add the cup of chopped walnuts and continue boiling over high heat until pretty much all of the maple syrup has evaporated and the mixture starts to get sticky. Pour onto a piece of parchment paper and allow to cool completely.

4. Put the cooled walnuts (the ones you toasted in the oven), ghee, and ½ teaspoon of salt in the bowl of a food processor and blitz them for 6 to 8 minutes, until smooth and creamy.

5. Transfer to a large mixing bowl and gently stir in the 2 tablespoons of maple syrup, then break the candied walnuts into bite-sized pieces and mix them into the nut butter.

6. Transfer the spread to an airtight glass container and let sit for 24 hours to allow the flavors to meld, then store in the refrigerator, where it will keep for up to a few months.

NUTRITIONAL FACTS (per tablespoon)

Calories: 101 Total fat: 9.6 g Total carbs: 3.8 g Net carbs: 3.0 g Protein: 3.0 g

quick & easy · squeaky clean · plan ahead · keto friendly · make ahead · egg-free

Makes about 2 cups (525 g)

- 1 tablespoon ghee
- ¼ teaspoon Himalayan salt
- ½ cup (66 g) raw sunflower seeds
- 1 cup (260 g) All-Natural Toasted Almond Butter (page 288)
- ¼ cup (60 g) tahini
- 2 tablespoons coconut aminos
- 1 teaspoon smoked paprika
- 1 teaspoon onion powder
- ½ teaspoon garlic powder
- ½ teaspoon freshly ground black pepper
- ½ teaspoon Himalayan salt
- ¼ teaspoon cayenne pepper
- 2 or 3 drops all-natural liquid smoke
- 1 to 2 tablespoons avocado oil, if needed

BBQ "PEANUT" SPREAD

Do you sometimes miss the crazy eruption of flavor that eating a big handful of barbecued peanuts would bring to your taste buds? You know, that unique hit of intense seasoning and spiciness, so bold that it almost seemed like it wanted to invade your entire brain and body? Well, that's exactly what you get with this nut butter: all the intensity of barbecued peanuts in a peanutless spread.

1. In a medium skillet set over medium heat, melt the ghee and salt, then add the sunflower seeds and toast, stirring almost constantly, until they turn slightly golden and become fragrant, 4 to 5 minutes. Turn off the heat and let cool for a few minutes.

2. In the meantime, place the rest of the ingredients, except for the avocado oil, in a large mixing bowl and mix with a wooden spoon or rubber spatula until well combined.

3. Stir in the toasted sunflower seeds and, if necessary, adjust the consistency by adding 1 to 2 tablespoons of avocado oil.

4. Transfer the spread to an airtight glass container and store in a cool, dark, dry place, where it will keep for up to a few months.

NUTRITIONAL FACTS (per tablespoon)

Calories: 73 · Total fat: 6.6 g · Total carbs: 2.1 g · Net carbs: 1.9 g · Protein: 2.1 g

under 30

 egg-free

 make ahead

Makes about 3 cups (875 g)

PRALINE AND CREAM NUT BUTTER

This nut butter is at its best when kept in the refrigerator. Its texture becomes nice and firm like that of cookie dough, with a flavor profile worthy of the fanciest ice creams. You'll probably need to keep this one under lock and key, to be honest. While the recipe makes a fairly large batch, I'm sure you won't regret having made that much; if you do find that you have a bit too much to consume it all yourself, find a very good friend and offer up a jar. They will love you forever!

For the praline

- 1 cup (100 g) raw pecans
- 1 cup (140 g) raw almonds
- 1 cup (240 ml) pure maple syrup (dark color or Canadian Medium)
- ¼ cup (55 g) ghee
- 1 teaspoon pure vanilla extract, homemade (page 84) or store-bought
- ½ teaspoon Himalayan salt
- ½ teaspoon baking soda

For the nut butter base

- 2 cups (240 g) raw cashew pieces
- 1 cup (140 g) blanched raw almonds
- 2 tablespoons macadamia nut oil or coconut oil
- ½ teaspoon Himalayan salt

1. Preheat the oven to 350°F (177°C).

2. Make the praline: Spread the pecans and almonds in a single layer on a large rimmed baking sheet and toast in the oven for about 10 minutes or until fragrant. Move the nuts around a few times as they toast.

3. Remove the nuts from the oven and transfer to a bowl to cool. Line the baking sheet with parchment paper.

4. Bring the maple syrup to a boil in a large saucepan set over high heat (seriously, you want a *large* saucepan here, as the syrup bubbles up quite a lot!) and let it boil vigorously for 5 minutes. Add the ghee, vanilla extract, and salt and boil while stirring for an additional 30 seconds or until well combined. Stir in the baking soda and, as soon as it's incorporated, throw in the toasted nuts and stir well.

5. Quickly transfer the praline onto the prepared baking sheet and spread it lightly. Set aside to cool and harden.

6. Meanwhile, make the nut butter base: Place the cashew pieces, blanched almonds, macadamia nut oil, and salt in the bowl of a food processor and process until it turns into a creamy butter, which should take about 8 to 10 minutes. You will have to stop and scrape the sides of the bowl a few times.

7. Break the cooled praline into pieces and reserve about half. Add the rest to the food processor and process for about 5 minutes, until it's completely incorporated into the nut butter.

8. Add the remainder of the praline and pulse a few times, just so the candied nuts get very coarsely chopped. You want big chunks of praline to remain in the butter.

9. Transfer to one or two airtight glass containers and store in the refrigerator for up to a few months.

NUTRITIONAL FACTS (per tablespoon)

Calories: 100 | Total fat: 7.5 g | Total carbs: 7.4 g | Net carbs: 6.5 g | Protein: 1.9 g

Makes about 2½ cups (685 g)

RUM RAISIN NUT SPREAD

Yes, you read that right. I've included real alcohol in this recipe, and honestly, even though I'm not big on the idea of consuming alcohol myself, I absolutely, positively would not leave it out. After all, very little gets used, and it does so much for the flavor of this intoxicating nut spread. I say go ahead and splurge. I promise I'll look the other way!

For the rum raisin mixture

- 1 cup (105 g) raw walnuts, chopped
- ½ cup (72 g) raisins
- ¼ cup (60 ml) good-quality dark rum
- 2 tablespoons pure maple syrup (dark color or Canadian Medium)
- 1 teaspoon pure vanilla extract, homemade (page 84) or store-bought

For the nut butter base

- 2 cups (240 g) raw cashew pieces
- ½ cup (70 g) blanched raw almonds
- ½ cup (70 g) raw macadamia nuts
- ¼ cup (55 g) ghee
- 1 teaspoon Himalayan salt

1. Put the walnuts, raisins, rum, maple syrup, and vanilla extract in a nonreactive container and let soak for 24 hours, or at least overnight, until the raisins and nuts have completely absorbed the liquid.

2. Make the nut butter base: Place the cashew pieces, blanched almonds, macadamia nuts, ghee, and salt in the bowl of a food processor and process for 8 to 10 minutes, until smooth, stopping to scrape the sides of the bowl from time to time.

3. Pour the nut butter base over the rum-infused nut and raisin mixture and stir gently until well combined.

4. Transfer to an airtight glass container and store in the refrigerator for up to a month.

NUTRITIONAL FACTS (per tablespoon)

Calories: 91 | Total fat: 7.2 g | Total carbs: 4.7 g | Net carbs: 4.0 g | Protein: 2.0 g

SMOKY BACON AND DARK CHOCOLATE NUT SPREAD

Makes about 2½ cups (655 g)

This nut butter would qualify as evil in a jar. Of all the nut butters I've created, it's by far my favorite. I'd never been entirely sold on the bacon-chocolate combination until I came up with this wicked devilishness. I would bet lots of money that just a tiny spoonful of this stuff will have you convinced as well!

- 4 thick slices bacon
- ½ cup (70 g) raw almonds, coarsely chopped

For the chocolate chunks
- 2¾ ounces (78 g) cacao paste, finely chopped
- 1 tablespoon raw honey
- 1 teaspoon coconut oil
- ⅛ teaspoon ancho chili powder
- ⅛ teaspoon Himalayan salt

For the nut butter base
- 2 cups (240 g) raw cashew pieces
- 1 cup (140 g) blanched raw almonds
- ½ cup (70 g) Smooth and Silky Coconut Butter (page 297) or store-bought coconut butter
- ¼ cup (55 g) ghee
- ½ teaspoon Himalayan salt
- ¼ teaspoon vanilla powder
- 2 tablespoons pure maple syrup (dark color or Canadian Medium)

1. Cook the bacon in a skillet until crispy, then remove it to a plate to cool. Add the chopped almonds to the hot bacon drippings and toast them over medium heat until golden and fragrant. Set aside to cool.

2. Make the chocolate chunks: Line a rimmed baking sheet with parchment paper. Melt the cacao paste in the microwave in 25- to 30-second intervals, stirring for a good 10 to 15 seconds after each interval, until it's completely melted. Add the honey, coconut oil, chili powder, and salt and stir gently until smooth. Pour the chocolate onto the prepared baking sheet and place in the fridge to chill for about 30 minutes. When set, chop coarsely into small chunks.

3. Make the nut butter base: Put the cashew pieces, blanched almonds, coconut butter, ghee, salt, and vanilla powder in the bowl of a food processor and process until smooth, stopping to scrape the sides of the bowl from time to time. This should take no longer than 8 to 10 minutes. Add the maple syrup and resume processing for about 30 seconds, until just incorporated.

4. Transfer the nut butter to a mixing bowl and place it in the refrigerator to cool for 30 to 45 minutes. It needs to be cool enough that the chocolate will not melt when you mix it in, but not so cold that it will have had time to set up, making the task of mixing anything in impossible.

5. Crumble the bacon and add it to the chilled nut butter along with the toasted almonds and chocolate chunks, then stir gently until well combined.

6. Transfer to an airtight glass container and store in the refrigerator for up to a month.

NUTRITIONAL FACTS (per tablespoon)

Calories: 119 | Total fat: 10.3 g | Total carbs: 5.3 g | Net carbs: 3.9 g | Protein: 2.6 g

Makes about 2 cups (525 g)

- 2 cups (200 g) raw pecans
- 1 cup (85 g) unsweetened toasted coconut flakes
- 1 tablespoon ground Ceylon cinnamon
- 1 teaspoon vanilla powder
- 1 teaspoon ginger powder
- 1 teaspoon Himalayan salt
- ¼ teaspoon freshly grated nutmeg
- ¼ teaspoon ground cardamom
- ⅛ teaspoon ground clove
- ¾ cup (225 g) pumpkin puree
- ¼ cup (75 g) Date Paste (page 82)
- 1 tablespoon blackstrap molasses
- 2 tablespoons raisins
- 2 tablespoons chopped raw pecans

SPICED PUMPKIN PECAN SPREAD

Deliciously sweet and spicy, lusciously creamy and velvety, this spread is a thousand times better than pumpkin pie filling! Make jars and jars of it and offer them to your friends and family at Thanksgiving. You'll be in their hearts forever!

1. Put the 2 cups (200 g) of pecans, toasted coconut flakes, cinnamon, vanilla powder, ginger, salt, nutmeg, cardamom, and clove in the bowl of a food processor and process for about 10 minutes, until smooth, stopping to scrape the sides of the bowl from time to time.

2. Add the pumpkin puree, date paste, and molasses and resume processing until combined.

3. Pulse in the raisins and 2 tablespoons of chopped pecans just to combine.

4. Transfer to an airtight glass container and store in the refrigerator for up to a month.

NUTRITIONAL FACTS (per tablespoon)

Calories: 69 | Total fat: 5.8 g | Total carbs: 4.2 g | Net carbs: 2.8 g | Protein: 0.9 g

Makes about 1½ cups (425 g)

WHITE CHOCOLATE MACADAMIA NUT BUTTER

If it's particularly warm out, there's a chance that this nut butter will remain fairly liquidy even after resting for a full day. To help it get to its rightful, creamy consistency, place it in the fridge for a couple of hours and give it a good stir. Then it should remain nice and stable for you, with a thick, frostinglike texture that will have you coming back for more!

For the nut butter base

- 1 cup (120 g) raw cashew pieces
- 1 cup (140 g) raw macadamia nut pieces
- ½ teaspoon Himalayan salt
- Pinch of vanilla powder

For the white chocolate

- ¼ cup (35 g) finely chopped cacao butter
- 2 tablespoons Smooth and Silky Coconut Butter (page 297) or store-bought coconut butter
- 2 tablespoons raw honey

For the add-ins

- ½ cup (70 g) raw macadamia nut pieces
- ¼ cup (35 g) chopped cacao butter

1. Make the nut butter base: Place the cashew pieces, macadamia nut pieces, salt, and vanilla powder in the bowl of a food processor and process until smooth and creamy. You may have to stop the motor and scrape the sides of the bowl a few times, but the butter should come together rather quickly due to the high fat content of the macadamia nuts.

2. While the nut butter is processing, make the white chocolate: Put the finely chopped cacao butter in a small microwave-safe bowl and heat on high in 30-second to 1-minute intervals, mixing well between intervals, until completely melted, 2 to 3 minutes total.

3. In a separate microwave-safe bowl, mix together the coconut butter and honey and melt on high, which shouldn't take much more than 30 seconds to 1 minute. Add the melted cacao butter to the coconut butter mixture one-third at a time, whisking each addition until well combined.

4. Add the white chocolate to the nut butter by pouring it down the feeding tube while the food processor is running. Continue processing until well incorporated.

5. Stop the motor, add the add-ins, and pulse a few times just to mix them in, no more.

6. Transfer to an airtight glass container and allow to rest for at least 24 hours before eating. Store in a cool, dark, dry place, where it will keep for up to a few months.

NUTRITIONAL FACTS (per tablespoon)

Calories: 120 | Total fat: 11.4 g | Total carbs: 4.8 g | Net carbs: 3.7 g | Protein: 1.6 g

CHAPTER 11

sweets and treats

make ahead freezer friendly

BLUEBERRY MUFFINS

Makes 1 dozen muffins

Quite simply put, these muffins taste exactly like what you'd expect a good classic blueberry muffin to taste like, only better. If you're a fan of blueberry muffins, I can predict that you'll get to know this recipe by heart in no time.

- ¾ cup (90 g) coconut flour
- ¼ cup (30 g) almond flour
- 2 tablespoons tapioca starch
- 1 teaspoon baking soda
- ½ teaspoon cream of tartar
- ¼ teaspoon Himalayan salt
- Grated zest of 1 lemon
- 1 cup (135 g) fresh blueberries
- 6 large eggs
- 2 large egg whites
- ½ cup (104 g) coconut oil
- ½ cup (170 g) raw honey
- ¼ cup (55 g) ghee
- ½ cup (120 ml) full-fat coconut milk

1. Preheat the oven to 425°F (220°C) and line a 12-cup muffin pan with parchment paper cups.

2. In a large bowl, combine the flours, tapioca starch, baking soda, cream of tartar, salt, and lemon zest and mix well with a whisk until fully combined. Gently stir in the blueberries.

3. In a separate bowl, beat the eggs and egg whites with a hand mixer on high speed until slightly frothy, about 2 minutes, then set aside.

4. In a third bowl, beat the coconut oil, honey, and ghee with the hand mixer on medium-high speed until smooth and creamy. Add the coconut milk and beat until well incorporated. Add the eggs and beat until fully incorporated. Do not panic if the mixture tends to break a little bit; it will come together when the flour is added.

5. Pour the egg mixture over the flour mixture and mix gently with a wooden spoon or rubber spatula until just combined, taking care not to break the blueberries. Divide the batter equally among the prepared muffin cups, filling each about three-quarters full.

6. Bake for 5 minutes, then lower the heat to 375°F (190°C) and continue baking for about 15 minutes, until a toothpick inserted in the center of a muffin comes out clean.

7. As soon as the muffins are cool enough to handle, transfer them to a wire rack and let cool completely. Store the muffins in the refrigerator in an airtight container for up to a week.

Tip: *For entirely sugar-free muffins, you could use unsweetened applesauce instead of honey, or even go half and half (¼ cup/ 85 g honey and ¼ cup/62 g unsweetened applesauce).*

NUTRITIONAL FACTS (per muffin)

| Calories: 269 | Total fat: 18.8 g | Total carbs: 19.4 g | Net carbs: 16.5 g | Protein: 5.7 g |

make ahead freezer friendly

Makes 1 dozen muffins

APPLE CINNAMON SPICE MUFFINS

With just the right mix of spicy and sweet, these muffins are best eaten warm with a generous dollop of All-Natural Toasted Almond Butter (page 288). For me, they make a great breakfast treat, served alongside a couple of pan-fried eggs and a few slices of crispy bacon.

- 2 cups (300 g) unsweetened applesauce
- 4 large eggs
- ¼ cup (52 g) coconut oil, melted but not hot
- 1½ cups (172 g) almond flour, sifted
- ½ cup (57 g) tapioca starch
- ¼ cup (30 g) coconut flour, sifted
- 2 tablespoons ground Ceylon cinnamon
- 1½ teaspoons baking soda
- 1 teaspoon cream of tartar
- ½ teaspoon Himalayan salt
- ¼ teaspoon freshly grated nutmeg
- 1 cup (85 g) diced dried apples
- ½ cup (50 g) raw pecans, chopped
- ½ cup (72 g) raisins

For the crumble topping
- 2 tablespoons unsweetened shredded coconut
- 2 tablespoons chopped raw pecans
- 2 tablespoons raisins, chopped

1. Preheat the oven to 425°F (220°C) and line a 12-cup muffin pan with parchment paper cups.

2. In a mixing bowl, combine the applesauce, eggs, and coconut oil and whisk until well combined and slightly frothy; set aside.

3. In a separate large bowl, combine the almond flour, tapioca starch, coconut flour, cinnamon, baking soda, cream of tartar, salt, and nutmeg and mix well with a whisk until fully combined. Stir in the dried apples, pecans, and raisins.

4. Add the applesauce mixture to the flour mixture and mix gently with a wooden spoon or rubber spatula to combine, taking care not to overmix the batter. Divide the batter equally among the prepared muffin cups, filling each about three-quarters full.

5. Mix together the ingredients for the crumble topping and sprinkle some over the top of each muffin.

6. Bake for 5 minutes, then lower the heat to 375°F (190°C) and continue baking for 15 to 18 minutes, until a toothpick inserted in the center of a muffin comes out clean.

7. As soon as the muffins are cool enough to handle, transfer them to a wire rack and let cool completely. Store the muffins in the refrigerator in an airtight container for up to a week.

NUTRITIONAL FACTS (per muffin)

Calories: 216 · Total fat: 13.6 g · Total carbs: 22.1 g · Net carbs: 18.2 g · Protein: 4.3 g

BANANA BREAD

Makes 1 loaf, serves 16

So you bought a bunch of beautiful bright yellow bananas, but before you had the chance to eat even one or two, the whole bunch turned brown on you. Hmpft! How did that happen so quickly, right? And now you're left wondering what in the world you are going to do with all those overripe bananas. After you make this bread, you will never again ask yourself that question! In fact, this banana bread is so perfect in every possible way, you'll probably start "forgetting" those bananas on the counter on purpose.

- ¾ cup (90 g) coconut flour
- ½ cup (60 g) almond flour
- ¼ cup (28 g) tapioca starch
- 2 teaspoons ground Ceylon cinnamon
- 2 teaspoons baking soda
- 1 teaspoon cream of tartar
- ¼ teaspoon Himalayan salt
- ½ cup (52 g) chopped raw walnuts
- ½ cup (80 g) chopped dates
- 2 cups (520 g) mashed overripe bananas (about 4 medium)
- 3 large eggs, beaten
- ½ cup (125 g) unsweetened applesauce
- ¼ cup (60 ml) almond milk or other nut milk, or full-fat coconut milk
- ¼ cup (55 g) ghee, melted
- 1 teaspoon pure vanilla extract, homemade (page 84) or store-bought
- 5 or 6 drops pure almond extract

For the topping
- ¼ cup (28 g) chopped raw walnuts
- ¼ cup (40 g) chopped dates

1. Preheat the oven to 350°F (177°C). Grease a 9 by 5-inch (23 by 12.75-cm) loaf pan with ghee or coconut oil and line it with parchment paper; set aside.

2. In a large mixing bowl, combine the flours, tapioca starch, cinnamon, baking soda, cream of tartar, and salt and mix well with a whisk. Add the walnuts and dates and stir until well coated; set aside.

3. In a separate bowl, beat the mashed bananas with a whisk until light and airy. Add the eggs, applesauce, almond milk, ghee, vanilla extract, and almond extract and whisk until well combined.

4. Add the banana mixture to the flour mixture and mix with a rubber spatula just until well incorporated, no more.

5. Pour the batter into the prepared loaf pan and sprinkle the chopped walnuts and dates on top. Bake for 70 to 75 minutes, until the top is golden and firm to the touch and a toothpick inserted in the middle of the loaf comes out clean.

6. Set the pan on a wire rack and let the bread cool in the pan for about 5 minutes before unmolding it. Let it finish cooling on the rack, then transfer to the refrigerator to chill completely before serving, for easier slicing.

7. This bread will keep in the refrigerator for up to a week and toasts brilliantly well.

NUTRITIONAL FACTS (per serving)

Calories: 153   Total fat: 7.4 g   Total carbs: 20.4 g   Net carbs: 16.2 g   Protein: 3.3 g

plan ahead · egg-free

make ahead

DARK CHOCOLATE HAZELNUT TART

Makes one 9-inch (23-cm) tart, serves 12

Silky smooth, ridiculously creamy, and intensely chocolaty, this tart will send you straight to seventh heaven with the very first bite! Of all the desserts I've created, this one sits really high on my list of favorites. Don't let the long list of ingredients scare you: It is surprisingly quick and simple to make and can be prepared well ahead of time.

For the crust

- 1 cup (80 g) unsweetened shredded coconut
- 1 cup (115 g) almond flour
- 2 tablespoons ghee
- 2 tablespoons raw honey
- ¼ teaspoon Himalayan salt

For the hazelnut butter layer

- 1 cup (260 g) All-Natural Toasted Hazelnut Butter (page 292)
- 2 tablespoons Date Paste (page 82)
- ¼ cup (60 ml) full-fat coconut milk
- 1 tablespoon pure vanilla extract, homemade (page 84) or store-bought
- ¼ cup (60 ml) warm water, plus more if needed

For the ganache

- 8 ounces (225 g) cacao paste, finely chopped
- 1 cup (240 ml) full-fat coconut milk
- ¼ cup (55 g) ghee
- ¼ cup (85 g) raw honey
- 1 teaspoon pure vanilla extract, homemade (page 84) or store-bought
- 3 to 5 tablespoons warm water (if needed)

For garnish

- ½ cup (70 g) coarsely chopped hazelnuts, toasted
- 2 tablespoons unsweetened toasted coconut flakes
- Pinch of fleur de sel

To make the crust:

1. Preheat the oven to 350°F (177°C). Grease a 9-inch (23-cm) round tart pan with a removable bottom with lard.

2. In a large bowl, mix together all the crust ingredients. Transfer the mixture to the greased tart pan and press firmly into the bottom and up the sides of the pan to form a crust.

3. Bake for about 10 minutes or until golden; set aside to cool.

To make the hazelnut butter layer:

1. Place the hazelnut butter, date paste, coconut milk, and vanilla extract in the bowl of a food processor and process until well combined. With the motor running, slowly add the water through the feeding tube until the mixture is smooth and creamy. If it still isn't smooth, add more water, a tablespoon at a time, until it becomes really smooth and creamy.

2. Pour the hazelnut butter mixture into the prebaked pie crust and spread it gently all the way to the edges. Set aside.

To make the ganache:

1. Place the cacao paste in a large heatproof mixing bowl.

2. Bring the coconut milk, ghee, and honey to a simmer in a saucepan over medium heat, then pour it over the cacao paste. Leave this undisturbed for 5 minutes, letting the hot milk slowly take care of melting the chocolate.

3. After 5 minutes, stir the ganache very gently with a whisk until smooth. If it separates, which it tends to do when you use coconut milk, add warm water, a tablespoon at a time, whisking after each addition, until it becomes smooth again.

To assemble the tart:

1. Pour the ganache over the hazelnut butter layer and spread it all the way to the edges. Garnish with chopped hazelnuts and toasted coconut and sprinkle lightly with fleur de sel.

2. Place in the refrigerator until set, at least 6 hours but preferably overnight.

3. This tart will keep in the refrigerator for up to 5 days.

NUTRITIONAL FACTS (per serving)

Calories: 443 · Total fat: 37.3 g · Total carbs: 20.9 g · Net carbs: 14.8 g · Protein: 5.3 g

plan ahead

egg-free

make ahead

HONEY PECAN APPLE CRUMBLE

Serves 8

We all get them from time to time: apples that have seen better days. You know what I'm talking about, right? Fruits that were "forgotten" in the back of the crisper drawer and seem to have lost most of their crispness and, well, all form of appeal? Well, I've got good news for you: Never again will you wonder what to do with those poor neglected apples!

For the apples

- ¼ cup (55 g) ghee
- ¼ cup (85 g) raw honey
- 8 to 10 cooking apples, peeled and sliced
- 1 vanilla bean, seeds scraped
- ¼ teaspoon Himalayan salt

For the crumble

- ½ cup (104 g) coconut oil
- ¼ cup (75 g) Date Paste (page 82)
- ¼ cup (85 g) raw honey
- 1 tablespoon pure vanilla extract, homemade (page 84) or store-bought
- ½ cup (60 g) coconut flour
- ¼ cup (28 g) tapioca starch
- ½ cup (65 g) sliced almonds, chopped very finely
- ½ cup (50 g) raw pecans, chopped
- ½ teaspoon baking soda
- ½ teaspoon ground Ceylon cinnamon
- ¼ teaspoon Himalayan salt

1. Preheat the oven to 350°F (177°C).

2. In a large, heavy skillet set over medium heat, melt the ghee and honey until hot and bubbly. Add the apples and cook until slightly caramelized and golden, about 5 minutes. Add the vanilla seeds and salt, stir well, and then transfer to a 9-inch (23-cm) round baking dish.

3. Make the crumble: In a large bowl, combine the coconut oil, date paste, honey, and vanilla extract and beat with a hand mixer on high speed until light and creamy.

4. In a separate bowl, mix together the coconut flour, tapioca starch, chopped almonds, chopped pecans, baking soda, cinnamon, and salt until well combined. Add this dry mixture to the creamed coconut oil mixture and mix with the electric mixer on low speed until just incorporated.

5. Drop the crumble by the tablespoonful over the caramelized apples.

6. Bake for 25 to 30 minutes, until the crumble top gets nice and golden and the apples are bubbling. Serve warm or cold.

7. This crumble will keep refrigerated for up to a week; reheat slightly in the microwave, if desired.

NUTRITIONAL FACTS (per serving)

Calories: 475 · Total fat: 28.8 g · Total carbs: 54.2 g · Net carbs: 45.8 g · Protein: 3.5 g

Makes one 2-layer, 9-inch
(23-cm) cake, serves 16

BUTTER PECAN CAKE

This cake may seem like a lot of work, but just one bite will make you forget about all that time you spent in the kitchen! The buttercream is so fluffy, light, and dreamy, you simply won't believe your taste buds.

Equipment needed:

Candy thermometer

Dry ingredients for the cake

- 2 cups (230 g) almond flour
- ½ cup (57 g) tapioca starch
- ¼ cup (30 g) coconut flour
- 1 teaspoon Himalayan salt
- 1½ teaspoons baking soda
- 1 teaspoon cream of tartar
- 1 teaspoon ground Ceylon cinnamon
- ½ teaspoon freshly grated nutmeg
- 1 cup (100 g) raw pecans, coarsely chopped and lightly toasted

Wet ingredients for the cake

- 1 cup (220 g) ghee
- ½ cup (104 g) coconut oil, solid but not cold
- 1 cup (300 g) Date Paste (page 82)
- 4 large eggs
- 1 (14-ounce/415-ml) can full-fat coconut milk
- ½ cup (120 ml) warm water
- 2 teaspoons pure vanilla extract, homemade (page 84) or store-bought

For the buttercream

- 6 large egg whites
- ¾ cup (180 ml) pure maple syrup (dark color or Canadian Medium)
- 1¾ cups plus 1 tablespoon (400 g) ghee, at room temperature
- 1½ teaspoons pure vanilla extract, homemade (page 84) or store-bought
- ½ teaspoon Himalayan salt
- ½ teaspoon ground Ceylon cinnamon
- ¼ teaspoon freshly ground nutmeg
- 1½ cups (365 g) Toasted Butter Pecan Spread, at room temperature (page 312)

For garnish

- Pecan halves

To make the cake:

1. Preheat the oven to 350°F (177°C). Grease two 9-inch (23-cm) round cake pans with ghee or lard and line the bottoms with parchment paper cut into circles.

2. In a large mixing bowl, combine all of the dry ingredients except for the chopped nuts. Mix well with a whisk, then sift to make sure that no lumps remain and to make the flour "fluffier." Add the chopped nuts and whisk to combine. Set aside.

3. Place the ghee, coconut oil, and date paste in the bowl of a stand mixer equipped with the paddle attachment and beat on high speed until light and creamy. Add the eggs, one at a time, and beat on medium speed until fully incorporated before adding another. Add the coconut milk, warm water, and vanilla extract and resume beating on medium-low speed until well incorporated. Don't be overly concerned if the mixture breaks a little bit; it will come together when the flour is added.

4. Add the dry ingredients and mix them in on low speed until just incorporated, no more.

5. Divide the batter between the prepared cake pans, spread it out evenly, and bake for 28 to 30 minutes, until the cakes are fully set, the tops are golden, and a toothpick inserted in the middle comes out clean.

6. Remove the cakes from the oven and leave them in the pans to cool on a wire rack, then transfer them (in the pans) to the refrigerator until completely chilled, at least 6 hours but preferably overnight.

To make the buttercream:

1. Place the egg whites in the well-cleaned bowl of the stand mixer equipped with the whisk attachment and beat on high speed for about 5 minutes, until they become really airy.

2. Meanwhile, bring the maple syrup to a boil over high heat. Let it to boil until it reaches 250°F (120°C) on a candy thermometer, 5 to 8 minutes. While the egg whites are being whisked on high speed, pour the hot maple syrup down the side of the bowl in a slow, steady stream (be careful not to hit the beater with the syrup). Continue beating on high speed for 2 more minutes, then lower the mixer speed to medium and continue whisking until the meringue cools to room temperature, 5 to 10 minutes.

3. With the mixer running, add the ghee to the meringue, about ½ cup (110 g) at a time, allowing each addition to be fully incorporated before adding the next. Once all the ghee has been added, throw in the vanilla extract, cinnamon, salt, and nutmeg, then crank up the speed to high and continue whipping until the buttercream fluffs up and becomes stiff enough to spread, about 2 minutes.

4. Lower the speed to medium and add the pecan spread as you did the ghee, ½ cup (110 g) at a time, then mix on high speed one final time for about 30 seconds.

5. If you find that the buttercream is a little too soft to be used immediately, chill it for 15 to 20 minutes, then give it a good stir to make it pliable again.

To assemble the cake:

1. The cakes may be a bit fragile, so be careful when unmolding them. Run a knife around the edge first, and make sure to support the cake with your entire hand as you take it out of the pan.

2. Place one of the cakes on a cake plate or board and spoon about one-quarter of the buttercream on top. Spread the frosting evenly all the way to the edge, then place the second cake, bottom side up, on top of the first layer. Cover the entire cake with the rest of the buttercream, creating little swirls with your spatula as you go. Garnish the frosted cake with pecan halves.

3. Keep the cake in the refrigerator for up to 5 days. However, it is best served at room temperature, so take it out at least 3 hours before serving.

NUTRITIONAL FACTS (per serving)

Calories: 860　·　Total fat: 80.4 g　·　Total carbs: 32.9 g　·　Net carbs: 28.8 g　·　Protein: 7.3 g

MAPLE SYRUP MOUSSE CAKE

Makes one 1-layer, 9 inch (23-cm) cake, serves 12

Wow your guests' eyes and taste buds with this maple syrup masterpiece. Granted, this cake doesn't come together quickly or easily, but it does come with guaranteed ooohs and aaahs.

For the cake

- 1½ cups (172 g) almond flour, sifted
- ¼ cup (30 g) coconut flour, sifted
- ¼ cup (85 g) raw honey
- 4 large eggs, divided in use
- 2 tablespoons coconut oil, melted but not hot
- 4 large egg whites
- ½ teaspoon cream of tartar

For the assembly

- 10 to 12 large picture-perfect strawberries
- Cake trimmings
- 6 strawberries, stems removed, chopped

For the mousse

- 8 full gelatin sheets (½ ounce/ 14 g; see Note, page 350)
- 4 large egg whites
- ½ teaspoon cream of tartar
- 1 (14-ounce/415-ml) can full-fat coconut milk, refrigerated overnight
- 1 cup (240 ml) pure maple syrup (dark color or Canadian Medium)
- 8 large egg yolks

For the chocolate topping

- 5¼ ounces (150 g) cacao paste, chopped extremely finely
- ⅔ cup (160 ml) full-fat coconut milk
- 2 tablespoons raw honey
- 1 tablespoon coconut oil
- Pinch of Himalayan salt
- Pinch of ancho chile powder

For garnish

- 6 to 8 large picture-perfect strawberries, stems intact, cut in half
- ¼ cup (34 g) fresh blueberries
- ¼ cup (30 g) fresh raspberries
- 8 lychees, peeled, pitted, and cut in half
- 1 to 2 tablespoons raw honey
- Fresh mint leaves

Equipment needed:

9½-inch (24 cm) by 2½-inch (6.5-cm)-deep cake ring (you could also use a springform pan, but your cake may not unmold quite as easily)

To make the cake:

1. Preheat the oven to 450°F (232°C). Grease a 13 by 9-inch (33 by 23-cm) rimmed baking sheet (sometimes called a quarter sheet pan) with coconut oil, then line it with a piece of parchment paper cut to fit perfectly inside it. Make sure that the parchment paper adheres to the entire surface, especially around the edges.

2. Put the flours, honey, and 2 of the eggs in the bowl of a stand mixer equipped with the paddle attachment and mix on medium speed until well combined. Add the 2 remaining eggs and resume mixing for about 5 minutes, until slightly emulsified and lighter in color. Transfer to a large bowl, gently stir in the coconut oil with a rubber spatula, and set aside.

3. Thoroughly wash the bowl of your stand mixer and equip the mixer with the whisk attachment. Beat the egg whites and cream of tartar on high speed until the mixture becomes light and fluffy and soft peaks form, 5 to 6 minutes.

4. With a rubber spatula, gently fold the flour mixture into the beaten egg whites in 3 or 4 motions.

5. Spread the batter as evenly as possible onto the prepared baking sheet and bake for 8 to 10 minutes or until the top turns golden brown.

6. Turn the cake over onto a cooling rack as soon as it comes out of the oven, but do not remove the parchment paper just yet. Set aside to cool for a few minutes.

7. Place a 9½-inch (24-cm) by 2½-inch (6.5-cm) cake ring on a flat cake plate or board. Remove the parchment paper from the cake and cut out an 8½-inch (21.5-cm) circle of cake. Place the cake circle in the center of the cake ring. Cut the trimmings into bite-sized chunks and set them aside; you're going to need them later.

8. Hull the 10 to 12 picture-perfect strawberries (listed under "For the assembly") and slice them in half lengthwise, then remove the rounded edges so you have nice flat slices. Again, hold onto those trimmings; you'll be putting them to good use!

9. Arrange your perfect slices vertically, narrow tips facing up, around the perimeter of the cake circle with the nicer side facing out, as this side will be revealed once the cake ring is removed. Press them lightly to ensure good contact with the metal ring. Set the ring aside.

To make the mousse:

1. Soak the gelatin sheets in ice-cold water for 15 to 20 minutes.

2. Meanwhile, in the well-cleaned bowl of your stand mixer, whisk the egg whites and cream of tartar until the mixture becomes light and fluffy and soft peaks form, about 5 to 6 minutes. Transfer to a bowl and set aside.

3. Turn the chilled can of coconut milk upside down and open it. Drain the liquid that's on top and add the solid cream to the bowl of your stand mixer. Beat on high speed for about 5 minutes, until it becomes nice and airy. Transfer to a separate bowl and set aside.

4. Bring the maple syrup to a boil, then remove the pan from the heat. Squeeze the gelatin sheets to remove as much water as you can, then add them to the hot maple syrup. Stir gently until completely dissolved.

5. Put the egg yolks in the bowl of your stand mixer equipped with the whisk attachment, and turn it on to high speed. Pour the maple syrup down the side of the bowl in a slow, steady stream (be careful not to hit the whisk with the syrup) and continue beating on high for about 2 minutes, then lower the speed to medium and whisk until the egg mixture cools to room temperature, about 5 minutes.

6. With the help of a rubber spatula, gently fold the whipped coconut cream into this egg mixture, followed by the whipped egg whites.

7. Pour half of the mousse onto the prepared cake circle lined with strawberries and spread it all the way to the edge. Make sure to fill in the cracks between the strawberries.

8. Distribute the reserved cake and strawberry trimmings plus the 6 chopped strawberries listed under "For the assembly" over the top of the mousse. Pour the rest of the mousse over this (but make sure that you still have a little bit of room left for the chocolate topping) and spread it as smoothly as you can, again pushing it all the way to the edge and filling in the cracks between the strawberries. Put the cake in the fridge to set for a few hours.

9. Take a look around. Now might be a good time to clean the kitchen.

To make the chocolate topping:

1. Place the finely chopped cacao paste in a medium heatproof mixing bowl. Place the rest of the ingredients for the topping in a small saucepan and bring to a simmer over medium heat. Do not let it boil. As soon as it starts to simmer, pour the mixture over the chopped cacao paste and let it stand for about 5 minutes to melt the chocolate, then mix very gently with a whisk until smooth.

2. Pour the topping over the chilled cake, spread it as smoothly and evenly as possible, and refrigerate until set, about an hour, before serving. The cake will keep for 3 to 4 days in the refrigerator.

To serve:

1. Remove the ring from around the cake (see Tips below).

2. In a large mixing bowl, gently toss together the honey and fruits listed under "For garnish."

3. Arrange the fruit mixture nicely in the center of the cake and garnish with a few fresh mint leaves. Slice using a warmed knife blade (see Tips below).

Tips: Warming the cake circle slightly with a propane torch really helps to release the cake from the ring cleanly. Hold the torch a few inches (7.5 cm) from the cake and go around to warm the entire perimeter. Be careful not to get too close; you don't want to melt your cake.

Likewise, if you want really clean slices, cut your cake with a warm blade. Run your knife quickly through an open flame (I hope you didn't put that propane torch away!) or dip it in hot water and then wipe it dry. Make sure to wipe the blade clean between cuts.

Note: Gelatin sheets work best for this recipe, but if you can't get your hands on them, you can use 1½ tablespoons (½ ounce/ 14 g) of powdered gelatin instead. Just make sure to bloom the gelatin first. To do that, sprinkle the powder lightly over the surface of ¼ cup (60 ml) of water and let it stand for 8 to 10 minutes. Do not dump the gelatin in one big pile, as the granules in the middle wouldn't soak up any liquid. Once all the gelatin is rehydrated, add it, along with the blooming water if there's any left, to the hot maple syrup and stir gently until completely dissolved.

NUTRITIONAL FACTS (per serving)

| Calories: 494 | Total fat: 24.8 g | Total carbs: 57.8 g | Net carbs: 49.6 g | Protein: 14.6 g |

POUDING CHÔMEUR

Serves 6 to 8

Pouding chômeur, which basically means "unemployed man's pudding," is a staple here in Québec. This popular dessert, born out of necessity, was allegedly created by female factory workers during the Great Depression. Traditionally, it's made of a basic cake batter onto which a hot syrup, usually maple, is poured. The cake then bakes and rises through the syrup, which settles at the bottom at the pan and mixes with the batter, creating a thick caramel-like sauce underneath the cake. Needless to say, it is a bit of a sugar overload, so even though this Paleo version is free of grains and refined sugar, it's something you'll want to treat yourself to on very rare occasions. I must admit, though, that if you have a sweet tooth, it's well worth the splurge.

For the cake

- ½ cup (56 g) lard
- ¼ cup (55 g) ghee
- ½ cup (170 g) raw honey
- 4 large eggs
- 1¼ cups (145 g) almond flour
- ¼ cup (30 g) coconut flour
- 2 tablespoons arrowroot flour
- 1 teaspoon baking soda
- ½ teaspoon cream of tartar
- ¼ teaspoon Himalayan salt
- ¼ teaspoon ground Ceylon cinnamon
- ½ cup (120 ml) full-fat coconut milk
- ½ teaspoon vanilla powder or 1 teaspoon pure vanilla extract, homemade (page 84) or store-bought

For the syrup

- 2 cups (475 ml) pure maple syrup (dark color or Canadian Medium)
- ¼ cup (55 g) ghee
- ½ teaspoon Himalayan salt
- ¾ cup (180 ml) full-fat coconut milk
- ¼ teaspoon vanilla powder or ½ teaspoon pure vanilla extract, homemade (page 84) or store-bought

For garnish

- ¼ teaspoon fleur de sel

1. Make the cake batter: Combine the lard, ghee, and honey in a large bowl and cream with a hand mixer on high speed. Add the eggs, one at a time, and beat on medium speed until each addition is completely incorporated.

2. In a separate mixing bowl, combine the flours, baking soda, cream of tartar, salt, and cinnamon and whisk until fully combined. Sift this dry mixture to ensure even distribution and to remove any lumps.

3. Add half of the dry mixture to the wet mixture and beat on low speed until the dry mixture is completely incorporated. Add the coconut milk and vanilla powder and beat well, then add the rest of the dry mixture. Beat one final time on low speed until just incorporated.

4. Divide the batter among 6 to 8 individual (1-cup/240-ml) ramekins and refrigerate for a few hours.

5. Meanwhile, make the syrup: Bring the maple syrup, ghee, and salt to a boil in a heavy saucepan. Add the coconut milk and bring back up to a boil, whisking constantly. When the mixture starts to boil again, stop whisking and let it boil for a full minute. Keep a close eye on the syrup, as it may rise and spill over. If it starts to rise too much, give it a quick stir to help it settle back down. Turn off the heat, whisk in the vanilla powder, and set aside to cool, then transfer to the refrigerator to cool completely.

6. Preheat the oven to 375°F (190°C). Place the ramekins on a large rimmed baking sheet.

7. Pour the syrup over the chilled batter, dividing it equally among the ramekins. Make sure that the ramekins aren't more than three-quarters full.

8. Put the cakes in the oven and immediately lower the temperature to 350°F (177°C). Bake for 22 to 25 minutes, until the cakes are golden brown.

9. Let cool for about 30 minutes, then sprinkle with fleur de sel. Serve warm with a strong cup of coffee, mild tea, or a humongous glass of water!

10. The cakes will keep in the fridge for up to 3 to 4 days; reheat slightly in the microwave, if desired.

NUTRITIONAL FACTS (per serving, based on 8 servings)

| Calories: 638 | Total fat: 37.0 g | Total carbs: 74.8 g | Net carbs: 73.0 g | Protein: 5.4 g |

Makes one 2-layer, 9-inch (23-cm) cake, serves 16

CARROT CAKE

Cream cheese icing has always been my favorite part of carrot cake. As such, I was convinced that it would be impossible to make a decent dairy-free carrot cake. Well, not anymore! This dairy-free icing is as close to the real deal as it gets. And the cake itself is so moist and dense and sweet and spicy, I'm afraid I can no longer say that the icing is my favorite part…but it sure is a fantastic complement!

Dry ingredients for the cake

- 1¾ cups (200 g) almond flour
- ¾ cup (90 g) coconut flour
- ½ cup (60 g) arrowroot flour
- 2 teaspoons baking soda
- 1 teaspoon cream of tartar
- 1 teaspoon Himalayan salt
- 2 tablespoons ground Ceylon cinnamon
- 1 teaspoon ginger powder
- ½ teaspoon ground clove
- ½ teaspoon ground allspice
- ½ teaspoon freshly grated nutmeg

Wet ingredients for the cake

- 4 cups (13 ounces/370 g) finely grated carrots
- 1 (15¼-ounce/432-g) can crushed pineapple in unsweetened pineapple juice, or 1 cup (280 g) very finely chopped fresh pineapple and ½ cup (120 ml) unsweetened natural pineapple juice
- 1 cup (240 ml) full-fat coconut milk
- ¾ cup (187 g) unsweetened applesauce
- 4 large eggs, lightly beaten
- 2 tablespoons minced fresh ginger
- Grated zest of 1 lemon
- Juice of 1 lemon

Add-ins for the cake

- ⅔ cup (70 g) raw walnuts, coarsely chopped
- ½ cup (75 g) dried apricots, chopped
- ¾ cup (108 g) raisins

For the icing

- 2 cups (280 g) raw cashew pieces, soaked for at least 8 hours
- Juice of 1 lemon
- Grated zest of 1 lemon
- ¾ teaspoon Himalayan salt, divided
- 1 cup (140 g) Smooth and Silky Coconut Butter (page 297) or store-bought coconut butter
- 1 cup (220 g) ghee
- ½ cup (170 g) raw honey
- 1 tablespoon pure vanilla extract, homemade (page 84) or store-bought
- ⅛ teaspoon freshly grated nutmeg

For garnish

- ½ cup (52 g) chopped raw walnuts
- 1 carrot (for carrot ribbons)
- Handful of raw walnut halves

To make the cake:

1. Preheat the oven to 375°F (190°C). Grease two 9-inch (23-cm) round cake pans and line the bottoms with parchment paper. This step is absolutely crucial; do not skip it! (That is, unless your idea of fun is to spend hours trying to figure out how to get two relatively fragile cakes out of their pans without destroying them.)

2. In a large bowl, combine the dry ingredients and mix well with a large whisk until fully incorporated—or, better yet, sift them through a large flour sieve. Set aside.

3. In a separate bowl, combine the wet ingredients and stir until evenly mixed. Pour the wet ingredients into the dry ingredients and stir with a rubber spatula until well combined. Gently mix in the walnuts, apricots, and raisins.

4. Divide the batter equally between the 2 prepared pans and even out the tops. Bake for 55 to 60 minutes or until the edges take on a nice golden color and a toothpick inserted in the center comes out clean.

5. Leave the cakes in the pans to cool on a wire rack, then transfer them (in the pans) to the refrigerator until completely chilled, at least 4 to 6 hours or, better yet, overnight.

To make the icing:

1. Drain and rinse the cashews and put them in a food processor or high-speed blender. Process on the highest possible setting until creamy, then add the lemon juice and resume processing until super smooth; blitz in the lemon zest and ½ teaspoon of the salt and set aside.

2. In a separate bowl, beat the coconut butter and ghee with a hand mixer on high speed until light and fluffy. Add the honey, vanilla extract, nutmeg, and remaining ¼ teaspoon of salt and resume beating until well incorporated. Add the cashew mixture and beat on high speed once more to combine.

3. Place the icing in the refrigerator and let it firm up for a few hours or overnight.

To assemble the cake:

1. When you are ready to assemble the cake, take the icing out of the refrigerator and give it a final beating with the hand mixer to fluff it up again.

2. Delicately run a knife or small metal spatula around the edges of the cakes to help detach them from the pans, then carefully unmold them.

3. Place one of the cakes, bottom side up, on a cake plate or board and spoon a generous mound of icing on top. Spread the icing evenly over the top of the cake, all the way to the edge. Place the second cake (again, bottom side up) on top and cover the entire cake with the rest of the icing.

4. Press the chopped walnuts all around the side of the cake (see Tip).

5. Use a vegetable peeler to make a handful of carrot ribbons and place them on top of the cake, along with a few walnut halves.

6. Store the cake in an airtight container in the refrigerator for up to a week.

Tip: The easiest way to coat the sides of a cake with chopped nuts is to put the cake on a board that's slightly smaller than the cake and put the nuts in a large plate or bowl. Then, while holding the cake in one hand, press the chopped nuts against the side with your other hand, letting the excess fall back into the bowl. Repeat, carefully turning the cake, until the sides are completely coated.

NUTRITIONAL FACTS (per serving)

Calories: 188　Total fat: 45.6 g　Total carbs: 40.2 g　Net carbs: 30.9 g　Protein: 11.9 g

make ahead freezer friendly

Makes 2 dozen cookies

BACON AND CHOCOLATE CHUNK COOKIES

If you're a fan of sweet and salty but have yet to try the bacon-chocolate combo, this is definitely the place to start. Other than that, I've but one thing to say: THESE ARE THE BEST DARN CHOCOLATE CHUNK COOKIES EVER! Adding anything else would be totally useless.

For the add-ins

- 4 slices bacon
- 1 cup (135 g) finely chopped cacao paste
- 2 tablespoons raw honey, melted
- Pinch of Himalayan salt
- ½ cup (50 g) raw pecans

- 2 cups (230 g) almond flour
- ¼ cup (28 g) tapioca starch
- 2 tablespoons coconut flour
- 1 teaspoon baking soda
- ½ teaspoon cream of tartar
- ¼ teaspoon Himalayan salt
- ¼ cup (56 g) lard
- 2 tablespoons chilled bacon drippings (from above)
- 2 tablespoons ghee
- 3 tablespoons raw honey
- 1 large egg
- 1 tablespoon pure vanilla extract, homemade (page 84) or store-bought

Tip: To save time, make a huge batch of chocolate chunks ahead of time so you have some on hand when a craving for these cookies strikes! Or, if you don't want to go to the trouble of making your own chocolate chunks, you can use good-quality store-bought chocolate (at least 80 percent cacao).

1. Prepare the add-ins: Cook the bacon until crispy, then place on paper towels to drain. Place the drippings in the refrigerator to chill (you will use them for the cookie batter).

2. Melt the cacao paste in the microwave in 25- to 30-second sessions, stirring for a good 10 to 15 seconds after each session until it's completely melted. Add the honey and salt and stir gently until smooth.

3. Pour the chocolate into a rimmed baking sheet lined with parchment paper and place in the fridge to chill for about 30 minutes. When set, chop coarsely into small chunks. Chop the pecans. Crumble the cooked bacon.

4. Sift together the almond flour, tapioca starch, coconut flour, baking soda, cream of tartar, and salt over a large bowl. Set aside.

5. Place the lard, reserved bacon drippings, ghee, and honey in the bowl of a stand mixer equipped with the paddle attachment and beat on medium speed until combined and creamy. Increase the speed to high and beat for 3 to 4 minutes, until the mixture gets fluffy and lighter in color. Add the egg and vanilla extract and mix on medium speed until well combined.

6. Add the flour mixture and mix on low speed until just incorporated. Stir in the crumbled bacon, chocolate chunks, and chopped pecans, then refrigerate the dough for at least an hour, until firm.

7. Preheat the oven to 350°F (177°C). Line a baking sheet with parchment paper.

8. Drop the dough by the tablespoonful onto the prepared baking sheet, leaving about 1½ inches (4 cm) between cookies. With your fingers, gently press down on the balls of dough to give them a cookielike shape.

9. Bake for about 9 minutes, until the cookies puff up and take on a light golden color. Let cool on the baking sheet for 5 minutes, then gently transfer to a wire rack and allow to cool completely.

10. Store the cookies in an airtight container in the refrigerator for up to a week.

NUTRITIONAL FACTS (per cookie)

Calories: 135   Total fat: 10.7 g   Total carbs: 7.5 g   Net carbs: 6.1 g   Protein: 2.7 g

plan ahead · freezer friendly · make ahead

Makes 2 dozen cookies

DOUBLE DARK CHOCOLATE COOKIES

Can you say fudgy, dense, and intensely chocolaty? This is exactly what these cookies are all about. Just one bite and you'll find yourself in chocolate heaven!

- ¾ cup (86 g) almond flour
- ¾ cup (67 g) cacao powder
- 2 tablespoons coconut flour
- 2 tablespoons tapioca starch
- 1 teaspoon baking soda
- ¼ teaspoon Himalayan salt
- ¼ cup (55 g) ghee
- ¼ cup (55 g) lard
- ½ cup (150 g) Date Paste (page 82)
- 1 large egg
- 1 teaspoon vanilla extract, homemade (page 84) or store-bought

For the add-ins

- 1 cup (168 g) Extra Dark Chocolate Chips (page 80)
- ⅓ cup (35 g) dried goji berries
- ¼ cup (28 g) finely chopped raw pecans

1. Sift together the almond flour, cacao powder, coconut flour, tapioca starch, baking soda, and salt over a large bowl. Set aside.

2. Place the ghee, lard, and date paste in the bowl of a stand mixer equipped with the paddle attachment and beat on medium speed until combined and creamy. Increase the speed to high and beat for 3 to 4 minutes, until the mixture gets fluffy and lighter in color. Add the egg and vanilla extract and mix on medium speed until well combined.

3. Add the flour mixture and mix on low speed until just incorporated. Stir in the chocolate chips, goji berries, and chopped pecans, then refrigerate the dough for a few hours, until firm.

4. Preheat the oven to 350°F (177°C). Line a baking sheet with parchment paper.

5. Drop the dough by the tablespoonful onto the prepared baking sheet, leaving about 1½ inches (4 cm) between cookies. Help form the cookies with your fingers, as they won't really change shape in the oven.

6. Bake for about 8 minutes, until the cookies look like they're barely baked. Let cool on the baking sheet for a minute or two, then carefully transfer to a wire rack and allow to cool completely.

7. Store the cookies in an airtight container in the refrigerator for up to a week.

NUTRITIONAL FACTS (per cookie)

Calories: 115 · Total fat: 8.6 g · Total carbs: 7.9 g · Net carbs: 6.0 g · Protein: 1.9 g

Makes 40 cookies

HONEY COCONUT MACAROONS

I have a funny habit of squishing down my macaroons before I eat them. For some reason, I like them when they are in really tight little balls. Obviously, the stickier they are, the tighter those balls get and the more I appreciate them. On a stickiness scale of one to ten, these probably score a twelve! Oh yeah, they're seriously sticky. And the not-so-subtle flavor of honey goes so perfectly with that of the coconut. A definite winner!

For the macaroons

- 1 cup (240 ml) full-fat coconut milk
- ½ cup (170 g) raw honey
- 1 teaspoon pure vanilla extract, homemade (page 84) or store-bought
- ¼ teaspoon Himalayan salt
- 4 cups (380 g) unsweetened finely shredded "macaroon" coconut
- 3 large egg whites

For the chocolate drizzle

- 2 ounces (55 g) cacao paste, finely chopped
- 1 tablespoon raw honey
- ½ teaspoon coconut oil

1. Preheat the oven to 350°F (177°C) and line a baking sheet with parchment paper.

2. In a large skillet set over high heat, bring the coconut milk, honey, vanilla extract, and salt to a boil while stirring constantly with a wooden spoon or spatula. Don't worry if the liquids don't seem to want to combine at first; eventually they will come together nicely. Just keep stirring. Let the mixture boil vigorously for 3 to 5 minutes, until it starts to turn a light caramel color.

3. Lower the heat to medium-high and add the shredded coconut; mix well and cook, stirring almost constantly, until the mixture gets dry and sticky, about 2 minutes. Set aside to cool for about 10 minutes.

4. Meanwhile, in a bowl, beat the egg whites with a hand mixer to stiff peaks. Gently stir in the coconut mixture with a large spoon or rubber spatula, then drop the batter by the tablespoonful onto the prepared baking sheet. A small spring-loaded ice cream scoop is the perfect tool for this task.

5. Bake for 12 to 15 minutes or until the macaroons are a nice golden color. Let cool completely on the pan.

6. Make the chocolate drizzle: Melt the cacao paste in the microwave, 25 to 30 seconds at a time, stirring well and often until it's completely melted. Add the honey and coconut oil and stir gently until smooth. Transfer the chocolate mixture to a small squirt bottle or resealable plastic bag with a corner cut off and drizzle some over each macaroon.

7. Refrigerate the cookies until ready to serve. They will keep in the refrigerator for up to a week.

NUTRITIONAL FACTS (per cookie)

Calories: 119	Total fat: 9.6 g	Total carbs: 7.3 g	Net carbs: 7.3 g	Protein: 1.2 g

under 30

 egg-free

 make ahead

CANDIED MAPLE SPICED MIXED NUTS

Makes about 3 cups (385 g)

These nuts are dangerous to have around the house. Very dangerous! Consider yourself warned.

- 3 cups (420 g) mixed raw nuts (see Note)
- 1 teaspoon Himalayan salt
- ½ teaspoon ground Ceylon cinnamon
- ¼ teaspoon freshly grated nutmeg
- ⅛ teaspoon ground clove
- ½ teaspoon red pepper flakes
- ¼ cup (60 ml) pure maple syrup (dark color or Canadian Medium)
- 1 tablespoon ghee
- Fleur de sel

1. Preheat the oven to 350°F (177°C).

2. Place the nuts in a single layer on a rimmed baking sheet, place in the oven, and toast until fragrant, 7 to 8 minutes.

3. Meanwhile, in a large bowl, mix together the salt, cinnamon, nutmeg, clove, and red pepper flakes; set aside.

4. In a large saucepan set over medium-high heat, bring the maple syrup and ghee to a boil. Add the toasted nuts and cook, stirring constantly, until most of the liquid has adhered to the nuts, 1 to 2 minutes. Remove from the heat and stir in the mixed spices.

5. Line the baking sheet (the one you used to toast the nuts) with parchment paper, then spread the nuts evenly over the baking sheet and return to the oven for 8 to 10 minutes, until the nuts appear golden and crunchy.

6. Remove the nuts from the oven and sprinkle with fleur de sel. Let cool completely before serving.

7. Store the nuts in an airtight container for up to a few weeks.

Note: *I used a combination of almonds, pecans, walnuts, macadamia nuts, and Brazil nuts.*

NUTRITIONAL FACTS (per ¼ cup/32 g serving)

| Calories: 193 | Total fat: 16.9 g | Total carbs: 8.4 g | Net carbs: 5.7 g | Protein: 5.0 g |

DARK CHOCOLATE MANONS

Makes 32 manons

Finally, a chocolate that you can eat without so much as an ounce of guilt! These really are not sweet, but frankly, they are so tasty that you won't miss the sugar hit at all.

For the chocolate centers

- 1 cup (108 g) toasted homemade coconut butter (see Notes)
- ½ cup (130 g) All-Natural Toasted Cashew Butter (page 290)
- ¼ cup (22 g) cacao powder
- ¼ teaspoon ground Ceylon cinnamon
- ⅓ cup (45 g) raw macadamia nuts, finely chopped
- ¼ cup (23 g) unsweetened finely shredded "macaroon" coconut, plus more for garnish
- ¼ cup (30 g) cacao nibs

For the chocolate coating

- 5½ ounces (155 g) cacao paste, very finely chopped
- 3 tablespoons raw honey, melted

1. Line a rimmed baking sheet with parchment paper.

2. Put the coconut butter, cashew butter, cacao powder, and cinnamon in a large mixing bowl and beat with a hand mixer until well combined and slightly fluffy. Throw in the macadamia nuts, shredded coconut, and cacao nibs and resume mixing until just incorporated.

3. Transfer the mixture to a piping bag (see Notes) equipped with a ½-inch (1.25-cm) round tip and pipe 32 little dollops about 1 inch (2.5 cm) in diameter onto the prepared baking sheet. Put the centers in the fridge to chill while you work on the chocolate coating.

4. Melt the cacao paste in the microwave in 25- to 30-second intervals, stirring well for an equal amount of time after each interval, until it's completely melted. Do not allow the chocolate to become hot: It should never get much warmer than body temperature.

5. When the chocolate is fully melted, add the honey and stir gently to combine.

6. Place a chocolate center on a fork and dip it in the melted chocolate. Pull the center back out, gently tap the fork against the side of the bowl to remove the excess chocolate, and place the manon on the baking sheet. Repeat with the remaining centers. Put the manons in the fridge to set for 10 to 15 minutes, then dip them a second time. If the chocolate coating has become too firm for dipping, warm it for a few seconds in the microwave. Sprinkle a little shredded coconut on top of each manon and return the manons to the fridge until completely set.

7. Place the finished manons in small paper cups and store them in a cool, dry place in an airtight container for up to a month.

Notes: To make toasted coconut butter, follow the instructions for making coconut butter on pages 296 to 298, using Method 1, 2, or 3, but use toasted coconut flakes instead of unsweetened shredded coconut. You could also use regular, untoasted coconut butter (homemade or store-bought), but the flavor would be slightly different.

If you don't have a piping bag, you can chill the mixture and then scoop out little balls using a small spring-loaded ice cream scoop. Then shape the centers by rolling them between your palms and pressing them down lightly.

NUTRITIONAL FACTS (per manon)

Calories: 129 | Total fat: 10.7 g | Total carbs: 7.4 g | Net carbs: 4.2 g | Protein: 2.3 g

quick & easy

 egg-free

 make ahead

nut-free

Makes about 2 cups (475 ml)

- 1½ cups (210 g) coconut sugar, divided
- ¼ cup (60 ml) water
- 1 cup (240 ml) full-fat coconut milk
- ¼ cup (85 g) raw honey
- 3 tablespoons ghee
- 1 vanilla bean, seeds scraped
- ½ teaspoon fleur de sel

SALTED CARAMEL

This caramel means business. Its flavor is as bold and intense as its color is dark. It's particularly delicious with apples, but chances are you'll want to have some on everything and probably eat it by the spoonful, too.

1. In a medium saucepan, combine 1 cup (140 g) of the coconut sugar and the water and bring to a boil over medium-high heat. Let the mixture boil for about 5 minutes, until the sugar becomes smooth, takes on a dark caramel color, and starts to thicken.

2. Meanwhile, in a separate saucepan set over medium heat, combine the coconut milk, remaining ½ cup (70 g) of coconut sugar, honey, ghee, and vanilla seeds and cook, stirring occasionally, until the mixture just barely starts to simmer, then kill the heat. Do not let it come to a full boil.

3. As soon as the coconut sugar and water mixture from Step 1 is ready, slowly pour in the warm coconut milk mixture while stirring constantly with a long-handled wooden spoon.

4. Once the milk is completely incorporated into the sugar, bring the caramel to a boil. Boil for 3 full minutes while stirring constantly, then turn off the heat and set aside to cool.

5. When the caramel has cooled to room temperature, stir in the fleur de sel.

6. Store the caramel in an airtight container in the refrigerator for up to a month. It will become firm when chilled, but you can gently reheat it to bring it back to its liquid form.

NUTRITIONAL FACTS (per tablespoon)

Calories: 69 | Total fat: 3.1 g | Total carbs: 11.2 g | Net carbs: 11.2 g | Protein: 0.1 g

ACKNOWLEDGMENTS

First and foremost, I want to thank Tasha, my favorite daughter ever and bestest friend in the entire universe, without whom this book would probably have never seen the light of day. You see, some years ago, she coaxed me into creating this thing called a blog, which I knew absolutely nothing about, so I could post a picture of some dish I'd made and photographed that day, just for the hell of it. Even though I thought the pictures were pretty ordinary, she believed that they were totally awesome and worthy of being shared with the rest of world. She was so insistent, I eventually gave in and with her help created the blog and made my very first post that night. Little did I know that it would mark the beginning of an extraordinary and wonderful adventure for me, one that would totally change the course of my life. Had it not been for Tasha, that picture probably would have fallen into oblivion, lost amongst a bunch of other insignificant files on my hard drive. I most definitely wouldn't be here writing these very words today. Tasha, thank you so much for being my number-one fan all these years, for supporting me always, for giving me the little push that I needed when things weren't going all that well, for taste-testing my recipes and proofreading my writings, and for giving me your honest opinion on them. Thank you for being such a great daughter and amazing friend. You're the best thing that ever happened to me.

To my mom and late father, the best parents I could've hoped for. I will never be able to thank you enough for supporting me, for being there for me no matter what, for standing behind my decisions even when you didn't quite agree with them or thought they weren't the wisest *(and yeah, more often than not you were right!)*, for lending me your ears and shoulders when I needed them, for loving me unconditionally, and, most of all, for shaping me into the person I am today. I am proud to be your daughter; I love you and adore you with all my heart. And Dad…words can't even start to express how much I miss you. What I wouldn't give to hand you a copy of this book right now. You'll always be my hero. Always.

To my son, Felix, and his girlfriend, Karoe, thank you for being such amazing kids, for being so understanding when I invade the kitchen and squat the dining room table, for being such good company, and for putting up with all my crazy stuff…you both totally rock! My life would be so very incomplete without the two of you.

Huge shout-out to the most important man in my life right now, my personal trainer and amazing coach, Charles-Alexandre Trudel, who expertly sees to it that I remain physically fit and strong by creating such awesome programs for me that I actually look forward to getting out of bed in the morning and lifting all kinds of heavy stuff. Charles, you inspire me daily and have impacted my life in such a positive way; for that I will be forever thankful. And hey, I really look forward to training at *your* gym someday!

Many many thanks to:

Erich at Victory Belt Publishing, for seeing potential in me and for believing in my success. Thank you for all your kind words of guidance and encouragement and for turning my dream into a reality.

Pierre Ouellet, my former boss, for being such a good sport and putting up with my crap for so long. I'm especially thankful for you eventually giving me the boot, forcing me to spread my wings and take flight. You are by far the most amazing boss anyone could ever hope to have, and I will forever feel honored to have been chosen by you to be a part of your team. Thank you so much for everything you've done for me.

Pierre St-Laurent, my former co-worker, for reading me all these years, for showing interest in my work, for your constant words of encouragement, and for always believing in me. Thank you, Pierre. You are big!

Special thanks to my beloved dogs, my faithful and loyal companions, who always stand behind me *(literally)* and accept me and love me for who I truly am *(even more so when they get to taste the food that I make…)*. Now if they only knew how to read!

Last but not least…

To all my readers and followers, and to all of you out there who are currently holding this book and reading these very lines:

Thank you, thank you, thank you! My life just wouldn't be the same without you all.

Living a healthy lifestyle, coming up with clean and tasty recipes, and staying physically active day in, day out isn't always easy. I'm only human, and yes, even after all this time, there are still days when I feel like giving it all up; but knowing that you are all there standing behind me, reading me, trying my recipes, getting inspired by them, counting on them even, and providing awesome support and feedback in return—that's what keeps me going!

I wouldn't be where, or who, I am today without each and every one of you guys.

Thanks to you, this book was made possible.

YOU MAKE A DIFFERENCE! Don't ever forget that.

RESOURCES

RECOMMENDED BOOKS

Ballantyne, Sarah. *The Paleo Approach: Reverse Autoimmune Disease and Heal Your Body.* Las Vegas, NV: Victory Belt Publishing, 2013.

Connell, Heather. *Powerful Paleo Superfoods: The Best Primal-Friendly Foods for Burning Fat, Building Muscle, and Optimal Health.* Lions Bay, BC: Fair Winds Press, 2014.

Hartwig, Dallas, and Melissa Hartwig. *It Starts with Food: Discover the Whole30 and Change Your Life in Unexpected Ways.* Las Vegas, NV: Victory Belt Publishing, 2012.

Perlmutter, David. *Grain Brain: The Surprising Truth about Wheat, Carbs, and Sugar—Your Brain's Silent Killers.* Boston: Little, Brown and Company, 2013.

Sanfilippo, Diane. *Practical Paleo: A Customized Approach to Health and a Whole-Foods Lifestyle.* Las Vegas, NV: Victory Belt Publishing, 2012.

Sanfilippo, Diane. *The 21-Day Sugar Detox: Bust Sugar and Carb Cravings Naturally.* Las Vegas, NV: Victory Belt Publishing, 2013.

Seib, Jason. *The Paleo Coach: Expert Advice for Extraordinary Health, Sustainable Fat Loss, and an Incredible Body.* Las Vegas, NV: Victory Belt Publishing, 2013.

Sisson, Mark. *The Primal Blueprint: Reprogram Your Genes for Effortless Weight Loss, Vibrant Health and Boundless Energy.* Malibu, CA: Primal Nutrition, Inc., 2009.

Wolf, Robb. *The Paleo Solution: The Original Human Diet.* Las Vegas, NV: Victory Belt Publishing, 2010.

Wolfe, Liz. *Eat the Yolks: Discover Paleo, Fight Food Lies, and Reclaim Your Health.* Las Vegas, NV: Victory Belt Publishing, 2013.

RECOMMENDED BLOGS AND WEBSITES

The Healthy Foodie
thehealthyfoodie.com

Against All Grain
againstallgrain.com

Balanced Bites
balancedbites.com

Civilized Caveman Cooking
civilizedcavemancooking.com

The Clothes Make the Girl
theclothesmakethegirl.com

The Domestic Man
thedomesticman.com

Health-Bent
health-bent.com

I Breathe...I'm Hungry
ibreatheimhungry.com

Nom Nom Paleo
nomnompaleo.com

Paleo Cupboard
paleocupboard.com

Paleo Foodie Kitchen
paleofoodiekitchen.com

Paleo Grubs
paleogrubs.com

PaleOMG
paleomg.com

Popular Paleo
popularpaleo.com

Ruled.me
ruled.me

Slim Palate
slimpalate.com

Stupid Easy Paleo
stupideasypaleo.com

Whole9
whole9life.com

RECOMMENDED BRANDS AND PRODUCTS

Bob's Red Mill
www.bobsredmill.com
- *Nut flours*
- *Coconut flour*
- *Tapioca starch*
- *Unsweetened shredded coconut*

Coconut Secret
www.coconutsecret.com
- *Coconut aminos*

Edward & Sons–Let's Do... Organic
www.edwardandsons.com
- *Coconut flour*
- *Shredded coconut*
- *Toasted coconut flakes*
- *Unsweetened coconut flakes*

Great Lakes
www.greatlakesgelatin.com
- *Grass-fed beef gelatin powder*
  Sadly very hard to procure in Canada

Navitas Naturals
www.navitasnaturals.com
- *Raw cacao powder*
- *Cacao paste/liquor*
- *Cacao butter*
- *Cacao beans and nibs*

NOW Foods
www.nowfoods.com
- *Organic beef gelatin powder*
  A very good alternative to Great Lakes for Canadian residents

OMGhee
www.omghee.com
- *Organic non-GMO ghee from pastured cows, handmade in small batches*
  Sadly not available in Canada

Purity Farms
www.purityfarms.com
- *Organic non-GMO ghee from pastured cows*
  A very good alternative to OMGhee for Canadian residents

Red Boat
www.redboatfishsauce.com
- *Fish sauce*

Simply Organic
www.simplyorganic.com
- *Organic herbs and spices*

Wild Planet
www.wildplanetfoods.com
- *Sustainably caught wild seafood*
- *Canned tuna*
- *Canned salmon*
- *Canned sardines*
- *Canned anchovies*

SHOPPING

Amazon
For everything and anything, Amazon carries a vast assortment of organic grocery products and kitchen equipment. Their customer service is excellent; shipping is often free and super fast. All in all, Amazon is a fabulous online shopping resource.

Costco
Costco offers tons of great finds for the avid Paleo shopper! They have a wide variety of organic nuts and dried fruits in bulk, as well as good deals on organic meats, fresh produce, and grocery products such as extra-virgin olive oil, avocado oil, and coconut oil.

eBay
eBay is a great place to find novelty items, such as vanilla pods in bulk, small kitchen appliances at great bargain prices, and vintage cutlery items. And there are quite a few hidden treasures to be found.

Vitacost.com
Vitacost.com is a fantastic online shopping resource and is especially great for Canadians. Shipping across the border is very affordable, and they carry products that are typically very hard for us Canadians to source, such as Purity Farms Ghee and Red Boat Fish Sauce. Excellent service and prices, too!

Julienned Carrot and Rutabaga Salad / 124

Grilled Caesar Salad / 126

Cucumber and Sweet Red Pepper Salad / 128

Spicy Mango Cucumber Salad / 130

Marinated Mushroom Salad / 132

Shaved Fennel, Orange, and Pistachio Salad / 134

Baked Eggs with Creamed Spinach / 138

Simple Egg Salad / 140

Creamy Egg and Spinach Casserole / 142

Quiche Florentine / 144

Smoked Ham and Asparagus Omelette / 146

Portobello Stuffed with Scrambled Eggs and Prosciutto / 148

Spinach and Chicken Omelette Lasagna / 150

Basic Grilled Chicken / 154

Buffalo Wings / 156

Chicken Fingers with Spicy Honey Dijon Dipping Sauce / 158

Honey Sesame Chicken / 160

Szechuan Chicken / 162

Spicy Indian Chicken Stew / 164

Creamy Coconut Chicken Stew / 166

Olive and Lemon Roast Chicken / 168

Asian Beef and Broccoli / 174

Beef Tartare / 176

Easy Braised Beef / 178

Montreal-Style Corned Beef / 180

Corned Beef and Sweet Potato Hash / 182

Grilled Beef Liver / 184

Ground Beef Breakfast Hash / 186

Moroccan Grilled Skirt Steak / 188

Meatloaf with Sour Cherry Sauce / 190

Shish Kebabs / 192

Filet Mignon with Beurre Maître d'Hôtel / 194

Hearty Meatballs in Wild Mushroom Sauce / 196

Paleo Moussaka / 198

Orange Rosemary Braised Leg of Lamb / 200

Apricot Pistachio Lamb Stew / 202

Shepherd's Pie / 204

Classic Lamb Roast / 206

Greek-Style Braised Lamb / 208

Bacon-Wrapped Pork Loin / 212

Cretons à la Québécoise / 214

Maple Balsamic Pulled Pork / 216

Breakfast Sausage / 218

Spicy Ginger Lemon Pork Stir-Fry / 220

Pork Souvlaki / 222

Ras el Hanout and Lime Pork Carnitas / 224

Fig and Prosciutto–Wrapped Pork Kebabs / 226

Pork Scaloppine Roll-Ups / 228

French Canadian Meat Pie / 230

Curried Coconut Shrimp / 236

Fatty Fish Patties / 238

Lobster Meat Crusted Salmon Fillets / 240

Scallop, Fennel, and Strawberry Salad / 242

Orange Ginger Salmon Tataki / 244

Easy Tuna Salad for One / 246

Pan-Seared Scallops with Balsamic Reduction / 248

Tuna and Pink Grapefruit Tartare with Sweet Potato Straws / 250

Cauliflower Fritters / 254

Basic Cauli-Rice / 256

Classic Creamy Coleslaw / 258

Oven-Roasted Glazed Carrots / 260

Grilled Avocado / 262

Grilled Cauliflower / 264

Grilled Endives / 266

Skewered Grilled Veggies / 268

Kaleslaw / 270

Lemony Brussels Sprouts Almandine / 272

Oven-Roasted Vegetables / 274

Rustic Acorn Squash Mash / 276

Roasted Garlic Cauliflower Mash / 278

Zucchini Carpaccio with Walnut Pesto / 280

All-Natural Toasted Almond Butter / 288

All-Natural Toasted
Cashew Butter / 290

All-Natural Toasted
Hazelnut Butter / 292

All-Natural Toasted
Sunflower Seed
Butter / 294

Coconut Butter / 296

A Taste of India
Seed Butter / 300

Apple Crumble
Nut Butter / 302

Baklava Nut Butter
/ 304

Chai Nut Clusters
and Date Swirl
Nut Butter / 306

Cinnamon Roll
Nut Butter / 308

Dark Chocolate
Hazelnut Spread / 310

Toasted Butter Pecan
Spread / 312

Crunchy Smoked
Almond Butter / 314

Maple Chai Candied
Nut Spread / 316

Maple Walnut Spread
/ 318

BBQ "Peanut"
Spread / 320

Praline and Cream
Nut Butter / 322

Rum Raisin
Nut Spread / 324

Smoky Bacon and
Dark Chocolate
Nut Spread / 326

Spiced Pumpkin
Pecan Spread / 328

White Chocolate
Macadamia
Nut Butter / 330

Blueberry Muffins
/ 334

Apple Cinnamon
Spice Muffins / 336

Banana Bread / 338

Dark Chocolate
Hazelnut Tart / 340

Honey Pecan
Apple Crumble / 342

Butter Pecan Cake
/ 344

Maple Syrup
Mousse Cake / 348

Pouding Chômeur
/ 352

Carrot Cake / 354

Bacon and Chocolate
Chunk Cookies / 358

Double Dark
Chocolate Cookies
/ 360

Honey Coconut
Macaroons / 362

Candied Maple Spiced
Mixed Nuts / 364

Dark Chocolate
Manons / 366

Salted Caramel / 368

INDEX